SOMERSET FOLKLORE

LLANERCH/FOLK-LORE SOCIETY

[CXIV]

COUNTY FOLKLORE
VOLUME VIII

SOMERSET FOLKLORE

BY

R. L. TONGUE

EDITED BY

K. M. BRIGGS

ISBN 1 897853 78 5

First published by
FOLK-LORE SOCIETY, 1965
Facsimile Reprint by
LLANERCH PUBLISHERS, 1995

Printed in Great Britain by
Robert MacLehose and Company Limited
The University Press, Glasgow

DEDICATED TO

THE MEMORY OF 'ANNIE'S GRANNY'

INTRODUCTION

The word "folklore" was invented almost 150 years ago, on August 22 1846, when the antiquarian W. J. Thoms appealed in the *Athenæum* for readers to join in recording"... what we in England designate as Popular Antiquities or Popular Literature (though by-the-by it is more a Lore than a Literature, and would be most aptly described by a good Saxon compound, Folk-lore) ...". The word was new, but the subject was not; for two hundred years antiquarians had been fascinated by local and seasonal customs, popular tales, traditions, beliefs which did not conform to official rellizion or science. Such material appears sporadically in the writings of William Camden (1551-1623), and far more abundantly in those of John Aubrey (1626-97). Some decades later came Henry Bourne's *Antiquitates Vulgares* (1725), a fierce attack against popular rel-ligious observances such as Christmas carols or visiting holy wells, because they were originally Roman Catholic, "the invention of indolent monks", and so un-doubtedly diabolical and heathen. His book, ignored at the time, was incorporated in 1777 into a much larger and more influential work, John Brand's *Observations on Popular Antiquities*. Brand agreed that most folk customs dated from before the Reformation, but he was free from the Puritan intolerance which equated Catholicism with paganism, and he enjoyed historical research for its own sake. He went on gathering mat-erial till his death in 1806, mostly by copying from books and journals, but sometimes by personal observ-ation. After he died, his book was reissued in a greatly enlarged edition, incorporating the later notes by Henry Ellis (1815). It had grown into a vast, confused scrap-book: local historians pounced upon it and used it as a model for their own researches.

In the course of the nineteenth century, many scholars boldly tried to formulate some all-embracing theory which would explain the origin and significance of myths, folktales, superstitions and magical beliefs, and the more picturesque folk customs, especially those connected with agriculture. The explanations offered went far beyond medieval Catholicism. Some suggested origins in pre-Christian Germanic or Celtic cultures; others, noting similarities with beliefs and rituals found among "primitive" non-European peoples, argued that folklore consisted of survivals from a prehistoric "savage" stage in human social development. The debate between these and other conflicting theories was carried on energetically at a high scholarly level, and attracted much public interest. It has been well described in Richard M. Dorson's *The British Folklorists: A History* (1968). And although modern scholars agree that all these Victorian attempts to find "a key to all mythologies" ended in failure, due to over-simplifications of the highly complex topics, some of the theories then launched are still to be found recycled in popular form: prehistoric paganism and Celtic paganism, separately or combined, are currently enjoying a fashionable revival in the mass market.

By the 1890s the Folklore Society, which had been founded in 1878, saw a need for systematic and accurate documentation of traditions within specific localities: huge unwieldy compilations like Brand's would not do. Between 1895 and 1914 seven volumes of *County Folklore: Printed Extracts* were published by the Society. The first covered three counties: *Gloucestershire* by E. S. Hartland, *Suffolk* by Lady Camilla Eveline Gurdon, and *Leicestershire and Rutland* by C. J. Billson. The rest covered one region apiece: *The North Riding of Yorkshire, and the Ainsty* by Eliza Gutch; *Orkney and Shetland Islands* by George Black, ed. N. W. Thomas; *Northumberland* by M. C. Balfour, ed. N. W. Thomas; *Lincolnshire* by Eliza Gutch and Mabel Peacock; *The East Riding of Yorkshire* by Eliza Gutch; and *Fife* by J. E. Simpkins. The 1914 war then interrupted the project.

These books may seem strange today because, like Brand's, they consist almost entirely of extracts from previously printed books and journals. Fieldwork, i.e. gathering information through interviews or by tape-recording, filming, and personal observation, is central to a present-day folklorist's technique, and was already practised in Victorian times by means of the simple

INTRODUCTION

The word "folklore" was invented almost 150 years ago, on August 22 1846, when the antiquarian W. J. Thoms appealed in the *Athenæum* for readers to join in recording"... what we in England designate as Popular Antiquities or Popular Literature (though by-the-by it is more a Lore than a Literature, and would be most aptly described by a good Saxon compound, Folk-lore) ...". The word was new, but the subject was not; for two hundred years antiquarians had been fascinated by local and seasonal customs, popular tales, traditions, beliefs which did not conform to official relligion or science. Such material appears sporadically in the writings of William Camden (1551-1623), and far more abundantly in those of John Aubrey (1626-97). Some decades later came Henry Bourne's *Antiquitates Vulgares* (1725), a fierce attack against popular relligious observances such as Christmas carols or visiting holy wells, because they were originally Roman Catholic, "the invention of indolent monks", and so undoubtedly diabolical and heathen. His book, ignored at the time, was incorporated in 1777 into a much larger and more influential work, John Brand's *Observations on Popular Antiquities*. Brand agreed that most folk customs dated from before the Reformation, but he was free from the Puritan intolerance which equated Catholicism with paganism, and he enjoyed historical research for its own sake. He went on gathering material till his death in 1806, mostly by copying from books and journals, but sometimes by personal observation. After he died, his book was reissued in a greatly enlarged edition, incorporating the later notes by Henry Ellis (1815). It had grown into a vast, confused scrapbook: local historians pounced upon it and used it as a model for their own researches.

In the course of the nineteenth century, many scholars boldly tried to formulate some all-embracing theory which would explain the origin and significance of myths, folktales, superstitions and magical beliefs, and the more picturesque folk customs, especially those connected with agriculture. The explanations offered went far beyond medieval Catholicism. Some suggested origins in pre-Christian Germanic or Celtic cultures; others, noting similarities with beliefs and rituals found among "primitive" non-European peoples, argued that folklore consisted of survivals from a prehistoric "savage" stage in human social development. The debate between these and other conflicting theories was carried on energetically at a high scholarly level, and attracted much public interest. It has been well described in Richard M. Dorson's *The British Folklorists: A History* (1968). And although modern scholars agree that all these Victorian attempts to find "a key to all mythologies" ended in failure, due to over-simplifications of the highly complex topics, some of the theories then launched are still to be found recycled in popular form: prehistoric paganism and Celtic paganism, separately or combined, are currently enjoying a fashionable revival in the mass market.

By the 1890s the Folklore Society, which had been founded in 1878, saw a need for systematic and accurate documentation of traditions within specific localities: huge unwieldy compilations like Brand's would not do. Between 1895 and 1914 seven volumes of *County Folklore: Printed Extracts* were published by the Society. The first covered three counties: *Gloucestershire* by E. S. Hartland, *Suffolk* by Lady Camilla Eveline Gurdon, and *Leicestershire and Rutland* by C. J. Billson. The rest covered one region apiece: *The North Riding of Yorkshire, and the Ainsty* by Eliza Gutch; *Orkney and Shetland Islands* by George Black, ed. N. W. Thomas; *Northumberland* by M. C. Balfour, ed. N. W. Thomas; *Lincolnshire* by Eliza Gutch and Mabel Peacock; *The East Riding of Yorkshire* by Eliza Gutch; and *Fife* by J. E. Simpkins. The 1914 war then interrupted the project.

These books may seem strange today because, like Brand's, they consist almost entirely of extracts from previously printed books and journals. Fieldwork, i.e. gathering information through interviews or by tape-recording, filming, and personal observation, is central to a present-day folklorist's technique, and was already practised in Victorian times by means of the simple notebook. Yet from these books it is virtually absent; editorial theorising and interpretation are also minimal. It must be stressed that the "Printed Extracts" series was never intended to stand alone, but to be a starting point for further study of the contemporary lore of each area. In his preface to the Gloucestershire volume, Hartland made "suggestions for systematic collection of folklore" to be undertaken by university students, school teachers, clergy, doctors, local historians and others. Plenty of his contemporaries were already working in this way; the purpose of reprinting old material was to provide historical perspectives and a set of securely dated benchmarks, from which to measure later developments, innovations or losses.

Another century has passed, and the County Folklore series is being reprinted in the 1990s, a period of nostalgia for an idealized rural past, seen as a time of idyllic simplicity and closeness to nature. Readers will find ample encouragement for nostalgia here: picturesque accounts of harvest customs, Christmas customs, fairs and festivals; old tales of ghosts, giants, fairies, boggarts, witches, heroes, bandits; healing charms, divinations, omens, spells; customs at marriage, birth or death. It is only too easy to see in all this mere quaintness and charm. To get a more historically balanced picture one needs to remember also the harsh social and economic conditions affecting very many rural workers: one may well wonder, for instance, whether a good harvest supper really compensated for low wages during the other 51 weeks of the year. The "printed extracts", like old photographs, offer facts, but facts selected and presented according to the viewpoint of the observers who recorded them. Now, in the 1990s, we inevitably add interpretative viewpoints of our own, conditioned by the cultural assumptions of our age.

The eighth volume in the series, Ruth Tongue's *The Folklore of Somerset*, appeared much later, in 1965, and is wholly different in spirit and method. She quotes no historical or literary texts, but weaves together innumerable tales and statements she has been told orally by country-dwellers since the beginning of this century. She was also, however, a creative performer, who delighted audiences in Women's Institutes by retelling the stories in a dramatic manner and a picturesque Somerset idiom - learnt by deliberate imitation, for she was not by birth a dialect speaker. Her renderings are thus personal re-creations, though on a basis of tradition. This is a phenomenon which does not fit easily with folklore scholarship, but which is quite familiar nowadays among folksingers of the popular revival movement, Her storytelling skills, and her passionate love of her native county, still give vivid pleasure.

Folklore is an ongoing process, in which every custom, story or belief (if it survives) is constantly re-modelled by social pressures so that it remains in some way relevant to changing conditions. Books written a hundred or two hundred years ago are in no sense a final word on the topic, nor are the versions of a story or custom which they contain necessarily "better" than the current ones - they merely pinpoint what it was like in one phase of its existence. Moreover, anything that is passed on through oral tradition exists in multiple versions, each differing in some degree from the next, and each equally valid. What is the "true" story about that haunted tree? What is the "right" way to dispose of Christmas decorations, and on what date? What "should" children do at Halloween? Are black cats lucky (UK), or unlucky (USA)? We shall never find definitive answers to such questions, but it is fascinating to compile our own observations about them, and to compare with writers who went hunting along the same tracks long before us.

Jacqueline Simpson,
President,
The Folklore Society,
February, 1994.

Foreword

THE general arrangement of this book on Somerset Folklore follows that of the books on County Folk-Lore published from 1895 to 1912, but there is an important difference. The earlier books drew almost exclusively upon already published matter, while Miss Tongue's consists chiefly of oral traditions collected by herself. There was originally quite an amount of literary matter in her collection, but it has been crowded out for want of room, for, useful as it may be to have already published matter collected and classified, it is obviously of far more importance to secure what has never hitherto been printed and may, therefore, disappear for ever if it is not at once recorded. Every day old people die and are forgotten, each one of whom may be the last to remember an almost lost tradition or story or song.

Originally Miss Tongue illustrated her traditional matter with quotations and citations from earlier books, but considerations of space have made it necessary to omit most of these. A list of the books that she has referred to is, however, given at the end. The amount of fairy lore surviving in Miss Tongue's collections will probably surprise the folklorist, who is accustomed to think the fairy beliefs as dead as Reginald Scot thought them in the sixteenth century.

Miss Tongue's method of collection is nearer to that employed by Dr. Campbell in *Cloud-Walking Country* than to the tape-recording of the modern folklorist. In skilful hands this last may produce remarkable results, and can sometimes reproduce the manner and idiom of the folk narrator with scientific accuracy; but it is often too near laboratory conditions to catch the subtler aspects of the truth, and it can be observed that those telling a story to the microphone do not tell it in quite their ordinary manner. The tape records contain very valuable evidence, but they can usefully be checked by other methods. Miss Tongue's method of reporting a story cannot pretend to scientific accuracy, though she is careful to record the narrator or narrators of each tale and to make it clear when she has pieced a story together from fragments, but her long, intimate connection with the people of Somerset has made it possible for her to discover things carefully hidden from the 'foreign' collector. Her racy and vernacular use of the Somerset dialect opened many hearts to her, and both as a rider and a herb doctor she shares the free-masonry of the countryside, but she has another special qualification — she is a 'chimes child', that is one born between midnight and cockcrow on a Friday, who is credited with the power of seeing spirits. For this reason she was admitted into a good many secrets as a child, and knows a great deal more of the hidden background of country life than it is possible for most educated people to learn. In a sense she may be said to collect from herself, for her greatest wealth of lore, and particularly of songs, she acquired as a small child, hanging about the old men in Taunton Market or visiting her school-mates' grand-parents. But, thanks to this early knowledge, she has the password, and is still able to check and corroborate her memories from information which would be fully volunteered to no other stranger.

K. M. BRIGGS

ACKNOWLEDGMENTS

MAY I thank the following for their varied and valued assistance during more than sixty years of collecting: Many Somerset members of the National Federation of Women's Institutes; old friends in Taunton, Exmoor and Quantock; farmers and villagers of the Western Hills; Taunton Library; Somerset and Middlesex County Libraries; Correspondents from abroad and from all parts of England; Mrs. Geoffrey Luttrell, of Dunster Castle; the late Mr. H. W. Kille, of the West Somerset Archaeological Society; Mrs. Hallam, of the Somerset Archaeological Society; Mrs. C. Bryant, Kingston St. Mary, of the West Quantock Folk-Singers.

I should also like to thank members of the Folk-Lore Society, Miss V. Alford, Miss C. Hole, Miss Theo Brown, Miss M. Dean Smith, Mr. and Mrs. Peter Opie, and Mr. Douglas Kennedy, for their encouragement and help.

And to Dr. Katharine Briggs for her endless patience and devoted assistance, my lasting gratitude.

RUTH LYNDELL TONGUE

October 31, 1964

Contents

7

PART I

1

Natural and Inorganic Objects

STONES, BARROWS AND BURIED TREASURE

THERE are many stories about standing stones and barrows in
Somerset, as there are in Cornwall and in Brittany, and even where
there are no explicit stories there is a strong feeling that the stones
are uncanny and should be left alone. The position of some of
these stones is explained by the feats of local worthies, or more
often of the devil, some were said to be petrified human beings and
some had a sinister life of their own. Many of these guarded
treasure. There are many stories of the stones moving and dancing
at certain times. A few needed to be placated by offerings.

John Wood, in his *Particular Description of Bath*, 1750, I, p. 148,
says of the standing stones at Stanton Drew — 'No one, Say the
Country People about Stantondrue, was ever able to reckon the
Number of these metamorphosed Stones, or to take a Draught of
them, tho' several have attempted to do both, and proceeded until
they were either struck dead upon the Spot, or with such an illness
as soon carried them off.' A local tradition still persists to this
effect. At Orchardleigh in East Somerset the principal stone stands
ten feet out of the ground, and the local tale goes that when an
attempt was made to get to the base of it the workmen dug down
ten feet without any sign of reaching bottom.[1] A further version of
this tale told me by a North Somerset school friend in 1909 gives
the fate of one of the workmen. The great stone suddenly fell and
crushed him, and then returned immovable to its position.

I was told by four people — a coachman and his wife, a retired
blacksmith and a hedger from Ellicombe and Triscombe — that a
father and his three sons who took the capstone from a West
Somerset menhir all died soon after. One got a fever, one was
drowned coming home from market, and when the old man and
his youngest son tried to use the stone for their barn it fell and
crushed them both to death.

[1] *Somerset Year Book 1933*, p. 106.

Buried Treasure

Many of the stones and most of the barrows are supposed to have treasure buried under them or near them, but it is dangerous to look for it and there are many stories of foiled attempts. The Caractacus Stone, for instance, standing on Winsford Hill, Exmoor, is said to be haunted by a ghostly team and their foolhardy driver who tried to uproot and drag the stone away to get at the treasure it conceals. The stone overturned the waggon and team and crushed the greedy waggoner.[1] On foggy nights they are still to be heard and met.

Many of the treasure stones are lively. The Cock-Crow Stone near Wellington turns round every time a cock crows. If you are lucky enough to see it turning you can push it aside and get the gold hidden underneath it, but if it is not the right time or the right cock you may push and heave for ever, a team of horses could not move it. The Wimblestone, or lively stone, at Shipham, is even more active. It is said that a farmer took chains and two horses and tried all day to move it. Man and team exhausted themselves in vain, but that night the Wimblestone roamed over the Mendips to the Waterstone at Wrington, had a good drink and returned to Shipham. The Waterstone is one to which offerings of milk and primroses used to be made. There is a large hollow in the capstone which is supposed always to hold water. A school friend of eleven told me the following anecdote of the Wimblestone. It was told her by her Mendip great-grandmother, aged ninety.

The Wimblestone

Zebedee Fry were coming home late from the hay-making above Shipham. It were full moon, for they'd worked late to finish, and the crop was late being a hill field, so he had forgot what night 'twas. He thought he saw something big and dark moving in the field where the big stone stood but he was too bone-weary to go chasing any stray bullock. Then something huge and dark in field came rustling all alongside lane hedge, and Zebedee he up and dive into the brimmles in the ditch till it passed right along, and then he ran all a-tiptoe to reach Shipham — When he come to the field-gate he duck two-double and he rush past it. But, for all that, he see this gurt stone, twelve feet and more, a-dancing to itself in the moonlight over top-end of field. And where it always stood the

[1] A Bossington blacksmith, 1946, and a Hawkridge gardener, 1956.

moon were shining on a heap of gold money. But Zebedee he didn't stop for all that, not until he were safe at the inn at Shipham. They called he all sorts of fool for not getting his hand to the treasure — But nobody seemed anxious to have a try — not after he'd told them how nimble it danced round field. And nobody knows if 'twill dance again in a hundred years. Not till there's a full moon on Midsummer night.

The Barrows had a reputation even more sinister than the stones. Almost every one of them is regarded as haunted or unlucky. In 1908 E. Dauncey Tongue saw something near Hangley Cleeve Barrows which he believed to be a Barrow Guardian. Twenty years later, when he was an East African District Commissioner with a great reputation for coolness as a big-game hunter, he spoke of it as the most terrifying thing he had ever seen. He described it as a crouching form like a rock with matted hair all over it, and pale, flat eyes. Such an account makes one feel that the men who attempted to find the treasure at Robin Hood's Butts were lucky to get no worse than a fright.

Robin Hood's Butts

Robin Hood's Butts are two sets of round barrows right up on the very top of the Blackdown Hills. Under one of these barrows is a hoard of gold, but it is no use digging for it, everyone knows that. So when a rich man brought a lot of workmen to find the treasure everybody warned them what would happen. The rich man and his labourers just laughed. They worked hard that day; they dug huge trenches and carted away great loads of earth, and propped up the trenches with heavy timber, but every time they looked at the barrows they were still the same size. They left stakes to show how far they had gone, and went home tired out. The next day only half the diggers turned up, and when they climbed to Robin Hood's Butts to carry on with yesterday's work they found that there were no stakes, no trenches, no loads of earth, the gorse was growing on all the barrows. The diggers turned and ran, but the rich man was stubborn. He picked up a spade and began digging a trench again. When at last he stood up to look at his work there was no trench and the very hole his spade had made was not there any more. He burst into tears, and no one has looked for the treasure since then.[1]

[1] Local tradition.

Treasure digging is always attended with some hazard. A field near the old Roman Camp at North Petherton is called the Money Field. A plough turned up several coins here where the old market place once stood, and they say that somewhere close at hand is a buried treasure house with an iron door, which holds 'wealth untold'. If you are desperate enough to dig for it you must choose a night with a full moon, for it can only be seen then. But they also say that if you hear the thunder of chariot wheels and the crash of galloping hooves fast approaching to run you down — well, 'don't blame me.'[1]

The Castle Rach story is an example of an international treasure story with the taboo against speaking.

There was a vast treasure hidden on Castle Rach, and it was guarded by devils; but the men of Corfe were both valiant and poor and they determined to dig it up. They went to the priest and he promised to come with them, bringing some salt and holy water. The church bells were rung to drive away the devils and the digging began. It was highly successful. So vast a treasure did their spades uncover that one man swore in sheer surprise. At once the chest sank out of sight, the devils came back and every man, including the priest, died within a year.[2]

So much for the present character of the stones. Here are a few typical stories of their origin.

Simon's Barrow. Wellington.

The Devil's Lapful. The Blackdown Hills.

The Devil was carrying a load of stones to drop on Wellington Church. He had so many in his apron that he carried a few in his glove as well. Just on the top of the hills the strings of his leather apron broke, and the stones, scattered over an acre of ground, formed the Devil's Lapful, while in his flurry he dropped the rest, which formed the five small barrows known as the Devil's Glove. There is a crock of gold buried somewhere near, but no one has found it. Many have tried, just as many have taken away the stones to make walls and gateways; but the Devil always brings them back, and inflicts some terrible punishment for disturbing Simon's Barrow.[3]

---

[1] Oral tradition. [2] Oral collection, gardener, Corfe.
[3] Oral tradition, Taunton, Miss R. Clatworthy, 1906–10.

Hurdlestone Wood. Stoke St. Michael and Cranmore.

There is a farm near Wrington called Hailstones Farm, but some folk say it should really be Hurlerstone Farm on account of the Devil picking up a great rock lying there and throwing it right over the Mendips to hit Cranmore Church. Of course, he missed, but it was a tidy throw even for 'the Old Boy'.

Some say it was a giant dropped it or made a bad shot of it. Anyhow the rock lies on the edge of a cliff in the woods and they call them Hurdlestone Woods. And there is a Giant's Grave there too.[1]

Various giants, are credited with stone-throwing, sometimes independently and sometimes in competition with the Devil. One of these is Sir John Hauteville, who lived at Norton Malreward in the thirteenth century. Various feats of strength are told of him. It is said that he once caught three sheep-stealers, and carried them all, one of them under each arm and the third in his teeth, up to the top of Norton Church tower, and threatened to throw them over it if they did not mend their ways. In 1938 he was still credited by oral tradition with having tossed a great rock from Maes Knoll to Stanton Drew, a mile and a half away. This was a rehearsal for a match with the Devil, which Sir John won, for he threw his rock from Shute Shelve to Compton Bishop — again a mile and a half — and the Devil's throw was three furlongs shorter.

Other barrows and stones are more soberly described as graves. Giant Gorme, said to have been the owner of a carved chair at Blaize Castle, has three graves ascribed to him, one on Charnborough Hill near Holcombe, one, now destroyed, at Combe St. Nicholas, and two groups on either side of Cam Brook, a branch of the Wellow.

'There is a place called the Devil's Stone at Ham Lane, and another at Combe St. Nicholas, but my parents always said it was the grave of a Giant who fought the Devil and got killed, and was buried where the roads meet to keep him from walking.'[2]

In Somerset, too, we find examples of the wide-spread story of human beings turned into stone because they had disobeyed some taboo.

---

[1] Mendip tradition collected from Frome and Cranmore during a riding tour in 1945.

[2] A W. I. member from Buckland St. Mary, May 1961.

There are three stone circles in Stanton Drew. The smallest is called 'The Fiddler and the Maids', but all three are marked as 'The Wedding' in Stachey's map of 1736. The story is that a wedding party gathered in the Church Field below Dundry Hill on a Saturday evening. The local harper played for them until nearly midnight, and then reminded them that it would soon be Sunday. They were very merry, however, and one of them cried out that they would go on dancing even if they had to get the Devil himself to play. The harper put up his harp and turned to go, but heard piping behind him, and looking back saw that a tall piper had joined the company. He piped faster and faster, so that they danced on, whether they wanted to or not. Their cries and shrieks and curses were heard during the night, but in the morning nothing was to be seen of them but the three rings of stones.[1]

This tale still survives in oral tradition.

The stones at the entrance of Wookey Hole near Wells are supposed to be the Witch of Wookey and her demons, turned to stone by a young monk from Glastonbury who sprinkled them with holy water. The Witch of Wookey belonged to the Medusa type of witch — a beautiful woman who had sold herself to the Devil and became progressively more hideous as she grew more wicked. She was feared all through Somerset, but her special malevolence was directed against lovers. The young monk who turned her to stone had had his marriage wrecked by her spells.[2]

These origin tales seem rather to belong to folk fiction than folk belief. It is doubtful if they were ever taken seriously.

Masonry and Building

Some trace is still to be found of the ancient belief that Earth requires a sacrifice before a man-made building will stand.

'I saw an old man building a stone bank when I was a child. He picked up a dead lizard wrapped in leaves and he put it in the hole. Then he said, "Yur 'tis then, yur's vor'ee." He tamped the earth and stones on the grave, then he said, "I've gived she a liddle asker, now her'll stand." '

This was told me by an old lady of eighty-five at Over Stowey in 1954, but I myself as a child had watched an old labourer putting a

---

[1] E. Boger, *Myths, Scenes and Worthies of Somerset.*
[2] Oral tradition. See also Poole, p. 140; *Somerset Year Book 1905*, Vol. IV, p. 193.

dead lizard into a stone wall. When he had filled in the hole he said to me, 'Now her'll stand come Judgement.'

The belief that a black dog must be sacrificed in a new graveyard (see Part III, Section 1) is part of the same body of belief.

BELLS

The art of bell-ringing is peculiarly English. On the Continent and in Scotland the mechanical carillon has superseded the hand-swung bells, but in England there is a tradition of many centuries whose continuity was only broken by the two World Wars, and even in the Second World War some attempt was made to bridge the gap by hand-bell ringing. In Crowcombe a hand-bell ringer went down the drang (alleyway) and rang church-goers to service, and at a neighbouring Quantock village hand-bells were rung in church instead of a peal. These two are typical of many churches. The object of the ringing was not only to keep the tradition alive but to hold the Devil at bay. A church without bells was felt to be an unblessed church.

It is natural that so ancient and traditional an art should have many strange beliefs attached to it, and the bell-ringers believe that the bells are uncanny things. They were cast to protect their churches from evil, and their power reaches as far as they can be heard. The weathercock and the gargoyles were also made to be guardians of the church, but the bells are felt to be more powerful, and each one assumes an individual identity for the bell-ringers. They have their likes and dislikes. The old men in Taunton Market told me that in one church volunteers were needed for the ringing and the man chosen was well liked by the ringers, but the bells would have none of him. 'He had to go,' they said. ''Twould have bin his death to stay.' And the bells were right, for he had to run away to sea to escape hanging for murder. Bells are often fastidious in this way about their ringers, who are called 'The Call-Men of Christ'. The bells obey them, and it is they who have to tell their charges if they have to be sent to the Bell Foundry to be recast.

There was a bell, however, in a Somerset Abbey that used to kill its ringers; 'a wicked bell 'twas till one day a brave man carved a criss-cross on the poor thing, which nobody had thought to do before, and after that it rang like a real Christian' (Taunton

B

Market). The theory is that it was a heathen bell, brought back from a Crusade perhaps. There are other bells yet being rung who are accounted sinister, and one church I know suffers from a bell with a most uncertain temper, which always misbehaves if there is occasion to ring a special peal. The ringers suggest quite seriously that the bell may be a foreigner, homesick for his own church. Even the mildest bells are dangerous to malefactors, and church robbers who try to hide themselves or their spoils in the belfry are often found dead in the churchyard. What killed them only the bells know.

The *Somerset Year Book of 1939* has a note on Ding Dong Darling of Stogursey.

'Ding Dong Darling, the ancient Curfew bell of Stogursey, is to ring again. The bell hangs over the Almshouses founded by Sir Wm. Poulet in the reign of Henry V. For 500 years it was rung daily at 6 A.M. and 6 P.M. Last year the eighty-year-old bell-ringer died, and the bell was silent, until another occupant has now been found for the bell-ringer's almshouses. The rope hangs down into the bedroom so that the ringer can do his work lying in bed.'

This was one of the bells said to have definite dislikes. In the old days it was a reference of the highest virtue to be its ringer. There is an old story that once in the Tudor days it refused to ring at all. 'No doubt the man didn't suit.'

Barlinch Bell. Dulverton

At Barlinch Priory they say there was a bell tower with several bells by which the Exmoor and Brendon folk ordered their remote lives and in which they took great pride. Then came the end of the Priory, and the bells were separated, and left their home of centuries. The Tenor Bell went to Dulverton, near its old home, and it still rings the sweetest note in the town, but Exeter Cathedral bought the Great Bell. It was loaded with immense difficulty behind a team of oxen and began its long journey into exile, and as the cart moved off it sent out one long, heart-breaking note so sweet and sad that Exmoor folk recall it with sorrow to this day. At last it arrived in Exeter, and with great excitement was placed in Exeter Cathedral. Crowds collected to hear the deep, sweet note so famous in West Somerset, but the Great Bell remained dumb. Silent it hung there until one day an exasperated ringer gave it so lusty a stroke that it spoke once more. So heavy and direful a note rolled from it that all the Devonshire cream in Exeter turned sour at the sound.[1]

Sayings about Bells

If the stroke of the passing bell is heavy there will be another funeral within a week.

> If bells or clocks sound very clear and gay,
> Good news is on the way.
>
> *Somerset.*

Bell-Ringers' Verses

Dulverton.

> Oliver Cromwell's dead and gone,
> He hung us in the tower;
> And every day we had to play
> For more than half an hour.
>
> *Dulverton boy, 1910.*

(Another version.)

> Old John Wesley's dead and gone,
> He left us in the tower;
> 'Twas his desire that we should play
> At eight and twelve and fower.

For other versions, see Snell, 1902.
Chew Magna.

> Twank a dilla, twank a dilla, twank a dilla,
> He that loves a pretty girl is a hearty good fellow.
> If a gentleman calls this fine sconce to see
> There's no harm in treating such ringers as we.
> We can ring bobs, singles, extremes and true blue.
> There's no ringers can compare with the ringers of Chew.
>
> *Story of Our Village*, Chew Magna W.I., 1935, p. 36.

[1] Local traditions, West Somerset. See also W. H. P. Greswell, *The Forests and Deer Parks of Somerset*, 1905, pp. 186–7.

Inscriptions on Bells

Brompton Ralph.

> Gabriel is my name
> In me find no blame.
>
> *Medieval Angelus Bell.*

Kilmersdon.

> You Ruddle and Cockey, come hither and see
> Which is the best workman of all us three.
> Thomas Bilbee cast me.
>
> *Eighteenth-century bell.*

Luxborough.

> Our merry peal is mainly due
> To Mr. & Mrs. Gerald Carew.
>
> *Nineteenth-century bell.*

Frome.

> God made Cockey,
> And Cockey made me
> In the Year of our Lord
> Seventeen forty three.
>
> *Eighteenth-century bell.*

RIVERS AND WELLS

There are more traditions of standing stones and rocks to be gathered in Somerset than of rivers. The people on the banks of the Severn and Parrett are reticent about their rivers, but some trace may be found of belief in the river spirit and its greed for human life. One rhyme, of which I found two variants, refers to the Parrett.

'Where's the farmer?'
Says the pump.
'Where's the mare?'
Says the well.
'I can tell you,'

'Where be measter?'
Say the river.
'Where be pony?'
Say the well.
'I've a took'n,'

| Says the River, | Say the water, |
| 'They do shiver-shake in Hell.' | 'They be drownded down to Hell.' |

These were collected in 1906 from a group of old men in Taunton Market, from whom I learned at various times more than a hundred folk-songs, rhymes, charms and stories. From the same source I obtained the even more brutal Dart rhyme:

> Dart, here's a man
> To chill
> Or to kill.
> Now let me over
> To go where I will.

It might be expected that the tradition would be dead by now, but a child was recently drowned near Langport, and the fatalism with which the disaster was discussed led me to suspect that Parrett was still expected to take its yearly due. In December of 1959 I learned that this was so, and that Parrett is supposed to take in turns a man, a woman and a child.

Other tributes may be offered and accepted by less dangerous waters. There is a well-known spring, for instance, now built over, on the foreshore between Weston-super-Mare and Steepholm, which is covered by the tides, but in between whiles used to supply the cottagers with fresh, sweet water. An old inhabitant told me in 1920 or thereabouts that it always would do so as long as the fishermen threw back the first of their catch. 'You look after they and they'll see you don't come to want.' It is doubtful whether 'they' are sea-people, or the spirits of the well, or of the two rivers which run out near Weston. The Manx fishermen were in the habit of throwing out the first of their catch to the sea-people to gain protection in storms, and it seems likely that the Weston men paid tribute to the same creatures, so that the tides should withdraw at the right time.

WELLS AND SPRINGS

Somerset is rich in wells and well traditions. The classification of the various types is difficult because they often overlap in function and properties, but they can be roughly divided according to their functions into magical and curative wells. Magical wells are wishing wells, dangerous wells and those bringing success to lovers. Curative wells are so various and often so specialized that it seems best to list them in an Appendix.[1] When we come, however, to the guardianship of the wells we cut across the functions. The wells at which some kind of tribute is paid to the guardian spirit are generally regarded as fairy wells, though some of them are credited with curative properties, as for instance Bathwater at Dulverton, for sore eyes, where a red rag has to be left behind. There are ten reputed fairy wells in the county, which may be distinguished from other wishing wells by having gifts left of rags, pins or coins for the Well Spirit. Some of these are healing and some wishing wells, and some have no definite properties, but it is thought unlucky to pass without leaving some tribute. Not all wishing wells have a known fairy guardian, and sometimes the objects dropped into them are used more as a means of divination than as a gift. If a pebble dropped into a well goes to the left your wish is thwarted, if to the right it is granted in part, if it falls straight, you will have all your desire. Pins that cross as they settle are unlucky, if they lie together it foretells a happy marriage, if they drift apart, so will you and your lover. As for coins, silver is the best, but farthings will do. It is lucky if the coins fall straight and lie flat. Coins must never be taken from a wishing well. The only two people known to have stolen from one were both hanged in later days, one at Ilchester and the other at Taunton. All wishes must be made in silence.

Nether Stowey Blind Well is a curative fairy well, where rags are left on a tree and pins dropped in the water. In 1935 I collected a story about two brothers which seems influenced by the widespread belief in the sympathy between twin brothers. It belongs to Stowey Blind Well in East Somerset.

'There was two brothers and they parted, but they promised to meet again down whoame in seven year. The one he was blinded in the Wars and the other he lost his sight, but for all that they set out. Folks helped them along times, and times they just travelled on in their darkness. And they heard their brother's voice asking for aid, and they both run, and they fell in the spring and it washed their sight back again. Wonderful good for the eyes 'tis.'

The efficacy of some of the wells is still believed in. In June of 1961 I collected two fragments about Skimmington Well, which is spoken of as a fairy well, though there is no mention of tribute in the following story.

[1] See Appendix I.

'There was a labouring man at Shapwick, and he had rheumatism so badly that he was crippled up. In the end he had to give up working, his limbs were useless. So he went to the old Witch. She looked at him, and she said, "Jack, my man, yew've no need to be this way. Yew go over to Skimmington Well. 'Tis on Rock Hill, over tew hawthorn hedges. Bathe in it at sunrise for dree mornings, and the use will come back to your limbs." So he went away to Curry Rivel and he bathed dree times, and he was cured of his ailments and worked for years afterwards.'[1]

The other fragment seems to contain some memory of revels at the well.

'Skimmington Well is where they go to dance on Midsummer Day and cure all their ills. 'Tis on Rock Hill.'[2]

Several of the dangerous wells were saints' wells, but some were associated with witches. There was, for instance, the Witches' Well at Pardlestone on the Quantocks, which has now ceased to be dreaded. I was told in 1950 that now ash trees grow round it it is safe. A few years earlier, however, I had been told more explicitly how it was sained.

'There was a well out over where they witches did go to meet times. 'Twas down a dark lane, and folks were feared to death to go by it and to let their stock drink. So they got a gifted man, and he said the right words and threw salt in it and drove 'em all away.'

Most of the saints' wells were curative, but there was a wishing well amongst them, and St. Agnes' Well at Cothelstone was resorted to by lovers. This is not surprising, for St. Agnes Eve was traditionally one for love divination, but St. David seems occasionally to have played the same part, if we may judge by the following story, told me by two old sisters who had been born in Bagborough and had returned there on a visit when I saw them.

'There were a maid-servant, see, and she were coming on in years and she do serve a farmer's wife as were high in station. Proper tackalackey she made of the dear soul, and she having no living kin. 'Twas pitiful, and her a-longing for a parcel of children underfoot, even if 'twas only to call her Auntie. But there, 'twadn't to be, and her with a heart so full a-drip with loving kindness as a honey comb. Oh, she were a proper mannerly maiden, no ways like her mistress who were just a old ewe dressed up lambs fashion

[1] 10/6/61, Weston Zoyland W. I. Farmer's wife, born at Shapwick.
[2] 9/6/61, Curry Mallet W. I. members.

and spending her days living two-three steps from nothing. But it didn't seem like the maiden couldn't never meet up with a proper man for her. She wadn't no summer morning to look at, poor soul, and her mistress kept her so thin as a·yard of pump water. But there Providence knows best! There were a old fellow over by Aisholt, and he were such a upstanding courageous man he'd a never got round to marrying, let alone finding the bravery to walk arm in crook with a maiden. Well o' course he were lonely like she. And it come to a St. Agnes Eve when maids creepy over to her well at Cothelstone and whisper their heart's desire when 'tis dark, and if St. Agnes do fancy the maiden she'll send a husband that year. Now the poor maid she were coming to the end of her days of womanhood and beginning to blossom about the head, and she were desperate unhappy about it. Her heart was all a-set on children, and she find bravery to slip out after farm's a-locked up. She didn't feel 'twere mannerly to worrit St. Agnes over one who was so on in years when there was young maidens as plentiful as blackberries, so what do the dear soul do but go down all in the dimmet to the Wishing Well in Seven Wells Coombe. Proper unket well 'tis, and hard tew find. But St. Agnes must ha' knowed, for she found'n though there wadn' but little moon, and old fellow he d'hear summat down in coombe and come to look-see. He were a wise old man and nothing hurted he, but he were shy of folks, seems like. Well, whether 'twere St. Agnes I can't say, but in a year the farm was sold up and the maid was a-wed to the old fellow. So quiet as a sheep the man was, wouldn' downarg no-one, but he made her a good husband. In a year or two she'd a babe in the cradle and one under her apron, and two clinging to her skirts, and they was all so happy as daisies in the sunshine, so they say. But there, "they say so is half a liar." '

SAYINGS AND BELIEFS ABOUT WATER

Running water is a holy thing. *Exmoor, 1951.*

Still water is dangerous to children. *Bridgewater, 1953.*

Water that is long coming to the boil has a devil in it. Stir him out with an iron spoon. *Lower Vexford, 1940.*

Spring water is best for the complexion and will cure all manner of ills. *North-east Somerset, 1950.*

When you get a pail of water from the spring always tip a few drops on the ground for good manners. *Lower Vexford, 1940.*

If you want something very badly go down to the spring at night and whisper it three times, then sign a criss-cross above the water and you will get what you asked for in some way, *but you may not like it. Farm labourer, Quantocks, about 1912.*

2

Trees, Plants and Leechcraft

A. TREES

THE remnants of ancient tree worship are clearly to be traced in the Somerset tree beliefs. Oak, ash, beech, holly and apple are all highly esteemed trees, though oaks are believed to be formidable. Hawthorn and elder are of doubtful character, walnut is the Devil's tree, and alder, willow and birch are all sinister. I have found tree traditions all over Somerset, but those about the oak are the most frequent. In Muchelney, about 1953, I was given a rhyme about trees.

> Ellum do grieve,
> Oak he do hate,
> Willow do walk
> If yew travels late.

The explanation of this is that the elm is believed to pine for its fellows. If two trees out of four are cut down the remaining two will soon die. Oak, on the other hand, resents cutting, and a coppice which has sprung from the stumps of cut-down oak trees is generally shunned. At Hookway near Oare Post there was a coppice of oaks which had been felled during the Second World War. Many of the Oare and Porlock people were much perturbed by the cutting, and the local blacksmith, who acted as chauffeur for me in 1945, refused to drive that way. It was quite clear that he felt that revengeful spirits were hovering about the place. There was an oak coppice, too, above Butterfly Combe at Holford, near Devils Gallop, where none of the local people would pick the whortle-berries, though some particularly fine ones grew there. I have heard it said several times in the Quantocks between 1905 and 1912 that if you cut down an oak you will hear it screaming and will die within the year, or at the best be taken very ill. Oak, however, will be your guardian if it likes you.[1]

---

[1] A farmer at Clatworthy.

The following story, which I was told by the old men at Taunton Market and have heard repeated several times since, illustrates the general tone of belief about the oak.

The Tree's Revenge

There was a old farmer, see, and he had two sons, and him and the eldest they was as cheese-paring a team as you'd a-meet outside Bristol City. Always getting a bit more on the sly they was, though farm were sizable enough to keep twenty men to work. 'Twas nothing but contrive and worrit to snip off a bit of hedge here and a plot of grass there from what wasn't theirs nohow. Seemed like they couldn't take their meals in contentment at the plenty they had, and the youngest he got so that he wouldn't agree at all. He was one that would sooner give with a kindly word. Now the farm lay by the forest, and the youngest son he'd always been the one as had gone to market through it, but he took care to start at sunrise and was back by sunset, and asked the great oak by the gate if he 'med go droo'. So when the old man begins to take away wood and cut timber without a word to anyone — though he'd fine coppices over-right the farm — youngest son he took himself away from hoame. Trees didn't say nothing — which was bad. If they do talk a bit you do get a warning, but if they'm dead still there's summat bad a-brewing. And zo 'twas. Be danged if gurt oak didn't drop a limb on cart and timber and farmer and eldest son. Killed they two stark dead outright, but when youngest came to rescue the dead the tree rustled fit to deafen he. Told he how 'twas I spose; nor it hadn't hurted the cart-hoss on account it was shod. So youngest he gets farm and gives back all the old man nicked, and puts fences to their rightful places, and prospers. And he drove the cart-hoss to market through forest all his days, and trees never followed 'n nor closed in about 'n, nor let drop branches. But he had a criss-cross of nails on each boot to make sure.

One of the few completely holy trees in the forest is the beech. If you are lost in a wood at night nothing can harm you if you sleep under a beech[1] tree, and if you say your prayers under a beech they will go straight up to Heaven.[2] If you swear under the beech tree the leaves will rustle, and a bough may even drop on you.[3]

[1] A maid-servant at Mells, 1925.   [2] Greenham, 1942.
[3] Broomfield, 1912, and W. I. Buckland St. Mary, 1961.

Ash and mountain ash or *wicken* are also protective trees. Carters' whip-stocks and drovers' gads were commonly cut from quicken or hazel to protect the beasts from spells, and quicken crosses were used against witches and stuck up in the bartons on Hallow's E'en. The ash shares the wicken's sanctity. An ash stick was the one to use against snakes, and in West Somerset it was the custom to hang a wreath of flowers on the ash tree nearest the farm to protect men and cattle against snake bites for the year. The ashen faggot, a bundle of ash twigs bound round with withies, was always burned on Christmas Eve, because it was said that Our Lady lay by an ash fire at Christmas, and the water to wash Our Lord was heated at it.

A strange Exmoor belief is that a wicken tree must never be planted near an apple, as one will kill the other.[1] The same is believed of the oak and walnut, but this is understandable, for the walnut is thought to be an evil tree, and the oak, however difficult its temper, is sacred, while the apple and the wicken are both good. There is, however, something ambivalent about the attitude to the apple tree. The apple was used as sanctuary in catching games when I was a child, but the Somerset children's rhyme might have another interpretation.

> 'Bogey, Bogey, don't catch me!
> Catch that girl in the apple tree!'

reminds one that in the early *Orfeo and Eurydice*, Eurydice was carried off to Fairyland because she slept under an apple tree, as Sir Lancelot was carried off by the four witch queens in Malory. The apple, too, is often the host of the mistletoe, a plant not allowed amongst the Christmas decorations in church. Yet in the orchard at least the apple is a benevolent character. The Apple Tree Man is the guardian spirit of the orchard and is said to reside in the oldest apple tree. A story relevant to this is *The Apple Tree Man*, to be found in *Folktales of England*.[2] When I was a child a schoolfellow showed me a very old apple tree in her orchard, and told me in a whisper that it was the Apple Tree Man. Other spirits attached to the orchard are the Colt Pixy and Lazy Lawrence.

A berried holly is a sacred tree which seems to belong to a male cult. The Holly Boy and the Ivy Girl are still spoken of at Christmas time. Holly must not be brought into the house before Christ-

---

[1] Exmoor, 1900. I heard the same from a Lancashire gardener in 1949.
[2] Briggs and Tongue. Routledge and Kegan Paul 1965.

mas Eve, and then only by a man.[1] Sterile holly is said to be
dangerous to man and beast,[2] and on a year when holly does not
berry it is wise to put a sprig of ivy or box into the holly wreath
to break the ill luck. There was a sterile holly near Robbers' Bridge
in the Weir Valley that cast a shadow in the moonlight like a hangman's noose. It was said that anyone who stepped over the shadow
would come to be hanged. The tree's ghost was as much dreaded
as the tree itself.

'There's ghosty tales about stoans 'n old trees. There war a big
holly bush between Oare 'n Hookway, where things was seed, 'n
arter they tooked he down there was terrible strange happenings,
— ah, proper queer they was. A gurt holly tree 'twas down to
Oare.'[3]

Another tree of a mixed character is the hawthorn. It is death to
bring the white hawthorn flower into the house. On the other hand,
though enemies of man, hawthorn trees are friendly to cattle, and
the stock always flourish if there are hawthorns in the field.[4] If
thorn bushes are ploughed up all the goodness leaves the land; the
trees should only be cut for healing. There are holy thorn trees,
cuttings from the Glastonbury Thorn, at Ilminster, West Buckland,
Whitstanton, Nailesbourne and Dursborough in Quantoxhead.
People used to gather round them on Christmas Eve to watch them
bud and flower. The belief was also associated with the kneeling of
the cattle, as this Ilminster legend shows.

The Beast's Thorn

A pilgrim who went from Ilminster to Glastonbury was asked
by the villagers to bring back some holy relic to bless the village.
They were all much disappointed when he brought back a single
thorn which might have been plucked from any hedge. He told
them that it was part of the Crown of Thorns, but no one believed
him. He planted it, however, and prayed beside it morning and
evening. The strange thing about the thorn was that it began to
shoot and grow at an uncanny rate, and people began to draw away
from the pilgrim and look at him with suspicion. The thorn still
grew, and by Christmas it was quite a little tree. The pilgrim
promised that it would bloom on Christmas day, but Christmas

[1] Fiddington, 1961; Kilve, 1960; Buckland St. Mary, 1961.
[2] Kingston St. Mary, 1938 and 1960.
[3] Walter Badcock, Triscombe, 1955.   [4] Tarr Ball, 1940.

day passed and nothing happend. But on Old Christmas Eve at night the whole village was wakened by a great clatter in the street. People threw on their clothes and ran to the windows, and there below them went all the sheep and cattle of the place, which had been securely shut in folds and bartons hours before. The richest farmer's master bullock was at the head of them. People tumbled out into the streets and followed their cattle. They went straight to the little thorn tree which stood blossoming white in the moonshine. The pilgrim was kneeling there already. Just as the crowd came up the first stroke of the midnight chime sounded. At that the great master bullock lowed aloud and knelt down on the frosty ground and every beast knelt with him. The stiff knees of the villagers were loosened and they knelt, too, among the beasts. And that is how Ilminster knows that it has a holy thorn.

A homelier version of this was told to L. Key in Taunton in 1948. The old man who told it has since died. His experience could be dated about 1888–90.

'When I was a bwoy we did make up our minds to take a look-see on Chrissmus Eve to find if the tree did bloom and cows come to kneel to 'en. So we went along lane to Nailesbourne like, and 'twas dark, couldn't see nothing at all. Proper black, and we had no light, zee, and all to a zudden there was breathings all around us, zeem-like, whichever way we'd turn. Thic lane were vull of cattle, and we just turn and run for it. No, we never zee no thorn blossom nor I wouldn't go now if I was asked. Vull of cows thic lane was.'

Elder is variously regarded as a witch tree or a fairy tree. Its leave must be asked before it is cut, and it must never be burnt or used for anything but healing. On the Blackdown Hills a man called Webber committed suicide, and though he was buried in the proper way at the cross-roads with a stake through his heart he still walked. In 1905 a Blackdown shepherd suggested to my brother that this was because the stake had been made of elder wood. The way the elder springs up again after it has been cut may have had something to do with this. The tree is loth to die. There is a vague story on the Quantox seaboard about a man who tried to cut down an elder which happened to be a disguised witch and which bled. This may only be a form of the wide-spread belief that elders bleed when they are cut down. The tree is more often connected with fairies than witches. On the Quantox seaboard it is said that anyone who stands under an elder tree on Midsummer Eve can see the fairies and get the wish of his heart, but he will die within the year. The same belief is held in Scandinavia.

The alder, the willow and the birch are all evil trees. If you venture into an alder holt alone you may never be seen again. 'They'll keep 'ee.'[1] The willow has a way of following one on a dark night muttering to itself,[2] and the birch, from which the witches cut their brooms, is traditionally the tree of death. 'The One with the White Hand' appears to be a birch tree, more especially as a version of the tale told by preparatory schoolboys to each other expressly mentions a birch.

The One with the White Hand

The One with the White Hand was a terrifying spirit who haunted the moorland near Taunton. It would rise at twilight out of a scrub of birch and oak and come drifting across the empty moor to lonely travellers so fast that they had no time to escape. She was deadly pale with clothes that rustled like dead leaves and her long, white, skinny hand looked like a blasted branch. Sometimes she pointed a finger at a man's head, and then he ran mad, but more often she laid her hand above his heart and he fell dead, with the impress of a white hand on his chest to show what had killed him.

At length a farmer who lived near determined that he would lay the spirit if he could, so he set out near sundown towards the moor with a slice of bread in one pocket and a good quantity of salt in the other. As the sun set he heard the rustling and saw the spirit sweeping towards him, but he stood firm with his hand in his pocket. The white hand came out towards him, but he thrust his own hand, full of salt, right in the thing's face.

'And yur's another white hand to match 'ee,' he said. A wind got up in a moment, and the thing vanished, and never troubled that stretch of moor again.

Hazel trees, like wickens, are protective, but they have not the magical, wisdom-giving qualities which hazel nuts have in Highland and Irish tradition. Their power is to bestow fertility. A girl who goes nutting on a Sunday will meet the Devil, and almost certainly the baby will come before the wedding. But fertility in

---

[1] West Somerset, 1952. [2] Muchelney, 1900.

wedlock is also the result of a plentiful nut harvest. The prolific show of catkins in 1958 made a gardener remark to me quite seriously, 'Ah, us'll see plenty of prams in village later on. 'Tis a good thing road'll be done by Easter, busy as Piccadilly Circus 'twill be.' And a common proverb is 'Plenty of catkins, plenty of prams'. In 1939 a West Somerset man told me a story that shows that this is a matter of general and practical belief.

A village girl who had returned from London to be married had brought some modern notions back with her. She openly said that she did not mean to be hampered with babies too soon, but was going to enjoy her freedom a little longer. This outraged the village morality, and when she got to her new home she found among the presents a large bag of nuts to which most of her neighbours had contributed. The prescription seems to have been successful, for in 1939 she already had four children.

Some brief collected sayings about trees are to be found in Appendix I, B.

B. PLANTS

I gathered many fragments of gardening tradition in the first quarter of this century, but I have noted fewer recently. Many of these fragments had to do with the virtues of plants and some with methods and times of planting. A good many plants were recommended for their protective qualities. For instance, houseleek, picturesquely called 'Welcome-home-husband-though-never-so-drunk', if it grew on the roof, protected the house from witches and from being struck by lightning; if herb bennet grew near the house the Devil could do nothing in it; a bunch of onions over the door kept away both witches and illnesses; fennel over the door prevented the house catching fire, and wormwood was used against the evil eye. St. John's wort was considered invaluable for many purposes.

> 'Blessed, blessed in the ditch,
> Cures the itch and the stitch,
> And drives away the witch.'[1]

Among the pieces of cultural advice I received, one of the most interesting was a cautionary one — never to take cuttings from an

[1] 1907–12.

old, disused garden. They never thrive, and they poison your own plot of land.[1] I was told, too, that the gardens where 'they old monks was tew' would flourish well if you refrained from swearing in them.[2] On the Blackdowns and Brendons a cross is still marked on the earth of cottage gardens after spring planting.

Different plants need different treatment. To ensure a good cabbage crop make a cross on the stump every time you cut one. Mint is shy, one should never look at it for a month after planting it, it needs time to settle down.[3] Mint is a valuable herb to have, a sprig in the milk keeps it from turning and mint rubbed over a new bee-hive will keep the bees from deserting. Parsley must be planted on a holy day or the fairies will get it, and broad beans must be set in the Candlemas waddle — that is, in the waning of the February moon, or they will not flourish. The ancient association with death hangs round the beans still, for a white bean flower foretells a death in the family, and to sniff the scent of a bean field is equally fatal.[4]

A flowering myrtle is one of the luckiest plants to have in one's window, but its culture is difficult. When setting it one should spread out the tail of one's gown and look proud.[5]

Many wild plants were esteemed for their magical properties. Cowslips, primroses and forgetmenots were to be carried when searching for treasure or venturing into the haunts of the fairies, but they must be the right number of flowers at the right time and the right place.[6] Primroses are still used for protection on lonely bartons on Midsummer Eve. Daisies are the woman's flower. Moon daisies are used in a spell to bring back an unfaithful lover, and ordinary daisy chains are sometimes felt to be a protection for children.[7] Mugwort is still considered to be one of the most powerful of all the plants. An old man in Brompton Ralph said to me in 1906, 'If yew do pick'n right there idn't nothing yew can't wish vor.' In Coles Herbal, 1657, it was recommended for running footmen and in 1930 I was told at Wincanton, 'Put mugwort in your shoes and you can run all day.' It is also esteemed as a herb. The rhyme goes,

[1] A Somerset gardner, *c.* 1925.   [2] West Somerset, 1930.
[3] A schoolfellow's grandmother.
[4] Trull, 1909; Martock, 1907.
[5] Borders of Devon and Somerset, 19th century.
[6] Willett, 1953.
[7] A maid from Bruton, 1907.

c

'If they would eat nettles in March
And Mugwort in May
So many young maidens
Would not turn to clay.'

The small, wild scabious is one of the most esteemed of the wild herbs. It is said that it gained its name of devil's bit because the Devil was so angry at all the good it did that he tried to gnaw the root away. The root spread out its tendrils, however, and twisted them round him so that he was almost strangled. It is sometimes called 'devil's guts' because of its twisted roots.

Wild thyme, which is used as a herb, is thought to be dangerous to keep in the house as it smells of death.[1]

The old popular connection between flowers and fairies has been so much sentimentalized in whimsical children's stories that it is apt to be discounted altogether, but it is preserved in the Somerset names for some of the wild flowers. Greater stitchwort is called 'pixies', and if you gather it you are likely to be pixy-led.[2] Herb Robert is called 'Robin Hood'. In the North its name is 'death-come-quickly', but in Somerset they merely say, 'If 'ee pick'n someone'll take 'ee,'[3] and the suggestion is rather of fairies than the Devil. Red Campion is another flower that is accounted unlucky to pick, and is called 'Robin Hood' or 'Robin flower'. A periwinkle is called 'sorcerer's violet'. I have not heard that word applied to witches, but one old woman in West Somerset once said to me, 'they sorcerers do dancey in gallitraps,' which makes it probable that she used the word to mean pixies.

C. LEECHCRAFT

The various cures which I shall list below seem to have four origins; the herbal cures come from a well-tried and old tradition. Many of them are to be found in Gerrard and Culpepper, and some maintain their places in the modern *materia medica*. I have tried many of them myself and found them valuable. A second class, a small one, seems to be founded on the idea that if one can hand on a disease one will get rid of it. An example of this is the passing through a flock of sheep to cure bronchitis. Quite a number

---

[1] A gipsy, 1944.   [2] Exmoor, 1948.
[3] Roebuck, Quantock Hills.

of cures rely on the effect of a sudden shock, such as the cure for jaundice, to give a patient a sandwich with lice in it and tell him about it afterwards. A few are pure magic, such as the silver necklace to be worn by an epileptic patient.

There are a few herbs which are almost universal specifics. St. John's Wort is one; an infusion of the leaves will cure catarrh, grow hair, heal cuts and make a poultice for sprains. An ointment made from it is good for burns. Nettles are much valued for their dietetic properties, an infusion of nettle seeds will cure consumption, and a sharp beating with green nettles is an effective counter-irritant for rheumatism. Among the non-vegetable cures adders are particularly helpful. The fat mixed with lard and peppermint is good against rheumatism, adder skin worn round the hat prevents headaches and a shed adder skin will heal an open cut. The other cures I have listed according to their ailments, adding the curious names by which these ailments are sometimes described.

AILMENTS

Abscess (Apse)

Poultice with chickweed steeped in boiling water. This will burst the swelling.

A poultice of marshmallow leaves is soothing and healing.

A poultice of arum (lords and ladies) will cure a swelling.
Tatworth W.I.; South and West Somerset, 1907–57.

Adder's bite

'Ashing tree, ashing tree,
Take this bite away from me.'

Suck the wound and spit, then say the charm. Do this three times. If you can make it bleed, so much the better. *Farm labourer, Ivyton, 1912.*

Apoplexy (Appleplexus)

Eat plenty of wallflower buds in salads and jams.

Arthritis (Arthuritis)

Beat it with a holly spray. *Triscombe, 1955.*

Asthma

Go out at dawn while the dew is still heavy and lie down in a sheep fold or where sheep have lain. *Roebuck, 1933.*

Bites

Boil some mourning bride (garden scabious) and make a poultice to draw the poison out of the bite. At Castle Neroche in 1901 this was done to my small brother after the sow bit him . . . the wound was deep but healed well.

Dog bites. Let the wound bleed well then wash with hot water in which scabious is steeped, which makes a strong disinfectant. Cover with scabious leaves and leave on to check bleeding and heal wound. *West Somerset.*

Insect bites. Rub with elder leaves and cover with same, the rough side for drawing, the smooth side for healing. *Hawkridge Gipsy; Norton Fitzwarren.*

Bleeding

Cover with yarrow, plantain or birdsfoot trefoil. These are ancient wound herbs and will check bleeding. I have used all three on horses and ponies with cut legs. *Tatworth W.I., 1961.*

For nose bleeding rub knot grass into the nostrils. *Quantock broom squire.*

Bleeding charm. Make a cross three times and pour cold water on the wrists, dab it on the back of the neck and drink a glass saying the Lord's Prayer between each swallow, or say:

> 'Christ upon the Tree
> Take this blood for me.'
>
> *Mid Somerset, 1920–5.*

Blisters

The juice of lesser spearwort will raise blisters on your hands. I have blistered a pony with this with good effect. *Quantocks, 1956*

Boils

Make a poultice of goosegrass (also known as sweethearts or cleavers). *Bicknoller.*

Make a tea of young alder blossom and drink a wine glass full for three days. Leave alone for three days and repeat twice more. This

will bring about a mild attack of boils and clear your blood for
life. *East Harptree.*

Bone Injuries

Poultice with comfrey at once and bones will knit. Comfrey was
carried in medieval times by soldiers. *West Somerset.*

Bone Shave (Sciatica)

> 'Boneshave right, boneshave straight
> As the water runs by the stave (willow bushes)
> So follows boneshave.'

The patient lies beside a stream running south and repeats this
three times. *Exmoor.*

Broken bones

Bind injured limbs wrapped in a poultice of comfrey and say
over it three times:

> 'Our Lord rade
> The foal slade,
> Sinew to sinew and bone to bone
> In the name of the Father, Son and Holy Spirit.'
>
> *Exmoor.*

Bronchitis (Brown titus or Brown Kitties)

Pour boiling water in a jug half filled with elder flowers and
blackberry leaves. Add sugar or honey and drink hot. *Tatworth W.I.,
1961; Weston Zoyland W.I., 1961.*

Always carry a blackberry shoot. Peel and nibble it if the cough
begins. *A Hedger, Bushpool, 1909.*

Drink elderberry syrup before going to bed. *Bagborough, 1906.*

A portion of honey from the comb three times a day. *Flaxpool,
1951.*

Eat raw limpets and snails. *Quantock and Polden Hills, 1955.*

Smoke dried coltsfoot and bramble leaves. *Exmoor gipsy, 1936.*

Make an ointment of lard and garlic and rub it on the soles of the
feet at night. *Halsway, 1957.*

Burns

Make a cross in spittle on the burn then cover with mallow
leaves. *Yeawe, 1952.*

Apply an ointment of fat and St. John's Wort. *Taunton, 1905–12.*

For a burned finger tip press hard on the lobe of your ear and the sting will go. *Crowcombe, 1955.*

Cancer

To ease cancer make a poultice of violet leaves and lay upon the swelling.

Eat violet buds in a salad.

Drink a tea made by pouring boiling water on violets or pansies, sweetened with honey. *Bathpool, 1905.*

It should be noted that violets are used by chemists for the alleviation of growths.

Corns

Soak an ivy leaf in vinegar and bind above corn. Repeat three days and the corn will come away. *Frome, 1957.*

Squeeze the juice of red campion on the corn several times. It will shrivel and come out. *Crowcombe, 1951.*

Rub it with the juice of greater celandine and it will come out with the blister. *Exmoor gipsy, 1942.*

Coughs and colds

Marsh mallow tea made from fresh leaves or sliced roots with the addition of a suitable paregoric. *Minehead area, 1950.*

Coltsfoot tea, as above, with blackberry buds. *Birchanger, 1937.*

Dried meadow-sweet added to a parsley infusion. *Pickney, 1912.*

To linseed tea add a heaped teaspoon of wild thyme and some sliced lemon. Take a tablespoonful every three hours to ease and cure a cough. *North Somerset, 1925.*

This is a most excellent cough remedy.

Cramp

Rub your feet with Jack in the Hedge (Garlic mustard). *Quantock woodman, 1912.*

Keep a tub of water under the bed.

Always go to sleep with your feet crossed. *A maid, Pitminster.*

Boil stems of periwinkle.

An infusion of dried powdered root of gladdon.

Rub your feet with the leaves of garlic mustard.

Bishops Lydeard W.I., 1958.

Yarrow worn inside your shoe.

Ear-Ache

Make a poultice of poppies and lay it against your ear. *Burnham-on-Sea, 1908.*

Heat an onion and place it in the ear. *Kingston St. Mary, 1959.*

Eczema

You may cure eczema in your stock by rubbing them with fox-glove leaves — *then wash your hands. A farmer, Hawkbridge, 1957.*

Eye troubles

Bruise the leaves of marsh mallow and lay them on sore or strained eyes. *Quantock broom squire, 1930.*

(I have found this very satisfactory.)

Boil chickweed and rose leaves and use as a lotion, or add unsalted lard and use as an ointment. *Farmer's wife, Stoke St. Mary, 1910.*

To clear your sight wash your eyes in dew. *Somerset, general.*

Wash the eyes in sea water then dry them on sphagnum moss. *Bossington, 1914.*

Make a decoction of birds eye and eye bright and dab tired eyes with it. *East Somerset.*

If you are troubled with the pin (cataract) a daily wash of eye-bright will help. *Western Hills.*

Go to the nearest Holy Well that cures sight and bring home a bottle of water in your left pocket. *Mid Somerset.*

Fits of Epilepsy (The falling sickness)

Cut the front paws off a live toad and hang on a red thread round the neck. *South Somerset, nineteenth century.*

Gold rings on every finger will cure the falling sickness. *A gipsy, Langley Marsh, 1920's.*

Wear a silver or gold ring on the first finger (the poisonous finger). *Mendips, 1925.*

Beg enough silver sixpences to make a necklace and always wear it. They must always be begged from the unmarried of the opposite sex. *Exmoor, 1904; North Petherton, 1910, 1911.*

Go round a Holy Well on your knees backwards at sunrise, and leave a red cloth on a tree with your sickness tied up in it. *Mid Somerset Moors, about 1910.*

Carry a bottle of water from Stogursey Well. *Stogursey, 1911.*

Crawl round the church at night and sleep on the altar steps. *Exmoor.*

Foot soreness

Infuse marigold flowers in warm water and bathe the feet.

Haemorrhage

Drink an infusion of dead nettle and bruised plantain leaves. *Old cottager near Cothelstone.*

Lie flat in the form of a cross and drink cold water. *Cottager, Cannington, 1905.*

Lie flat on your back with your hands crossed.

Bathe the back of the neck and forehead with cold water, or cover with wet leaves.

Drink cold water and say the Lord's Prayer three times, with three drinks of water between each prayer.

Western Hills, 1905–12.

Headache

An infusion of the leaves of viper's bugloss or of wood betony drunk hot, or an infusion of mint leaves, drunk hot or cold. *West Quantock Group W.I., 1959.*

Hiccups

Say the Lord's Prayer and take a sip of water from the wrong side of the mug between each sentence. *Washerwoman, Taunton, 1905.*

Hold your nose and close your mouth and count twenty backwards. *Schoolfellows, Taunton, 1905–12.*

Indigestion (Interjections)

Drink the juice of two juniper berries in hot water or eat the berries fasting, never more than ten berries a day. *Gipsy, Langley Marsh, about 1928.*

White poplar bark boiled and the infusion drunk will relieve night sweats and indigestion with flatulence. It is also good for fevers. *North-east Somerset.*

Inflammation (Infloration, or information)

Make a hot fomentation of stewed slugs. *Crowcombe, 1955.*

Give a decoction of sliced roots of heath milkwort. *Exmoor gipsy, 1945.*

Poultice with leaves of marsh mallow and give infusion of the same. 'Yew do dap'n on where pain's bad 'n yew do drink the water leaves was scalt 'n.' *West Somerset, 1910.*

Wrap the patient in a sheep's pelt, new flayed, or kill a lamb, cut it open and place the patient's feet in the warm corpse. *Farmer, Brendons, 1910.*

Insomnia

Drink an infusion of lime flowers and sleep on a pillow stuffed with lavender. *Taunton Deane.*

Jaundice

One louse from a lady's head boiled in milk. *Told to a district nurse by an old labourer, Crowcombe, 1952.*

Spread cattle lice between bread and butter and give to patient. Afterwards tell him what he ate. He may be sick, but he'll never have jaundice. *A quarryman, Triscombe, 1949.*

Lung trouble

Drink a bowl of snail broth every day for a month. *Taunton, 1907.*

Nursing troubles

Place a hot compress of peppermint leaves on the breasts to relieve the 'curdled milk'. *Cottager, Cothelstone, 1912.*

Pneumonia (New Harmoniums, Pewmoaner)

Wrap the patient in the fresh flayed pelt of a calf and place his feet on a bull's milt (spleen). *West Somerset.*
I was told of this being done successfully on a remote farm on Exmoor about 1942.

Rashes

Rub with dock leaves or plantain. *Tatworth W.I., 1961.*

Rheumatism (Screwmaticks or screws)

Carry a potato in your pocket.
Get stung by bees, then use plantain leaves to ease the stings.

Exmoor.

Make an infusion of traveller's joy leaves and drink a wineglassful every day. *Brendon gipsy.*

Beat it with a holly spray. *Minehead, 1956.*

Rupture

Split a maiden ash and pass a child through three times. Bind up tree with a hay band. *Blackdown Hills, 1900.*

This must be done on a Sunday at sunrise, from east to west. *Exmoor.*

Stings

Bee stings. Rub with plantain leaves. *Sampford Brett.*

Nettle stings. Rub with a dock leaf, elder or dandelion. *Lawford, 1954.*

The stitch

Touch your knee, spit and make a cross in spittle on your boot. *Bruton W.I., 1961.*

Swelling

Get someone of the opposite sex to cross it and say in secret:

> There came two angels out of the North
> One brought fire
> One brought frost
> In frost
> Out fire
> In the name of the Father, the Son and the Holy Ghost.

Gardener, Combe Florey, 1957.

Toothache

Chew tobacco or cloves. *Nailsbourne, 1959.*

Ulcers (Alices)

Make a poultice of chickweed. This does equally well for boils or hard swellings.

Bathe with an infusion made by pouring boiling water on mallow leaves.

Use mallow leaves as a poultice. *Kingston St. Mary, 1933.*

Varicose Veins

Crush mallow roots and make with unsalted lard into an ointment. Use also for sore feet. *Western Hills, 1905–12.*

Pour boiling water on marigolds, flowers or leaves and use at intervals. *Roebuck, 1954.*

Warts

Magical cures

Count pebbles to the same number as the warts and put them in a bag and throw them over your left shoulder. 'There was an old woman at Flaxpool charmed warts, she just counted them and didn't speak.' *Crowcombe W.I., 1948.*

Tie a white horsehair round them. *Taunton, 1905–25.*

Rub an elder root on them, cut as many dents in it as there are warts, bury it, and as it decays your warts will vanish. *Stoke St. Mary, 1905–12.*

Cut a cross in a potato and throw it away saying —

> 'One, two, three
> Warts go away from me,
> One, two three, four,
> Never come back no more.'

South Somerset, 1920's.

Tie as many pebbles in a bag as you have warts and 'drop'n in water then no-one else won't pick'n up and get 'n'. *West Somerset, 1952.*

Stick a pin in an ash tree up to the head and say:

> 'Ashy tree, ashy tree,
> Pray buy these warts off me.'

Quantocks, 1912.

Herbal Cures

Rub them with the wool inside a bean pod, or the milk from a scarlet pimpernel. *Crowcombe W.I., 1958.*

Dip ivy leaves in vinegar and tie over them. They will drop off. *Taunton, 1958.*

Rub them with — Greater celandine, sun-spurge, red campion, sow thistle, dandelion, buttercup, petty spurge, or navelwort. *Various W.I.'s, 1958–61.*

'My little girl had warts on her hands this year. All over them. Yes, she had sixty-four in the end and her teacher said, "Heather, your hands don't look clean." It made them look dirty, see, and she minded it badly. We tried all sorts of things and then I took her to the Wart Charmer. Well, he took a piece of elder and he touched every wart twice, crossed it, and then he muttered to himself the prayer and then he slapped his knee and did this (a flicking away gesture). And he said, "If they haven't gone by April come and see me again in May." Well, by the end of April the warts were still there, all sixty-four, but we were busy, see, then in May I said, "Heather, what about your warts?" And they'd all gone and there was just the pink new skin, it still shows a little now.

I have a big wart on my finger, see, so I rubbed with the plant they call eggs and bacon (yellow toadflax), but I couldn't have done it right so it hasn't gone completely. It should make a black mark all round it. I'll try rubbing it with a slug as you say, or with Robin Hood (red campion).' *Postmistress, Mrs Triggol, Lydeard St. Lawrence, 1959.*

Whooping Cough (Hoppy Cough)

Put a fried mouse in the child's shoes. *Mid Somerset.*

Pass the child over the back of a donkey and under its belly. *Milverton, about 1911; Bruton W.I., 1961.*

Take it to the rider of a piebald horse for a cure. *Quantocks, 1912; Bruton, 1961.*

3

Birds, Beasts and other Small Deer

In Somerset, as elsewhere in England, certain birds are regarded as more important and significant than the rest. There are some general sayings, as that bird song in January means snow in February,[1] or that all the birds are married on St. Valentine's Day and the church bells should be rung for them,[2] but on the whole the traditions cluster round the significant birds, robins, swallows, magpies, ravens, owls, pigeons, gulls, the cuckoo and the farmyard cock.

The robin is regarded as a sacred bird, though it is doubtful whether its sanctity goes back to pre-Christian times. The tales and rhymes about it have a Christian flavour. It is said, for instance, that the robin's breast was once white, but that he flew through the fires of Hell to bring a drop of water on his beak to Our Lord on the Cross, and that his breast was scorched red as he went through;[3] or, alternatively, that he tried to pull out the thorns from the crown of thorns, and his breast was dyed with the blood.[4]

In several sayings and rhymes Jenny Wren is coupled with Robin Redbreast, as in

> Robin Herdick and Jenny Wren
> Are God Almighty's cock and hen,[5]

and

> When Ruddick's breast be fiery red,
> Cracky Wren must beg her bread.[6]

This refers to a belief that specially bright plumage on the robin's breast foretells a stormy winter. I have found no trace of robin sacrifice, like the wren sacrifice in some Celtic countries, but the robin's nest is under special protection.

---

[1] The Postmaster, Crowcombe, 1960.
[3] Galmington and Taunton Deane, 1904–12.
[5] South-west Somerset.
[2] A Laundress, Taunton, 1904.
[4] Glastonbury 1905.
[6] Exmoor.

Who so robs the Ruddick's nest
Neither prospers nor is blest.[1]

If a pet robin dies it will mean a death in the family, and a strange robin flying into the house is a sign of death.[2] Otherwise the bird is lucky.

Swallows and martins are also lucky birds, with traditional notions attached to them. They are said to be husband and wife, and in 1909 an old labourer repeated to me the ancient belief that martins have no feet. It is considered lucky to have them nesting round the house.[3] In 1908 a maid said to me in Taunton, 'A swallow's nest brings health, wealth and happiness.' They are watched for weather auguries. When martins fly in a cloud look for a cold spell:[4]

'Swallows fly high, no rain in the sky;
Swallows fly low, 'tis likely to blow.'[5]

On the Severn coast they say that sand martins are fairy birds, though the only reason they give for this is that they build in hollow banks.

Magpies are the rustic augur's birds. If you see a magpie on your right hand as you go to market whatever business you do first will be very lucky. If it is on your left, turn round and go home, for nothing will prosper with you that day.[6] If you see a single magpie when you are on a journey spit over your left shoulder to break the ill luck;[7] an onion, however, carried in the pocket will make this unnecessary,[8] and the bird is only unlucky when one is travelling alone.[9] A magpie perched on the house is unlucky, it brings illness to the hale[10] and death to the sick.[11]

A Somerset version of the common magpie rhyme was overheard from a carter's boy about 1890.

One is sadness, two is joy,
Three a girl and four a bwoy,
Five a wedding, six a loss,
Pyatt, don't 'ee steal my hoss.

[1] Somerset (general).　　　[2] Yeovil, 1910.　　　[3] Taunton Deane, 1920.
[4] Maid-servant, Taunton, 1908.　　　[5] Galmington, 1907.
[6] Frome, 1909; South Petherton, 1906; Chelvey, 1920.
[7] Goathurst, 1904; Taunton, 1959.　　　[8] Weston-Super-Mare, *c.* 1926.
[9] Kingston St. Mary, 1960.　　　[10] Cranmore, 1948.
[11] Blackdown, 1913; Enmore, 1937.

The raven is an ominous bird in Somerset, as elsewhere, but some dim connection with King Arthur in the popular mind prevents it from being considered evil. It is considered unlucky to name one, and they are called 'black birds' or 'crawses'; if you name them you will summon them.[1] If you hear a raven bark three times, turn round the other way and cross your fingers or you will meet with bad luck.[2] If you rob a raven's nest it is believed that a baby will die in your farm or village. A very old Exmoor farmer near Yearnor told me in the 1930's that when he was a boy he and a friend had stolen a raven's egg for a collector. They had been well paid, but they would never do so again, for his friend's baby sister had died and the best cow on his father's farm had lost her calf.

The royalty of the raven is traditional through most of Somerset. A Mr. Bolton, a Londoner, told me in 1936 that he had once sighted a raven above Porlock Weir, and had with great difficulty made an old labourer look up at it. The old man took off his hat and said, 'He be King, so he be,' and went back doggedly to his work; and I myself was told in south-west Somerset as late as 1956, 'If a pair of ravens cross your path raise your hat and wish them well. They are a king and queen.'

Some friends in Bridgwater illustrated the ill luck that follows an attempt to injure a raven by this rather fragmentary tale:

Farmer Loscombe's Race. There was once a pig-headed old farmer called Loscombe who lived out to Northmoor Green, and he didn't believe in ill-luck, so when he saw a pair of ravens he took a shot at them. Well, the fairies they took hold of his old pony, and they forced him to ride a race all night long and left him lying in a swound in his own cow-yard. From the day those ravens crossed his path he was a changed man. He pined away to a natomy. There was a wise woman at Bridgwater, and his wife she got her to come to the farm and fed her well, and she charmed the evil away.

Owls are even more unlucky birds than ravens, and like ravens they should not be named. When they hoot it is a sign that ghosts are about, and it is wise to stay indoors. 'Never answer their cry, or they'll have 'ee.'[3] The man who said this evidently regarded an owl as a witch in disguise. No harm came to the tailor in the humorous anecdote of the Blackdown Hills of the Tailor who answered the Owl.

[1] West Somerset, 1935.   [2] King's Barton, 1909.   [3] West Somerset.

There was once a village tailor who was more than half a coward, like many tailors before him. One night his work had kept him late, and he had to go through a dark wood to get home. There was no moon, and he wandered round and round in the wood, until at last in despair he yelled out, 'Man a-lost! Man a-lost!' Immediately a hoarse voice answered him, 'Who? Who?' 'Please, zur, 'tis me, zur,' faltered the tailor. 'Who? Who?' 'Jacob Stone, zur.' 'Who? Who?' 'Honest tailor as ever lived, zur,' faltered the tailor, nearly dead with terror. At the next call he would have swooned outright, but just then a light came glimmering through the trees, and his old neighbour, the woodcutter, came towards him. 'I heard 'ee a-call,' he said. 'Proper dark and unket 'tis in wood; full up of owl-burds 'tis tew.'[1]

A nightjar is even more sinister than an owl. It is a witch in disguise and sucks the cows' milk. It can only be shot with a silver sixpence.[2]

Round the Somerset seaboard there are strong traditions about seagulls, which are believed to be the souls of drowned sailors.[3] The West Somerset folksong, *The Cold, Cold Sea*, has this theme. Round the Porlock to Lynmouth coast they warn you not to feed a seagull, and above all not to look it in the eyes. If you do, one day when you are clinging to a wreck, or perhaps only swimming, it will find you and peck out your eyes, and leave you to drown. At Taunton Deane they say that, though the young gulls come inland every winter, there will be bad storms if the old gulls come in in flocks.

There are a good many traditions about pigeons, both wild and tame. An old coachman at Minehead about 1893 used to say that stolen pigeons would never mate, but if they were sent home even after two years they would mate again. He also said that a swallow-tailed pigeon brings luck, particularly if it is a white one. This is unusual, for white creatures, and even white flowers, are generally considered ominous. A white pigeon is traditionally a death token in the Tongue family, and at Huish Barton a pigeon is said to dash itself against the windows when any great misfortune is about to occur to the inmates.[4] The Somerset tale about the pigeon's traditional cry is a fuller one than I have found elsewhere, though there

---

[1] See F. W. Mathews, *Tales of the Blackdown Borderland*, pp. 113–14.
[2] Farm children, Brompton Ralph, 1904–6.
[3] Blue Anchor, 1906; Watchet, 1955.
[4] Monksilver, 1956; Stogumber W.I., 1960.

is an anecdote in Gloucestershire about a sheep-stealer strangled by the sheep he had stolen as he got over a stile.[1] Evidently the pigeon that the second brother heard was a stock dove, which has a peculiar, purring note.

The Sheep-Stealers of the Blackdown Hills. From Sampford Arundel.

There was once a sheep-stealer who had just killed a fat ewe on Blackdown and tied a rope round it to drag it away, when he heard a wood-quest begin to talk. 'Take two-o—,' it said, 'Take two–o–o!' 'That's good advice,' said the thief, 'Two will balance easier nor one.'

So he killed another, and tied the two sheep together, and slung them round him, one in front and one behind, and away he went. He got on well enough until he came to the stile at Hangman's Stone, and then, as he was climbing over, the front sheep swung behind him and the rope slipped up round his neck, and there he hung, a hanged man.

Now this thief had a brother who was nearly as bad as he. For a time he kept straight after his brother had been hanged, but by and by he fell off into his old ways. One morning he went up to Blackdown, just where his brother had gone, and he was stealing up to one of the sheep when a wood-quest began to cry again. This time it said, 'Rope, r–r–rope! Hang the man!' When the sheep-stealer heard that he ran home as fast as he could pelt and never went sheep-stealing again.

There are almost more traditions about the cuckoo, the bird of Spring, than any other. In spite of his association with marital infidelity the cuckoo is, on the whole, a lucky bird, and many rites and beliefs are associated with first hearing him. He should be heard first on the 15th of April,[2] if he does not arrive until the end of the month the harvest will be poor and late. There are a number of things to be done on first hearing him. You should run out of the house and stand on the grass if you wish for a good hay harvest,[3] turn the money in your pocket and say,

'Cuckoo, cherry tree,
Catch a penny, give it me,'

[1] E. S. Hartland, *County Folk-Lore Gloucestershire*, 1892, p. 51.
[2] Crewkerne, 1925.　　　　　[3] East Somerset, 1950; Bath, 1916.

D

so as to be rich for the year,[1] count the number of calls he makes, so that you may have that number of lucky months,[2] and pick up the soil from under your right foot so that you may not be troubled by fleas or lice.[3]

Then you must burst into activity — 'Always bustley when yew do hear the gew-kew.'[4] But before starting work a maid should take off her right shoe, and if she finds a hair inside it it will be the same colour as her future husband's hair.[5] Anyone who hears the cuckoo after old Midsummer Day (July 7th) will never live to hear him again.[6]

A Somerset version of the well-known cuckoo rhyme is

> In April
> Come he will;
> In May
> He sings all day;
> In June
> He changes his tune;
> In July
> Away he'll fly;
> In August
> Go he must.
> If he stay until September
> 'Tis as much as the oldest man can remember.

The wryneck is sometimes described as the cuckoo's mate.

Of all domestic birds the farmyard cock is believed to have most magical virtues. Keep a watch dog to drive off humans and a cock to drive off ghosts and your stock will thrive.[7] A cock scares the devil, so he is set on the Church Tower to face the four ways the wind blows.[8] A cock crowing at night before midnight means that death is passing by.[9] A cock crowing three times foretells the arrival of a stranger; and so on. A black cock was often used by the witches for a sacrifice, and perhaps for this reason it was said that a black and a white cock should never be kept on a farm together. They would fight, and the stock would never thrive.[10] There seemed, however, to be prejudice against a black cock by itself.

[1] Crewkerne, 1951; Triscombe, 1925.　　[2] Mendips, 1954.
[3] Crewkerne, 1951.　　[4] Exmoor, 1904; Luccombe, 1937.
[5] Maidservant, Chard, 1908.　　[6] Birchanger, Exmoor, 1930.
[7] Moorlynch, 1947.　　[8] West Somerset.
[9] Holford, 1910; Picton, 1938.　　[10] Mark, Mid Somerset, 1924.

B. BEASTS

The Somerset traditions pay very little attention to wild animals. Rats, mice, hares, rabbits and weasels are all felt to be sinister and to have some connection with witchcraft. If a rat gets into a bedroom it can only be killed by a white dog and a black cat together. All three are uncanny animals.[1] Mice running over the legs of horses and cattle are supposed to give them quarter-ail (paralysis). To drive mice away from your buildings and land bury one in a split ash tree and bind it up with nine bands.[2] All through Somerset a rabbit seen near the cows is suspected of being a witch in disguise. This may be by association with hares, which are everywhere suspected of being sometimes witches. I was told in East Somerset that if you turn back three steps after meeting a hare this will break the ill-luck. This seems an easier way of getting out of it than going home altogether, as the fishermen do. Strangely enough, I have found no traditions about foxes or deer.

The numerous traditions about domestic animals show clearly what a farming community we have in Somerset. There are many beliefs and tales about the conduct, ailments and colour of domestic animals, some of them connected with certain lucky or unlucky seasons of the year.

May is an unlucky time for birth. May cats catch no mice,[3] and one is well advised to drown May kittens at birth,[4] for they will take toads and spiders into the house,[5] and those that do so are no natural cats, but witches in disguise.[6] Foals born in May are dangerous, and are never really broken to handle.[7] I was told, too, by Exmoor gipsies never to trust a wall-eyed horse in May. On the other hand, a foal born on Midsummer Day will always win a race or be the master-horse in the team.[8]

The Man who got into his Cart. Buckland St. Mary. South

One May I met and stopped to talk to an elderly carter in a Quantock lane. After mutual admiration of the hill pony I rode, and his solid Shire mare, we went on to discuss their ways. Yes, they had both been difficult that day, and so, all unasked for, out

---

[1] Annie's Granny, Trull, 1908.
[2] John Ash, carter, Bishop's Lydeard, 1908; East Lucott, 1946.
[3] Stogumber W.I., 1960.   [4] Halsway, 1957.
[5] Halsway, 1958.   [6] North Somerset, 1936.
[7] West Somerset.   [8] North Somerset.

came this tale. "'Tis May, you see,' said the carter, '*Always "trouble-some" they are then*. I don't never trust'n, not even the old 'oss yur. I've worked she twenty years tew. My wife she have an old uncle over to they Blackdowns and they was carting stones to *mend their Church*.[1] Uphill 'tis and a nasty piece of road — they was those days, all stones — and there was a bit of a bank down over. I'd a-walk any 'oss up there and down over but there was a carter, he did get intew the cart see — and *summat* give his 'osses a fright and he was killed outright. In May 'twas. There's a verse over at the Church there. No, I don't like May, never tell what a 'oss will take and do.' *1936, Quantock Hills.*

Christmas Eve is a time of great significance for animals, though Old Christmas is often the operative date. Horses and cattle go down on their knees at midnight on Christmas Eve, and the Master-bullock lows three times,[2] and all animals can talk for an hour after midnight.[3] Sometimes we are more vaguely told that all animals can understand the language of men, and on a certain night they can all speak it. The stupid old farmer in the tale told me by a Blackdown shepherd in 1905 had evidently struck inadvertently on the night.

The Farmer and his Ox

There were an old farmer had an ox that were always okkud, an' one night he says to it, 'Thee girt stupid fule! I'd a-like to know who taught 'ee to be so okkud. I'd larn en!'

And at that the ox said: 'Why, 'twas thee, thee stoopid, girt fule!'

An old village sexton told me a story when I was a child about a dog who used human speech, but he did not say if it was on Christmas Eve. The words seemed lent to the dog in its despair.

The Faithful Dog[4]

A wretched old pauper died, and was buried on the North side of the Church, and nobody mourned for him but his half-starved and ill-treated dog. He laid himself down on the grave all that day and

---

[1] The Other World preferred it to fall into ruin. *This is the 'verse' on a stone:* May all carters who read this take warning and never get into their carts. 1860.
[2] Spaxton, 1908; Crowcombe, 1958; Fiddington, 1961.
[3] Stogumber, 1948.   [4] Mid Somerset, *c.* 1908.

all that night and howled, and presently the town began to make out the words of his lament.

> 'I'll lie on my master's grave
> For lo–o–o–ve, for lo–o–o–ve.
> Because he was all I did ha–a–a–ve,
> Because I was all he did ha–a–a–ve
> To lo–o–o–ve, to lo–o–o–ve.'

As the night went on the howls grew fainter, and in the morning the sexton found the dog dead, and being a Christian soul he buried it beside its master and told no-one. So that Church has two Church Grims to guard it now, and no devils will come within miles of it.

Every horse must have a holiday on Old Christmas Day or it will play up during the year,[1] and Good Friday is also a beasts' holiday.[2]

The traditions about colour are even livelier. White is generally felt to be unlucky. The prejudice against white cattle seems particularly strong around Crowcombe. I was told by a land-owner there —'When I first came to Crowcombe in 1951 we had a pure white heifer born, and the cowman wanted it destroyed at once. The Major was horrified. It was a lovely, healthy little creature, but the cowman still persisted.' Someone else in the same Institute said,— 'The Druid Cattle were white.' A year earlier I had been told at Crowcombe that white cows are fairy cows and are unlucky, and I heard the same thing at Kingston St. Mary in 1960. In Crowcombe, too, and in several other places, I was told that white cattle were poor men's cattle and would never thrive, and again in Stogumber in 1949 they said that white cattle were 'wisht' and would only thrive under a 'gifted' cowman. At Nailesbourne I learned that round Broomfield and Goathurst and the lower Quantock slopes farmers would not keep white cattle.[3]

White dogs, especially those with red ears, are believed to be uncanny.[4] At Lawford in 1951 I was told that all white dogs must be shut up on New Year's Eve, for anyone seeing them on that night would die before the year was out. White cats are also

---

[1] Farmer, Wheddon Cross, 1937.   [2] Farmer, Oare, 1948.
[3] 1960.   [4] West Somerset 1905–50.

believed to be unlucky unless they have blue eyes. Black cats, on the other hand, are lucky, here as elsewhere.

Even white feet are unlucky on horses. Four white feet are unlucky everywhere, but in Somerset they say:

> Three white feet don't try it or buy it,
> If it's a present don't ride it yourself;
> Wrap it up in paper and put it on the shelf.[1]

A skewbald or piebald horse, however, is so lucky that its luck extends to the rider, who can cure whooping cough.[2] A wish formed on seeing a piebald or skewbald horse will be fulfilled if you link your little fingers and do not look at its tail. You must not speak until you have wished, and you must say this charm to yourself —

> Black's white, and white's black,
> Over the nag's back.
> Make my wish come true, wish come true,
> Wish come very, very true.[3]

Like a skewbald horse a tortoiseshell cat is thought to be lucky. One is recommended to keep them, as they will always be good mousers.[4] They are all supposed to be female, the males are brindled or ginger.

Horses, cats and dogs are all supposed to see ghosts; cats get on well with them, and can sometimes be seen purring and rubbing against them.[5] This is all part of the general uncanniness of the cats. It is never wise to discuss unket things when a cat is present, it knows too much already.[6] The suspicion of being a disguised witch hangs over all unknown cats. A West Somerset man told me in the 1930's that a strange cat must never be let in after dark — it will harm the children and curdle the milk. Unlike cats, dogs are the enemies of ghosts, and drive them away by barking. Horses are frightened of ghosts, and will always shy away from a place where a horse has been killed or blood has been shed, even if it was years ago.[7] Oxen and donkeys are both safe against ghosts and evil spirits because of their association with the Nativity. Where horses fail to deal with supernatural troubles oxen are resorted to. In the

---

[1] Lydeard St. Lawrence, Crowcombe W.I., 1957.
[2] This is generally believed throughout Somerset.
[3] Schoolfellows, Taunton Deane, 1908–18.
[4] Chedzoy, 1948.   [5] Taunton, 1908–48.
[6] South and Mid Somerset, 1928–50.
[7] An old groom, North Somerset, 1905.

traditions about Wiveliscombe Bottom which I collected between 1906 and 1952, the ghost of Sir John Popham was laid with the help of oxen.

Sir John Popham, the hanging judge, broke his neck in Wilscum Bottom, where there is a deep pit that is said to lead directly down to Hell. After his death an oak tree grew up there which was thought to contain his spirit, and the place grew so dangerous in the common estimation that the people of Wellington made a determined attempt to lay the ghost. They sent for a conjurer to advise them and he said that the oak must be uprooted. So the people got teams of horses and put chains of cold iron round the oak, covered their ears in case it might scream when it was uprooted, and began to haul. The conjuror must have been a doubtful character, for the chains snapped at first pull, and the teams and drivers ran home as fast as they could go. The chains were mended with the help of three blacksmiths for luck, but no one would risk the danger again till an old ploughman, who was very much respected for the sanctity of his life, went to one of the farmers and said that if he could have the help of ten oxen he would pull up the tree. He said he had seen the oxen kneeling on Christmas Eve, and he was sure no harm would come to them. They let him take the oxen, but they kept well away. He took a Bible in his pocket, and singing psalms so loudly that he could be heard from Wiveliscombe to Wellington, he wound the chains round the oak. Then he called to the oxen and the tree came out as easily as a carrot. It screamed loud enough as it came, but it did the ploughman no harm, nor the cattle, and the Wellington people covered their ears. The ghost escaped from the tree somehow, though, before it was burned, and took refuge in Wilscum Copse, but it had been so daunted that it did not trouble anyone for a hundred years.

The donkey is further hallowed by its association with Palm Sunday, when it is said to have received the cross upon its back. This story, which I was told by an Exmoor gipsy woman in 1938, well expresses the half-humorous veneration which is felt for the donkey.

The Liddle Dunk Foal

'There was a liddle small dunk foal and he wanted to go look-see at life, so when his old mammy weren't a-looking he trit-trotted off on his wankly liddle legs.

'First go off he met an old witch.

' "I'll have 'ee!" say she, but when her touch 'n her got burned. "Drat!" says she, "Born on a Zunday, I'll be bound!"

' "Like all dunks, my mammy d'say;" say the liddle small dunk foal, and he went on along. Then he met Bogey.

' "I'll have 'ee!" say Bogey, but when he grab'n his fistesses fried. "Yow!" say Bogey, "Yew've a criss-cross on yewr back, keep away vrom me!"

' "Like all dunks, my mammy d'say," say the liddle small dunk foal, and he went on along till he come to a gallitrap.[1]

' "Be off out of that!" say the Pixies. "Us can't ride 'ee, and now yur yew comes treading in our ring, and yew just seben days old!"

' "So was all dunks once, so my mammy d'say," say the liddle small dunk foal.

'Then they all says, "Be off whoame! Quick now!"

'So he trit-trotted back to his mammy. And furst she kicked 'n fur gooin' stray and then she gived 'un his dinner.'

The belief in the horseman's word, which, breathed into a horse's nostrils will ensure instant obedience, is strong in Somerset. It is referred to in the story of St. Aloys and the Lame Nag in Part III. There seems to be a trace of some similar word which can be spoken in healing cattle.

It is uncertain whether pigs are able to see ghosts, but they are gifted by tradition with the power of seeing the wind.[2] In old times the smallest pig of the litter, or 'nestle-tripe', was commonly dedicated to St. Anthony and given over to the town to feed until it was fat enough to be killed. There is, I believe, a Tantony Pig in a stained glass window in Langport Church, and as a child I was told this story about it, which is rather reminiscent of the medieval legend, *The Bell of Atri*.

The Tantony Pig

'There were a little nestle-tripe as were made a Tantony Pig, and everyone were that sorry for 'en that he grew twice so fast and fat with all he were gived to eat. There were a bell with a rope outzide clerk's cottage, and pig learned if he shook rope some'un 'ood come a-running to help, so when butcher time come along Tantony Pig he ups and daps along to rope and rings 'en hard for

---

[1] A fairy ring. [2] Brendons, 1943.

help. After that the town 'oodn't let 'en be bacon, so he runned
round and eat up all their rubbidge for 'en grateful, and a wur a
Tantony Pig all his days.'

C. INSECTS AND REPTILES

As might be expected there are more traditions about bees in
Somerset than about any other insects. In Somerset, as elsewhere,
bees must be told when the master of the house dies, and the hives
must be put into mourning. Some say that they must be turned
round.[1] Bees are believed to be weather prophets.

> 'If bees stay at home, rain will come soon,
> If they fly away, fine will be the day.'[2]

Bees are said to dislike anyone watching them while they drink, and
to bring bad luck on any one who does so.[3] A strange belief is that
after twenty years they will revolt against the bee-master and must
be sold before this happens.[4] An old woman in West Luccombe
told me a good deal about the bee traditions current in her part of
the country.

'Bees is strange mortals. There idn't many as bees'll take to. My
grand-dad he'd say his bees all knowed he when they met'n out to
his day's labour. Proper vine bee-master he were tew, but he d' give
his bees to my uncle afore the twenty years were up — ah, they
went willing. Come twenty year your bees will turn on 'ee, no
matter. So he do give they away willing, and they d' go willing.
Strange mortals is bees, yew d'need tew study their ways. Won't
never be seed drinking, bees won't. There were a girt fule wench
knowed this tew, but her were curious, see. She were dapping
along to Revel, so fine as a cow wi' tew tails and she see a tired bee
light down by edge of river. What does the fule do but her ups and
tiptoes and spies on 'n. Her wad'n no butterfly, so what does bee do
but sits down on her girt poking nose and let her have it. Twice her
size they say her nose was, and twad'n no mistaking it afore. Wad'n
no Revel for she.'

A wild bee is called a drumble-drone, and a wasp an apple-
drame.

[1] Crowcombe, 1954.   [2] East Somerset, 1946.
[4] Exmoor, 1948.   [3] Bishop's Hull, c. 1909.

'An apple-drame and a drumble-drone
Were all there wert to see.
The apple-drame lay dead in the snow
The drumble-drone in the tree.'[1]

In West Somerset a chirping cricket means news, but in the
North it is said to bring ill luck.

Here, as in the North, a certain sacredness attaches to the spider,
and one hears the rhyme,

'If that you would live and thrive
Let the spider run alive.'[2]

In spite of this the spider was a good deal used in folk medicine. In
Brean in 1900 a correspondent of mine was told, 'A spider cures
ague. Shut one in a box till he do curdley up.'

Snails were thought to have some control of the weather, and the
rhyme to call a snail out of its shell seems to have been used as a
rain charm. One, which I overheard from a village child near
Clevedon, in 1920, says so explicitly:

'Snail, snail, put out your horn,
We want some rain to grow our corn.
Out, horn, out.'

This was said while tapping the shell to imitate rain. Another
pleasant rhyme comes from the West Somerset Hills.

'Snarley orn put out your orn,
Vather and mother's daid,
Zester an' brother be at the back door,
A-begging for barley bread.'

Glow-worms cannot affect the weather, but they foretell it.

'When the glow-worms light their lamp,
Then the air is always damp.'

On the Western Hills in the first quarter of this century I was
told that you must chase the first butterfly you see in the year,—
"tis to drive 'en away, so 'ee won't come again.' 'Come again' is
generally used to mean haunting, and in some parts of the country
white moths are supposed to be the souls of unchristened children.

---

[1] Somerset Wilts Border.   [2] Exmoor, 1925.

There may be some faint trace here of a conflict between the ghosts of Winter and the forces of Spring. On the Devon Borders butterflies are called 'King Georges', which are here the protagonists in the Mummers Play.

Of the reptiles, toads lie under a strong suspicion of witchcraft, it is said that an adder will never bite a 'gifted' person, a slowworm is supposed to be blind, and if it is killed in the morning it cannot die till sunset.[1]

Other animal beliefs will be found embedded in the stories and in witchcraft and magical practices.

[1] Kinsford, Exmoor, 1906.

PART II

1

Witchcraft and Magic

From the witches
And the weasles
And the creeping things at hedge bottoms
Good Lord deliver us.

West Country Litany.

In popular belief there are three kinds of witches, although the judges at the witch trials refused to acknowledge the distinction. The white witches were those who did no evil and were devoted to healing and the discovery of black witches. The grey witches would heal if they were so disposed and had still their chance of salvation, but if they were offended were ready to use their powers against their enemies. The black witches were altogether given over to evil and served Satan wholeheartedly. It is probable that the white and grey witches have the longer lineage, and that the black witches date from the time when witchcraft began to be considered a Christian heresy. It will be readily seen that there is frequent debate as to whether a particular witch is black, white or grey. An example of this is shown in the Keenthorne Witch, who was credited with great and uncanny powers, beyond those of the ordinary white witch, but seems to have reserved her malice only for people of bad character.

Black, White or Grey?

Harriet, the Witch of Keenthorne

Harriet was a well-known witch who lived near Stogursey about 100 years ago. She was blind, and considered very dangerous, but she had her good days, and others when she was not too malicious. Here are three instances which I was told by the children and grand-children of the actual seekers.

White

'My gran when she were a young maid, she was wishful to know if my grandad did love she, and she got her courage up and she went by herself, see. She got so far as the path to Harriet's door and she daresn't go a step further. She could see Harriet squat down by the fire in the hearth ever so still, all in black. Then she turn and look at Gran and her eyes were white. Gran she couldn't stir a finger, and Harriet she say, "I d'know what you d'want, my maid. Go whoame and see who be by briar bush." Gran she turn and run and never mind the brambles, but when she got to whoame there stood my grandad by briar bush, and he axed her and her were that out of breath her couldn't think to say "no" the first time.' *An old cottage woman, 1920.*

Grey

'My mother used to tell me how one of her sisters was foolish as a maid and got herself into bad trouble. 'Twas terrible thought on those days, not like their shameful ways now, and she was so beside herself she went to Harriet to see could she buy summat to rid herself afore 'twas noticeable. When she got near door her courage failed her and she stood and shook all over. There were Harriet huddled adown by vireplace all in black, with white eyes, and her says, "I do know what you d'want. Go whoame, thee gurt fule, and tell'n tew marry 'ee." And my auntie done just that and he did, and my mother had sixteen cousins.' *An old hedger, 1960.*

Black

'Our grandad were a proper terror of a man, zo wicked a temper as he had no one daren't zo much as cross he. Led my Gran a sad life. His pigs was ailing and he took a notion 'twas Harriet's doing and she'd overlooked 'n. Well then, off he marches with a gurt stick and in at her door. Reckoned he were gwine to tan the hide off she and dust her backside like he done my Gran. And no salt to his pocket. Harriet she just sat there, quite still like and she turn her white eyes on he, and she say quiet and cold like spring water, "I d'know what yew want, now will 'ee walk or ride whoame?" And my Gran came and found 'n all a-sat right down in the midden all tore with thorns and twigs and so white as whey, and he were a-begging all "Where be I tew? O, where be I? I been a-vlying I have, over treetops and droo hedges. O, my dears, where be I?"

And my liddle old Gran she up and say quietly, "Yew be buried in your own dung-heap, and best place vor 'ee." ' *A labouring farm couple both told it, 1930–40.*

The grey witches were in some ways even more feared than the black, because their ambivalence made it doubtful what kind of treatment one would get from them. An old cottager who is very rich in traditional lore[1] warned me against wearing grey in October for fear I might be taken for a grey witch. Apparently October is the month in which all witches have to show their nature and colour.

There is no doubt that the belief in witchcraft and the fear of it is wide-spread in Somerset, and I have, even in the last few years, come across many countercharms against witchcraft and traces of most of those beliefs which we find explicitly mentioned in the seventeenth-century witch trials. The fear of sacrilege and the traditions about the stealing of the holy water are still alive. In old days the holy water was protected by the addition of salt and often by a chained and locked cover to the font. These are still to be found in at least eleven churches in Somerset — Berrow, Chelwood, Chewton Mendip, Locking, Nempnett Thrubwell and Hinton Blewitt in the North, Radstock in the East, East Pennard in Mid Somerset, Milverton in the West and Charlton Adam and Wheathill in the South. It is doubtful if any of them are now kept locked, but the tradition of sacrilege still remains. The simplest safeguard is a pair of crossed pins. I was once resting in the cool arch which covers the stone steps into Crowcombe Church House when I saw a highly respected village worthy go up to the church wall, push something into a cranny and then go quietly away. I went up to the place at once and found a pair of pins, pushed deeply in and crossed. I left them and asked no questions, but certain church visits did end almost from that day.

Grey witches can go to church, with precautions, but certain black witches are believed not to be able to go at all.

> 'So her stayed in her bed,
> And her covered her head,
> Vor fear
> She'd d' hear

[1] Eli Vellacott (80), Treborough, Brendons, 1951.

The Kirsmass bell,
Then her zoul 'ood a-go to Hell.'

This I was told by a parish clerk at a casual meeting on Dunkery
Beacon in 1955. And in Minehead in 1923 I heard an old woman
say, 'She was a witch, sure; if'n her missus took she along to
church her'd spew at church door and be all over quakey.'

Many of the witches, however, acquired a technique by which
they could go to church with impunity and say the Lord's Prayer
with the congregation, substituting 'Our Father which wert in
Heaven' for 'Our Father which art in Heaven', and pausing to
insert 'never' silently at the appropriate moments as Julian Cox did
at her Taunton Trial in the seventeenth century.[1] These witches,
however, were liable to make dangerous mistakes. A suspected
witch came out of church one Sunday with a prayer book tied up in
a red handkerchief. As she came out of the church porch her legs
crossed, and she could never uncross them again till she died. She
may have had a wafer concealed in her prayer book, but according
to the local belief it was sacrilegious enough to take a red handkerchief to church instead of a white one.[2]

Another hazard run by the witch was the rebounding of her
curses if they failed to make lodgement. It was apparently true of
her as of ordinary people that curses like chickens will come home
to roost. I was told by an old fisherman at Weston-super-Mare in
1907 about a Burnham witch who laid a curse on a boy who had
annoyed her, forgetting that he was Sunday born, and a first born
child at that. The curse could not lodge, and turned back on the
witch herself, who suffered for her incautious ill-temper.

At Kingston St. Mary in 1959 I was given a description of a
suspected witch which showed how easily anyone at all eccentric
would have come to be regarded as one in earlier days.

'But we've got an Irish one in the village now.'

'Do they call her a witch among themselves?' I asked.

'No, I've never heard anyone call her that, but that doesn't mean
they don't think so. She goes in for these books of predictions and
she's what I call a hermit.'

'A recluse?'

'She's crazy on horses, and bets on them every day. *Her eyes*

[1] Glanvil, *Saducifmus Triumphatus*, 1681, p. 198.
[2] South Somerset, local tradition. See also C. Walters, *Bygone Somerset*, p. 113.

blink all the time, and sometimes she'll talk on for a quarter of an hour with her eyes shut.'

'Perhaps it's night blindness?'

'No, I don't think so. Perhaps it's just done to frighten people. She used to come to our farm at midnight, after we were all in bed, and keep us talking till one or two. She could put a curse on you. My uncle said something to her she didn't like, and she said, "I'll curse you." He lost his watch and then he lost his signet ring, and then he had a crash — not a bad crash, mind you — all in three weeks.'

Another common belief cited in the witch trials is that the witches flew through the air on broomsticks. In 1664, for instance, there was a Stoke Trister witch who claimed to have flown on a broomstick. She was sentenced to death, but committed suicide in prison. Her name was Elizabeth Style.[1] Somewhere about 1912 an old man at Dodington said to me, 'Thic wicked old witch to Fiddington, she d' fly on broomsticks over they Quantocks, November night time she 'ood.'

The tradition of the hair tedder, or witch ladder, is still a lively one. In A. L. Humphrey's *History of Wellington* he tells of how a hidden attic room was found in a cob house which was demolished in 1887 in which there were six heather brooms, an armchair made of oak and ash and a rope with feathers twisted into it. The workmen said that these were all witches' belongings and called the rope 'a witch's ladder'. They said it would be used to cross the roof. It was a half-inch rope, five feet long, made of three strands and with a loop at one end. The feathers, goose, crow and rook, were woven into the rope at irregular intervals. The neighbouring old women were reticent about it, though they admitted that 'they witches' twisted their own ropes. A Devonshire woman called it 'a wishing rope'. It was exhibited at the meeting of the British Association in 1887.[2]

Tales about these witch ladders are still current. At Stoke St. Mary I was told in 1925,[3] 'If anything goes wrong for a witch she waves the ladder to and fro, muttering her request while it is still a-swing, and the matter will be righted.' The grand-mother of one of our maids at Corfe had a more usual tradition about it; she said

[1] Willis Watson, *Somerset Life and Character*, p. 67.
[2] A. L. Humphreys, *The History of Wellington*, p. 235.
[3] Mrs. Williams, a baker's wife.

that a Blackmoor witch hung the rope outside to draw the milk from her neighbours' cowsheds.

In the right hands the witch's ladder can be used for good as well as evil, for a farmer's wife at Staplehay, somewhere about 1908, told me that if a white witch suspects someone of witchcraft or crime she can summon him by hanging the ladder outside the door.[1]

The belief in the Evil Eye is more common than explicit. It may be most easily recognized by the countercharms against it, but I have several times come across explicit mention of it. In the nineties of the last century there lived a woman near Wellington who was dreaded because she had the Evil Eye.[2] I myself as a child, when picking flowers along the lanes, have been seized and rushed behind the hedge while a woman passed by. She had looked upon and praised the baby of our maid's sister. The child had died.

Traces still remain of the belief in the Devil's power over a witch at her death which is the climax of many witch stories. A Mendip maid told me in 1908 about a woman who did things with pigs. The neighbours were afraid to be with her when she died, for the nails would be drawn off from her hands and feet.

Occasionally a witch when she died left her familiars behind. This is surely the meaning of a reported fragment sent me from the Chard district about 1920 by a correspondent who is now dead.

'When my husband's granny died, that was close to her hundreds, his auntie did go a-rummagin' to clear all the old rubbish in the roof place, and she did find a dreadful thing with horns. She was a Methodist, was his auntie, and she knowed what 'twas. She picked un up wi' the tongs and burned un in kitchen fire. Terrible put about she was.'

The Methodists were not sceptical about diabolic powers, and they inherited the Puritan tradition about direct conflict with the Devil.

In 1959 I was told of another witches' meeting place.[3]

'There's a witches' cave at Hestercombe, and a underground passage runs from it to the Manor. There's log chairs and witches' figures made of wood there. It was all locked up, and no one knew 'twas there, but the Army had it and they found a way in. It's the Fire Station now, and no one can go and look.'

---

[1] Farmer's wife, Staplehay, 1906–12.   [2] Bruton, 1906.
[3] Mrs. J. Tucker (70), cottager, Kingston St. Mary.

Legends of underground passages leading from old houses to an outlet at some distance are common enough, but it is unusual to have them leading to a witches' cave.

The old traditions of the diabolic contract and direct meetings with the Devil still survive. In 1955 the Rev. Peter Birkett, the Rector of Crowcombe, told me, 'We once had a young maid-servant who shut herself in a dark cupboard and said the Lord's Prayer backwards three times whenever it thundered. This was supposed to call up the Devil.'

Curiously enough, this charm is also used to exorcise ghosts.

One comes across traditions and accounts of witches all over the place, sometimes a mere general description of a local character, like the following account from Mrs. Hill, Crowcombe, 1905, but more often with some definite case of ill-wishing or over-looking.

'There was a bad old man in Crowcombe, he lived in the cottage near Mrs. Branchflower, and he went to the old witch over at Kingston St. Mary, yes, the one that kept the toads, and got her to teach him what she knew. I was frightened of him because — I was living at the cottage then with Miss Carew — he said to me one day, "If you was going out and I knowed something bad would happen to 'ee I could stop you going and you'd never know." After that I was frightened of him, but Mrs. Branchflower, she kept a laundry then right next to him, she didn't mind him a bit. "Go on with you," she'd tell him, "You and your old ways." '

This old man seems to have been harmless enough, although he was feared. More serious allegations were made against an old blind weeding woman at West Buckland. A farmer in the neighbourhood annoyed her, and his cows began to pine and did not recover until he had contrived to get her moved to Wellington Union. This was in the 1870's and she died in 1890.

The refusal of a gift to a reputed witch was often considered to be the cause of subsequent misfortune, and many examples of this can be found in the published works on Somerset Folklore, Snell, Willis Watson, Mrs. Kettlewell and the *Somerset Year Book*.[1]

A Mendip witch made a habit of turning up after the week's baking was done and asking for a loaf. At last the farmer's wife lost patience, and replied roundly, 'I've none to give 'ee. I don't see why I should bake for 'ee.'

The witch went away, but that evening she was seen peering in

---

[1] See Selected List of Books.

at the window. The daughter who saw her had a withered hand afterwards.

Sometimes rather pixy-like pranks were played by the witches. There was a notorious witch at Nailesbourne, and someone crossed her and she told him 'he'd walk up and down water all night'. Mrs. Bailey, who lived opposite his cottage, saw him standing in the stream next morning, he had not been able to get out of it all night.[1] Anne Bodenham boasted of a similar trick,[2] but this was in a horse-pond; it is most unusual for witches to have any power over running water. The witch in this story was supposed to be a particularly evil one. In 1959 I took down a similar story from a farmer's wife at Kingston St. Mary.

The Man Who Was Cursed

'You know the Seven Kings. Well, a man went to have his drink, and he had some fish on his bike, and another man came out of the pub and defiled it. When the fish-man saw what had happened he asked who had done it. No one owned up. So he said, "The man that did it will not get home very easily tonight."

'So the man that did it tried to get home. He left the pub and he walked home — he lived at Nailesbourne. In fact, he lived where Mrs. Bailey lives now. Instead of being able to get through the gate — there is a stream on the left-hand side of the house — he was walking up and down the stream till the early hours of the morning unable to get indoors.'

Gipsies are often supposed to have special powers of cursing. A farmer's wife at Flaxpool Farm in the Quantocks said to me in 1959: 'I wouldn't let our three carthorses go to the slaughter house when we changed over to tractors. The gipsies came after them, but I wouldn't let them go, and the gipsy said, "You'll never do any good with them." Well, one of them ran a wire into her foot and had to be put down, and the other went and injured its back and we lost it, and the third was struck by lightning. It had to be sheltering under that one tree. If that wasn't a gipsy curse I don't know what was. It makes you think, doesn't it?'

The commonest tales of all about the witches still relate to shape-shifting, and the commonest shape taken by the witches was, in Somerset at least, that of the hare, though the rabbit runs it close.

[1] Nailesbourne, 1900.   [2] *Dr. Lamb's Darling*, 1653, pp. 4-5.

The cat and the toad were two other forms taken by witches, though these were more often thought to be the witches' familiars. No witch can change her shape to a lamb or a dove.[1] Occasionally the Black Dog, usually a devil or a ghost, was thought to be a witch.

At Combe Florey in the 1920's they said to me, 'There are only gifted people at Coombe Florey, but if you cross the Minehead road to Bagborough and Kingston St. Mary there are hares enough there. So us do know where all they black witches do bide.'

It is generally the white rabbits or black ones that are suspected of being witches. At Norton Fitzwarren I was told by the lodge-keeper in 1935, 'Never shoot a wild black rabbit, it is the soul of your grandmother.' And in the Quantocks in 1957 I came across a fine example of living superstition. 'White rabbits are witches. There were a pair running in Crowcombe Park but no one would shoot them. Perhaps we can't melt down a silver bullet out of present-day coinings, and no one wears silver buttons nowadays.'[2]

A vivid story of a witch hare was told me in 1955 by Walter Badcock, an old coachman, then about seventy-four. As the tale went on the old man's accent got broader and he lost sight of his tenses.

The Witch Hare

'No, I never heard of no ha'nting to Ellicombe Farm. Us lived to Ellicombe tew. There was the Ellicombe harnt, 'tis old tales, and the Ellicombe witch — but there, believe it or no 'tis all a sham.

'Well then, as I were going up whoame t'Ellicombe with the old pony, we did kip a pony for to drive t' Mine'd, and I seed a girt fat wold hare in behind a boosh — a fine one tew — and the two years of 'n stuck right up above boosh; 'n I said, "Yew bide theyur, my la–ady, 'n I'll have 'ee when I gets my gun."

'So I goes down whoame 'n gets my gun, 'twas a gude one tew, 'n I creeps up back, 'n there her two years was 'n I seed her yed. 'Twadn' more'n 20 yards, 'n I lifs the gun 'n lets vly! 'N her hops away so easy 'n slow I let's 'n have't agen, but didn't make no difference, I couldn't shoot 'ee. I takes gun whoame, 'n I puts up playing card down hurchet (orchard), 60 yards, 'n I hits 'n every time. Well, I telled a vuller 'bout 'n 'n how I couldn't shoot'n, 'n her said, "Nor yew won't never till 'ee puts zilver in yewer gun.

---

[1] West Somerset, 1955.　　　　[2] H. Follet, artisan gardener, 1/3/57.

'Tis a witch hare, 'n us all knows 'n yurabouts." No, I couldn't shoot 'ee.'

This tale was about Ellicombe, the district haunted by the notorious Joan Carne. The same man told me a rather similar story of a witch hare at Bratton Court.

The Bull-Dog Pistol and the Hare

'Well then, 'nother time when I were young I were working in gardens down to Bratton, 'n there were a bridge in gardens 'n 'ee went up along by a long haige, 'n I seed a vine hare a-sat down in haige, 'n her didn't never move, 'n I says, "Yew stay thur, my dear, 'n I'll have 'ee." Now, I tried with my gun same as Ellicombe, and bits of leaf 'n grass did vly up round whur her did quat, but her just upped 'n jump deown in ditch t'other side, not hurted a bit, though tree behind were marked. Well then, I says, "I'll have 'ee another day," an' next time I tooked a pistol, a heavy gurt thing they did call a bull-dog, took a bullet as big as a currant, from a Winchester gun, an' I goes down over bridge, 'n I do trip somehow, 'n blows end of me boo–ut raight off! Mid hev been me gurt twoe. No, I never seed hare no more, nor I 'oodn't want tew.'

There was an old woman who lived near Elworthy Barrows who was suspected of being a hare. Some labourers determined to course her, but she evaded the dogs and disappeared behind the cottage. When they marched up to the door boldly to take possession and burn it down the old lady herself opened it, and with one accord they all turned and ran. 'Her were turble short in her breathings, they d' say.'[1]

An earlier story of a witch who was generally thought to take the form of a black dog was told me of the same place by a friend who lived there in 1880. A farmer shot at a hare which got away, but this old woman was afterwards seen to be crippled, so it was supposed that she had used the hare form as well as the black dog one.

The *Somerset Year Book of 1934* recorded two stories of shape-shifting collected from Petronella O'Donell, both of which I have found in oral tradition. One was of a sailor coming back on leave,

[1] Brendon Hills, 1912.

to tell us, 'She were a witch right enough.' *From Mrs. R. Hill, Crowcombe, 4/3/37.*

Mrs. Hill hails from Pitminster and would have heard this story some sixty years ago. The old woman probably lived in the 1880's.

The Dung-Putt

There was an old witch over to Broomfield used to keep cats and toads and if she didn't like you she'd send the toads after you. She lived in the cottages at Rose Hill — they've fallen down now, and if anyone did anything she didn't like she'd say, 'I'll toad 'ee,' and people was all afraid I s'pose. I knew the carter who worked over to Ivyton Farm and he had to go to Bridgewater with the cart with a load of corn and she come to the door and asked him to bring her a couple of sacks of coals back. Well, he forgot and when he come to pass her cottage she came out for her coals, and she shook her fist at him and said, 'I'll set the toads on 'ee.' When he got to Ivyton, farmer asked him why he looked so bad and when he told him he said, 'I sooner have lost the wheat than you should ha' forgot they coals.' And after that if he had to take a load of dung, s'pose too, she'd come to the door of her cottage and cackle at him. And sure enough the pegs sprung and the dung putt tipped up. Then she'd cackle, 'That'll teach 'ee to forget my coals. I'll toad 'ee!' The carter told me he'd tie the pegs down with binder twine but 'twas no use. Every time he got to the cottage the twine broke, and the pegs sprung, and the old witch she'd come to her door, and stand there and cackle. *From Wilfred Chidley, artisan, Crowcombe, 21/2/57.*

The carter, who is a very old man, is still living but has moved.

Toad Messengers

There was a witch at Wedmore from whose mouth toads issued, and went thence upon her errands. Those of her victims who were thus 'hag-ridden' could only find safety if they had the courage to pick up the devilish messenger in the tongs and burn it in the fire.[1]

Toads on the Road

A farmer's wife I knew had words with a black witch who lived at Countisbury, just over the Devon Border. She was a redoubtable soul, and determined to outface the old woman, witch or no. She mounted the pony and rode across Lucott Moor, and to Wind-

[1] Mrs. Birkett, the Rector's mother, Wedmore, 6/9/55.

whistle Corner to County Gate. A little way beyond this the pony refused, and when she looked for a reason she found the road was swarming with toads. The further she tried to go the more there were. She turned the pony for home, and when she reached Yenworthy dismounted to get over her scare. A local tradesman's van drew up beside her, coming from Countisbury. Toads in the road? What toads? He'd seen her in the distance turn her pony back towards Porlock, and he'd caught her up in under five minutes, but there were no toads.

Apparently repeating this tale to me awakened her resentment again, for a little later I saw her in a lane, hammering a blacksmith's nail into a footprint in the dust, and went by discreetly on the other side of the hedge. I never mentioned the matter, and all I was told about it, some time later, was that the old witch was dead.[1]

The following stories are about white, grey and black witches, so far as they can be differentiated. It will be noticed that many of the witches are said to 'come again' after their death. This was always considered a danger unless the witch was burnt. Burning was not, however, the legal penalty for witchcraft in England, although the witches themselves sometimes asked for it in the belief that their witchcraft would not then be hereditary to their children. The only case in which a witch might legally be burnt was when she was condemned for petty treason — that is the murder of a husband or master. When, therefore, we find stories of witch burnings we may suspect that tradition has been busy and that we are dealing rather with folklore than history. Madam Joan Carne, one of the most dreaded of the Somerset witches, is an example rare in English tradition of a young and beautiful witch. In the Appendix will be found a few notes on some of the witches who were actually brought to trial in Somerset. The memory of these is still lively.

White Witches

White witches, or conjurors, are still resorted to in Somerset. Between 1949 and 1957 I gleaned a number of scraps of information about white witches still at work. At Alcombe in 1939 the blacksmith was a white witch; he could draw nails or thorns from a horse's hoof by a charm. The power was passed on to his daughter. There was a white witch at Hawkcombe in 1950, and one at King's Brompton recently, and I understand that one is still living at

[1] Lucott Moor, 1945.

Withypool. One of these can overpower the evil eye and cause the overlooked to thrive. A farmer's wife at Lawford told me about a godly old man at Monksilver who had cured one of their ponies of ringworm. He would take neither money nor gifts for his services.

Today in the Chard district there is a conjuror who charms away warts. He can cure without seeing his patient, and from miles away. These white witches were many of them specialists upon one ill, but the conjuror was generally consulted when some kind of witchcraft or overlooking was suspected.

A Taunton White Witch

'In a farm where granddad worked (Nailesbourne Farm, Mr. Biffin) they made cheese and butter. They had a lot of girls then, as they do, and every time they tried to make the butter it wouldn't come. Well, anyway, they sent to Taunton to Billy Brewer who lived in St. James Street and he came out and went to the farm, and they explained what had happened, the butter wouldn't come. And he had all the girls there that were working there, looked around and walked in, and said to the farmer (and said about a particular girl), 'You get rid of her. She's evil!' After this girl was gone everything was all right. No more trouble with the butter making.'[1]

The Horse-Collar

A Crewkerne conjuror met one of his would-be clients with the remark, 'I know who you be looking for, and I do know what you do want wi' 'en.' After which he used toads for his divination, sewed the charm securely in a horse-collar, and said it must never touch the ground.[2]

The Lucky Horse-Collar

There was a farmer whose finest cart horse was bewitched, and he could neither find the witch nor cure the horse, and then his cows and pigs began to pine; so off went his wife to the conjuror in a town miles away. When she came in all the conjuror would say was, 'I know what you have come for. Take this horse-collar *without touching it* and hang it on the wall of your kitchen. So long as no one ever touches it your man will prosper.'

[1] Mrs. Lowman, carter's wife (70), Kingston St. Mary, 1935.
[2] Mr. Wyatt, Chard, 1909.

Then he handed her the magic collar on the end of a hazel stick, and not another word did he utter.

So the farmer's wife drove home with the collar still on the stick across her knees, and when she got tò the farm she went in and straightway hung it on a peg above the clavel tack (mantelpiece), and she wouldn't speak till all was done. Then she told the farmer all about it, and sure enough the beasts were cured from that very day.

She sent the conjuror a great market basket of eggs and butter and chickens, for he would take no money ever. The farm grew richer and richer, and the family never allowed a soul to lay a finger on the horse-collar over the clavel tack, until one day a great foolish maid-servant lifted it down and dusted it. You can guess where their luck went after that.[1]

The Withypool Witch

A farmer who had lost some of his sheep and had seen a hare at the time of their deaths decided to consult the conjuror at Water-row. He was told before he had spoken a word what his trouble was, and then shown the witch responsible. He promised he would deal with her. This hag had an ill name for halting wagons and scaring horses, but she now began to pine till 'she was skin and bone hanged agin the wall'. She became so feeble that many a time she was taken for dead. Then suddenly she would be gone, and they would find her 'a-quat stark nekked in t'road or spinning around like a whirligig'. Eventually she recovered, but remained quite harmless, more even than her old husband, who was a notable quiet soul, and prayed as hard as the neighbours for her death-bed, but he had a pet gander who followed him about everywhere. This was regarded as rather suspicious. It may have been for protection against his wife, but it laid him under the suspicion of being at least a white witch himself.[2]

The Pig and the Butcher

A widow living near Chard was certain that her pig had been bewitched by someone passing late on Midsummer Eve, for it had never thriven since that date. She set out rather timidly to ask the local conjuror's help, and had hardly gone a quarter of a mile when she met him face to face. 'I know what you do want,' he said, 'and

---

[1] Blackdown Hills, local tradition.   [2] Mrs. Keal, Exmoor, 1945.

I'll tell 'ee what to do 'bout it, and not a penny for it. Take the pig to the butcher.'

Well, it was a great loss, but the widow thought she might save a little bacon, so off she went to the butcher. When the butcher saw her coming he turned pale, but when he saw the pig his eyes rolled in his head.

The widow had a good guess now who it was who had bewitched her pig, so she stood firm, whatever the butcher could say, and fairly forced him to take the knife to the pig. At the first cut such a sheet of flame came out of the beast's mouth, that everyone in the town came running. But all they ever found of the pig or the butcher were two cinders, so the widow was well rid of both of them.[1]

Grey Witches

The Harptree Witch

There was a celebrated witch at Harptree during the last century who had the power of healing and could cure the King's Evil. But she had other powers which rendered her formidable. She had second sight. Among her prophecies were the following: Water will one day cross Harptree Combe and treasure be found there. Bristol water pipes now cross it, and it is said that the workmen found buried silver.

Before a certain tree comes into leaf the Schoolmaster will be laid low in his grave. He died within the month.

A village mason was warned by her not to go to work, but 'bide in bed'. He went on and fell off his ladder and broke his arm.

The Vicar wanted to move the pulpit and was told, 'If you shift the pulpit you'll shift yourself.' He left the parish shortly after.

The Harptree witch was a nasty person to offend. A shopkeeper who asked for her long account to be settled was haunted by a rat in her bedroom until she died; a labourer disagreed with one of her sons and found that he could not take the straight way home. He had to make a long detour across the fields. These traditions come from Mendip friends about 1925 but they are also recorded in Mrs. Kettlewell's *Trinkum-Trinkums of Fifty Years*.

In the Chard story of The Pig and the Widow it is clear that the butcher was a black witch and the conjuror a white one. But there is

[1] Chard, 1909.

another version of the tale from Corfe in which the conjuror seems to have been a grey witch. The pig indeed went on fire when the butcher cut its throat, but it could only be quenched by the village blacksmith. A guess made about this failure of the conjuror is that he had taken money for his help. This seems automatically to turn a white witch into a grey one. In the late nineteenth century there was a Chard conjuror who received payment in money for his charms and spells, but he 'wasn't well thought of'. In other words, he was suspected of being a grey witch. The following story illustrates the belief.

'*Set the Dogs on Her*'

An Exmoor farmer had such ill luck with his stock that he went to visit a conjuror thirty miles away. He was told that the old hag who had overlooked him would visit him and that he must be ready to do just what the conjuror told him. The farmer paid the conjuror and returned home to have his revenge. Now, there was a queer old soul in a little cottage up the lane, and when she was seen passing by the farmer forgot all his instructions and yelled, 'Set the dogs on her!' Even as he shouted and the dogs rushed out, his chair, a stout oak chair, rose in the air with him in it until it touched the ceiling. The dogs rushed in again howling and the chair descended; but the farmer had suffered a 'fairy stroke', and never moved or spoke again for the rest of his life.[1]

Either the conjuror's charms rebounded on the farmer because he had accepted money, or the farmer in his rage had placed himself in danger by omitting any precautions. My informant, however, distrusted the conjuror. Her theory was that the old woman was a white witch, and the conjuror, being a black one, sought to destroy her through the farmer, but his magic rebounded. She was anxious to know if I could tell her what the conjuror's end was. She gave me his name, but as a branch of the family is still alive I cannot put it down.

Black Witches

Conjurors are generally credited with being either white or grey witches, but from his reappearances and from his dying commands to his wife it is pretty clear that George Beacham was a black one.

---

[1] Simons bath. See also F. Hancock, *The Parish of Selworthy*, p. 237.

The Conjuror's Boots

George Beacham was a cattle dealer and a conjuror. In spite of the fact that his house stood across the lane from the Quaker Meeting House he owned a wizard's staff and magic books. When his time came to die he was very unwilling to relinquish his power of plaguing his neighbours.

'Yew bury me to cross-roads,' he told his poor wife. 'I a'nt going to be under no churchyard soil, I tell 'ee. I wants to be where I can keep an eye on the neighbours' doings, so dig my grave to cross-roads. If 'ee don't I'll trouble 'ee.'

Whatever the widow might have done the neighbours were quite determined to be clear of the conjuror, and on July 27th, 1788, they buried him good and proper in Winscombe Churchyard. A year passed by without disturbance, but on July 27th, 1789, the quiet of the Quaker meeting was broken by screams from across the road. A passing woman had looked in at Widow Beacham's cottage and seen chairs and tables dancing with pots and pans, while the kneading trough rocked unaided.

The Friends went across to unravel the mystery, moving out of the way of a large armchair that was gliding across the room. As they stood there wondering the dead conjuror's boots clattered slowly downstairs and out into the kitchen to meet them.

Both Hannah More and Mr. Jones, the curate of Shipham, visited the cottage; but no naturalistic explanation of the phenomena has been found.[1]

The burial of suicides at cross-roads is generally supposed to be to prevent them from walking, but in Somerset this is believed to be ineffectual unless they are held down with an ash stake through the heart. Indeed, cross-roads are frequent places for hauntings. Even when the witch does not actually come again her spirit often hangs as an evil influence round the place of her death.

The Putrid Pool

A scholarly recluse lived with his daughter in Growly House, in the wood now called the Holts. They were well off and kept a man-servant, and exaggerated notions of their wealth got about. Alice Duke, the local witch, and her son, Abel, persuaded the man-servant to join with them in a robbery. He was to set fire to the

---

[1] Sidcot, local traditions. The historical details of the story are to be found in Knight, *The Heart of Mendip*, pp. 80–2.

F

house, Abel was to seize the daughter, and the witch was to secure the money. The servant's part of the work was done too thoroughly, the scholar and his money were burned together, and the daughter, who had escaped, ran back into the fire to save her father and died there too. The neighbours came too late to help them, but they caught Abel and hanged him out of hand, and drowned Alice Duke in a neighbouring pool. The pool still smells putrid and is never ruffled by any wind.[1]

Madam Joan Carne (died 1612)

Madam Joan Carne was an Elizabethan witch whose husbands died of suspected poisoning. Her restless spirit was condemned to stay in 'The Witch's Pool' half a mile away, but every year she comes one cock-stride nearer home.

There was a lass in Queen Elizabeth's days who was called Joan, and she had a smile and a way with her. It is not surprising that she won the heart of a farmer and got on in the world quite a bit. What was surprising was that in spite of her smile he died soon after and left her comfortable. It wasn't to be thought her taking ways would keep her a widow long, so next time she took a yeoman and he was richer than her first. Nobody knows how it was he died so soon though some could give a guess. And now the poor soul had lost two healthy, wealthy husbands in a year or two, and was richer than ever. They say luck goes in threes. So whether it was that smile of hers; or whether riches call to riches, it wasn't long before she became Madam Joan Carne of Sandhill Manor, wife to the wealthiest man in the neighbourhood. Would you believe it, in spite of all her care, that strong, hearty man was taken ill of a sudden and, for all the nursing his family gave him, and the watch his servants kept over him, and the broth his lady coaxed him to drink with a special smile, he too died. To be sure he had kept alive longer than the other two, but his family and friends had seen to that. And now Madam Joan Carne had Sandhill Manor for herself as well, and she was the best-served woman in Withycombe. Who knew if she'd smile at *them*!

When at last she died they made sure of her. They nailed her coffin with iron nails, they hurried her body off to the Church for Christian burial and when the service was over they came dancing

[1] A maidservant, Chard, 1909; Mr. Sanderson, Crewkerne, 1910. See also *Somerset Folk Series*, No. 3, 1924.

with joy back to Sandhill Manor. One of them flung open the kitchen door and there stood Madam Joan Carne frying eggs and bacon quite placidly. Then she turned her head and smiled at them. . . . Well, they sent post haste to Watchet for a priest who was hiding there — their own Parson had failed badly and Watchet had succeeded with another ghost. Now, the Priest must have known a lot about Madam Carne for he sent her wicked spirit into a pond not a mile away and she can only return by one cock-stride each year despite her smile.[1]

'We used to fish and get blackberries by the Witch's Pond but we were always ready to run for our lives.'[2]

'Our people are now saying that she turned into a hare and someone shot her with a silver bullet and lamed her, and that she is now a ghost. Some of our older men say she's about if things go wrong.'[3]

Nancy Camel

Nancy Camel lived in a cave and sold her soul to the Devil. He came to collect her one stormy night and left hoof-prints in stone on her cavern walls.

Old Nancy Camel lived in a cave in the woods. She was a stocking knitter and worked ceaselessly by day and at night by rushlight to gain a few more pence to add to her hoard. Then she began to work on a Sunday and people whispered together and looked sideways at her for a godless old miser.

It is not surprising then that one night the Devil visited her with a sack of gold to increase her hoarding.

And now she was really rich, but she still went on knitting to scrape in a few more pennies; folk dare not refuse to buy her stockings for they knew she was a witch.

When the seven years were nearly up she went in terror to the priest and confessed. He promised her pardon if she would throw away the Devil's gold but she found she couldn't bring herself to part with the last coin, and hid it. Then she went back to the priest and told a lie about it — and after that the pardon was no protection at all.

A fearful storm broke out that very night, and above the howling of the wind folk heard the rattle of wheels and the crack of a giant whip. Then a terrible scream rang out from the cave.

[1] See Withycombe Church Porch, local tradition.
[2] Mrs. Burgess, Withycombe, 1955.
[3] Mrs. Stevenson, Sandhill Manor, 6/10/59.

In the morning the priest and a few villagers went to find old Nancy. She was gone, but the deep marks of wheels and hooves on the rock of her cave are still there to show who carried her off.[1]

The Whistling Ghost of Quay-Town

Old Mrs. Leakey lived with her son and daughter-in-law at Minehead in the seventeenth century. Her son was a prosperous ship-owner with boats crossing to Ireland for cattle and to Wales for sea-coal. Old Mrs. Leakey was a cosy, comfortable old lady and her family seemed very fond of her. Only once she looked up with a queer twinkle and said that maybe if she came again she wouldn't be so welcome. They took it for a joke at the time, but then she died and they found that it wasn't a joke at all. For Mrs. Leakey came again, and in a most sinister way. She once met the Parson by the stile, and upon his trying to return her to the place she had left she kicked him over it. She strangled the baby in the cradle, and she went down to Quay-Town when her son's ships were sailing into port and whistled up storms which wrecked them. All attempts to lay her failed until at length an Irish bishop managed to banish her. Tradition says that he did not manage it completely, or that she left her familiar behind, for an evil spirit is still hanging about Culver Cliffs which has brought more than one picnic party to an abrupt end. The affair made a considerable stir at the time, and the King sent a Royal Commission to investigate it. Her ruined and unhappy son could swear that there was no trickery about it, and in the end the Commissioners decided that she must be a ghost. It is witches, however, that whistle for the wind.[2]

B. MAGIC AND SPELLS

Counter-charms

In the anecdotes of the White Witches we have already come across some examples of counter-charms. These are of two main sorts, there are the harmless and purely protective charms and the retaliatory charms designed to harm the witch. Halfway between these are the charms that take away the witch's power for ever.

Horse-shoes, crosses and wicken are the commonest of the pro-

---

[1] Shepton Mallet, local tradition.
[2] A full account of this can be found in F. Hancock's *History of Minehead*, pp. 394–402, but local tradition is still lively about Mrs. Leakey.

tective charms. Almost every Somerset farm has a horse-shoe nailed up over a barton or barn or a back door. Nowadays they are 'just left up there', but the cowmen still find a hidden satisfaction in their presence. On Exmoor and the Brendons, as in the Scottish Highlands, one can still see wicken crosses tied with red thread hung over the cowshed doors. But it is best not to comment on them, for to mention them breaks the luck. At Chelvey Court the wide Jacobean staircase has horse-shoes nailed on the bottom step. They were put there to prevent any witches who had somehow managed to slip into the house from getting upstairs.

Witch stones, or self-bored stones, such as used to hang in stables in Aubrey's time to prevent the horses from being hagridden are still vaguely considered lucky and are hung to the old, heavy stable-door keys.

Crosses were equally powerful. There is a crude stone cross upon the pier of Kentsford Bridge. This is an old pack-horse bridge near Watchett, Madam Joan Carne's neighbourhood. There is a tradition that the cross was put there to protect travellers from a particularly wicked witch against whom even running water was not a sufficient protection.

In Mrs. Kettlewell's *Trinkum-Trinkums of Fifty Years* an unusual protection is mentioned. A free Martin — that is a heifer who has not yet calved — was put into a team of horses that had been spell-bound and who were then able to move.[1]

Verses of Scripture are a more widespread nostrum, and if none come to memory any rhyme may serve the turn. I was told this in Stoke-sub-Hamdon in 1907, and the East Anglian tale told me by a Harwich schoolgirl of fourteen in 1955, is to the same effect.

Vinegar Tom

There was a man who was afraid to go past where Vinegar Tom was because he might get taken away, so they told him what to say, and then he couldn't do anything to him.

> "Vinegar Tom, Vinegar Tom,
> Where by the Powers do you come from?'

And he learned it. So when Vinegar Tom came out he said it, but he didn't say it right. He said:

[1] F. B. Kettlewell, *Trinkum-Trinkums of Forty Years*, p. 47.

Vinegar Tom, Vinegar Tom,
Where in the world do you come from?'

And it wasn't right but it rhymed, so Vinegar Tom only threw him over the wall.

Vinegar Tom was a familiar in the seventeenth-century East Anglian Witch Trials.

One curious protection against witches which I found current in the Quantocks between 1930 and 1945 is to carry a rabbit's foot in one's pocket, presumably because witches so often took the form of rabbits.

Of the more vindictive and retaliatory charms the drawing of blood is perhaps the most widespread. This belongs to the middle order of charm, that which deprives the witch of her power. Scraping above the breath with nails or a pin will free one from her ill-wishing. This was done at Chewton Mendip in 1900, and also to my own knowledge on Exmoor in 1942. There was a case in Bridgewater late last century where an old woman and her daughter were secretly attacked and scratched on their arms till the blood ran. The attacker was the father of a sick child who afterwards recovered.[1]

A more ferocious variant of the blooding charm occurs in a story I was told in the Brendon Hills. In a remote coombe there lived a very much dreaded old woman who was blamed when babies and pigs pined and grown-up people were taken unaccountably ill. Neither the parson nor the doctor seemed able to do anything against her, but a local road-man coveted the witch's power. He met her in a lonely lane with a bill-hook, wounded her and forced her into a deep drain by the roadside. There he kept her, between the peril of drowning and of being slashed to death, until she yielded her power to him. When the neighbours helped her out of the drain she was little better than a lunatic, and she died soon after, as harmless as a sheep. As for the road-man, he claimed to have become a conjuror — a white witch — but he was looked at askance. People said he had the evil eye. For a short time he was wealthy and moved to Taunton, but here his luck left him. His wife died, his daughter ran away from him, and no one was much surprised when he took his own life.

A milder method of breaking the witch's power is shown in the tale of the Magic Parcel, of which there are several variants.

[1] Told me as a child by old Bridgewater folk, 1905–12.

A child in one of the remote cottages on the Western Hills fell very ill, and daily grew worse in spite of all that his mother could do. At last she went the twelve miles over to Elworthy to consult a white witch there. He was a very godly old man, and after they had prayed together he gave the mother a small parcel carefully done up and told her to hand it to an old neighbour, who had been very assiduous in her enquiries, next time she came to ask after the child. This the mother did, and the old woman gave a wild scream and fell down. When she recovered her power was gone, and she tottered away. The child recovered.

In some versions of the tale the witch cries out, 'I am done!' as soon as she takes the parcel.

The mysterious 'Monksilver Murder', when three women, Elizabeth Conibeer and her two daughters, were found brutally cut about by a pair of tailor's shears, may have been a ritual blood-letting to break a spell, or may have started with that intention. At least I have heard it hinted in districts fifteen miles apart that these women had brought their killing upon themselves. The murderer was never found, but the local people knew who it was.

The nailing of a foot-print is an attempt to lame the witch by sympathetic magic. It is still a charm against witchcraft and the evil eye, and I have known it done in several instances, twice since the Second World War.

The Blacksmith's Nail

'There was a old woman to Porlock Weir, they d' call her a witch. She d' keep twoads in her bedroom and up on the shelves like. 'Twas so long ago I can't call it to mind, must be fifty year, but my sister she could tell 'ee. But thur was a woman whose pigs did always get out, no matter! whenever this old witch d' go by. Try how she could they'd always be out and running. So she went and drove a blacksmith's nail into her heel print in the ro–ad, 'n the old woman she were a-crippled all on a sudden, 'n they had tew half-carry her whoame.'[1]

Once I was so lucky as to get a hint from a blacksmith about the making of the nail. It is not often that they will betray their magical secrets. This was at Porlock in the 1940's.

'The nail must be specially made, yew see, by the blacksmith.

---

[1] Mrs. Badcock (late 70's), Triscombe, 1955.

I've a-knowed it done. 'Twas never touched by hand or 'twas no good.'

Another sinister piece of magic is the summoning which is one form óf the dreaded *Hate Charm*. A lock óf hair, a piece of clothing, a tooth, or anything else that has belonged to the witch is used. The conjuror puts the object into a shovel with burning salt and recites:

"Tis not this thing I wish to burn
But Mrs. (Priddy's) heart of (Wookey) I wish to turn.
Wishing thee neither to drink, sleep nor rest
Until thou dost come to me and do my request,
Or else the wrath of God may fall on thee
And cause thee to be consumed in a moment. Amen.'[1]

Hearts stuck with pins were both protective and malificent charms.

'When there was illness in the Court Flock our shepherd cut out the heart of a young sheep that had died and stuck it full of pins to keep the evil spirits away. I think it was horrible.'[2]

Hearts and Pins

'Witches can't come droo walls, but only down the chimbley, droo windows and doors.'— So a bullock's heart stuck full of pins, points outwards, was hung up the chimney to scratch her as she came down — no witch would risk this. Such hearts were found at Litton in the nineteenth century (Kettlewell, p. 39) and at Taunton and Wellington in old houses now pulled down. These were protective charms — but bullock or pigs' hearts and pins have been discovered put to a malignant use. In these cases the initials of the victim are formed by the pins, or the heart is nailed behind the clavel tack to suffer slow scorching and suffocating smoke, or it is placed in a sealed jar or jug and set beside the fire to roast. The destroying formula is that quoted in the Wellington version — "Tis not this heart I mean to burn' etc. As the heart roasted or suffocated or smothered so did the victim. The worst witches used to remove the jar at times and allow the sufferer a blissful surcease from agony — and then renew it by replacing the jar by the fire. Some hearts have been found cut from black cloth with pins across

[1] The Mendip Hills, 1894.
[2] The Hon. Mrs. Trollope-Bellew, Crowcombe Court, 1957.

them, and on the Blackdowns an onion stuck full of pins is as deadly as a heart. There are two of these bewitched hearts in Taunton Museum, one from Ashbrittle, Blackdown Hills, and one from East Quantoxhead, Quantock Hills, but in some farms there are still to be found the shepherd's charms already mentioned.

These are all known cases:

Litton	Mendips	1840
Taunton	Mid	1890
Wellington	South-West	1889
Ashbrittle	West	20th century
Bridgwater	West	1900
East Quantoxhead	Quantocks	20th century
Crowcombe	Quantocks	20th century

Amateur Magic

People who would not call themselves witches sometimes descended to black charms in an extremity. I collected two examples of the making of the waxen heart as late as 1960.

'There was a woman who lived near us and she was at odds with my mother, so she made an image of her and stuck pins in it, in the knees, and my mother suffered terrible after that with rheumatism in her legs.'[1]

'I know someone, she is a neighbour, and she said she didn't like a woman who lived near, so she was going back home to make a puppet of her and stick pins in it. I never dared ask if she did.'[2]

The Hate Charm was most commonly used by jealous girls deserted by their lovers.

Use a mutton shoulder bone and stab it with a knife or pin while every window is darkened and there is only firelight, or thrust it into the fire. Say:

> "Tis not this bone I mean to prick (or burn)
> But my false love's heart I mean to prick (or turn)
> Wishing him neither rest nor sleep
> Till he be dead and gone.'

After this he will pine away and die regardless of doctors' remedies.[3]

This charm was not only used by deserted lovers, but sometimes

---

[1] A member of the Stogumber W.I., 1960.
[2] Member of Clapton W.I., 1961. [3] A washerwoman, Taunton, 1905–12.

served other occasions of malice. Walter Raymond has a story of an unpopular tax collector spying through the chinks of a cottage shutter to see a hard-driven family working this spell with his name. His horror and indignation brought on a heart attack, and he fell down and died on the spot to the consternation of the family. I have been told that this story was founded on fact and occurred in South Somerset.

There are many pleasanter charms by which girls can summon their lovers or find out their future. Most of them are attached to certain seasons of the year and belong properly to the next part of this book, but a few may be used at any time. It may be that they all once belonged to a date, and the tradition of it has perished.

The Silent Supper, for instance, originally belonged to Midsummer Eve, but was described by Miss Alice King about 1860[1] without the mention of any special date. A man and a woman took part in this; they spread a table with bread and cheese and cider and sat down opposite each other with the Marriage Service open between them and in absolute silence. At midnight the wraiths of the future husband and wife will appear, eat the food and disappear again, all still in silence. In 1910 this tradition was still alive in the Quantocks, for a friend said to me about that date, 'If a coffin walks in bolt upright it is a sign of death within the year; if nothing happens eat the feast yourself and forget your disappointment.'

Summoning by even ash was a simple method of divination if one could find an ash leaf with an even number of leaflets. Then one held it in one's hand and went out, saying:

> 'This even ash I double in three,
> The first I meet my true-love shall be;
> If he be married, let him pass by,
> But if he be single let him draw nigh.'

Throw the leaf in the face of the person first met, and he will be the future husband.[2]

The Egg and Water Charm seems as if it might properly belong to Easter. Boil an egg hard and take it upstairs backwards, carrying a glass of water. Put them by the bed and get into bed backwards, saying:

---

[1] Quoted in Poole's *Customs, Superstitions and Legends*, pp. 14–16.
[2] West Luccombe, 1939. I was taught a similar rhyme by a maid's mother at Wellington in 1910.

"'Tis not this egg I mean to eat
But my true love's heart I mean to seek;
In his apparel and array,
As he wears it every day.'

The wraith of the lover will then appear and drink the water.[1]

To summon by sowing hempseed at midnight a girl goes out into the garden and pretends to scatter hempseed, saying:

'Hempseed I scatter
Hempseed I sow
He that is my true love
Come after me and mow.'

One unfortunate Exmoor maiden was overtaken by a suitor with no face. She went out of her mind, but lived for years. 'If 'twas her time come she'd ha' seed a natomy' (skeleton).[2]

A schoolfellow at Staplegrove taught me a pretty charm with running water in 1908. I also heard it at Over Stowey in 1920. Go out alone and fill a cup with running water. Drink it and say:

'Water, water, running free,
May my love run swift to me.'

There are a few singing games and counting-out rhymes which were thought unlucky and supposed to have some reference to witchcraft. Sally Go Round the Moon was one, and there was a witches' dance which none of the old people would let us play at. There was a counting-out rhyme which rather seems to refer to the witches' coven:

'One, two, three, four, five, six, seven,
Eight, nine, ten,
Eleven,
Twelve,
and THIRTEEN.'

We used to use this until we were warned that "'twas turble unlucky'.[3] Another that was thought equally ominous was:

---

[1] North Somerset.
[2] John Ash, carter, East Lucott, 1948; also Crowcombe, 1925.
[3] Staplegrove, 1905.

'Eena, deena, dina, dess,
Catla, weena, wina, wess.
Eggs, butter, cheese, bread;
Stick, stack, stone dead!'

There is certainly a sinister suggestion about this that it was used to select a victim.[1]

[1] Mrs. Key, Bath, 1906.

2

Supernatural Creatures

A. GHOSTS, WRAITHS AND WARNINGS

SOMERSET, like most other rural counties in England, abounds in ghost stories, and those that follow are only a very small selection from the material available. Many of these are universal types, but there is a large proportion of tales of the Wild Hunt, or the Yeth Hounds, and among the historical ghosts are many from The Duking Days, as Monmouth's Rebellion was called. I have arranged the tales in four divisions:

(a) *Spectral Lights and Warnings*, (b) *Dangerous Roads*, (c) *Historical Ghosts*, and (d) *Haunted Houses and Exorcisms*.

(a) *Spectral Lights and Warnings*

Corpse Candles

The tradition that spectral lights give a forewarning of death was examined by both Richard Baxter and John Aubrey in the seventeenth century, and the belief in them is still active in Somerset.

There was a suicide by drowning near Minehead in the 1940's, and the farmer's wife at East Lucott said, 'They'll zee the lights a-dancing now where he sank down.' When an old woman lay ill in the cottage above Nutscale Ford a neighbour going to nurse her saw the corpse-lights floating about in the cleeve and was terrified. They floated on before her to the cottage door. An hour later the old woman died. This I had from the neighbour herself.[1]

'I've heard tell of they down to Skilgate when I was a child. I do think someone seed they over to Winsford, but I can't call it to mind properly.'[2]

The Spunkies

Will o' the Wisps in Somerset are called *Spunkies* and are believed to be the souls of unbaptized children, doomed to wander

<hr>

[1] Tarr Ball, 1949.　　　　[2] Brendon Hills, 1888.

until Judgement Day. These are sometimes supposed to perform the same warning office as the corpse candles.

Stoke Pero Church is one of the places where 'they spunkies do come from all around' to guide this year's ghosts to their funeral service on Hallowe'en. One St. John's Eve, an old carter called me to watch from Ley Hill. The marsh lights were moving over by Stoke Pero and Dunkery. 'They'm away to church gate, zo they are. They'm gwaine to watch 'tis certain, they dead cannles be.'[1]

Midsummer Eve is the night on which the spunkies go to church to meet the newly dead, and also the night on which the spirits of those about to die may be seen entering the church.

Hammets Walk

Hammets Walk runs from Wilton Church to Upper High Street, Taunton, beside the Wilton stream behind Taunton Gaol. In my childhood this was haunted by a ghost with green hair. We children called this ghost *Spunky*. It is possible that there was a child murder by drowning there, though the green hair seems to suggest a water spirit. There is often, however, a confusion between the spirit of a river and its victim.

'As children we used to listen for the plop-plop footsteps of the fairy with green hair at Hammets Walk, and run away as scared as anything.'[2]

Such a ghost was also seen at French Weir after a boy was drowned at flood-time about 1906–7.[3]

'I've heard tell on'n many a time; my mother did say 'bout them.'[4]

A Death Warning. Wellington

Very late one night a workman called Marrish was on his way home down Tower Lane. As he came near to the church he saw that it was fully litten up. It was too late for any service, and so, fearing that evil-doers were robbing the parish box, he turned aside and hammered on the sexton's door. It took some time to rouse the sexton, and longer for him to dress and get the keys. When they reached the church, all was silent and dark. Nothing had been disturbed. A few nights later Marrish died suddenly at the very hour at which he had seen the strange light.[5]

[1] East Lucott Farm, 1942.
[2] Mrs. S., Rich's Holford, 1957.
[3] Personal memory, 1906–12.
[4] Mrs. L. (82), Crowcombe, 1955.
[5] Oral collection, 1909.

A Hawkridge Warning

'Our house was over by the church, and I was sat in the kitchen one night in the winter, and there came three knocks on the door, thundering great knocks tew. We think 'tis boys playing, so I go out arter'n, and there in the moonlight was a white shape moving, so I follow, see. It did move all round churchyard and come up to stile. I cudent move for my life's sake. Vicar told me later the words I shud ha' said — "Why troubles thou me, in the name of the Lord?" and it would ha' spoke and found peace. But I didn't know then, and I cudent ha' spoke for fright. So it went away all among the tombstones and disappeared. Talk about frightened, I was that all right.

'Next day we come to hear my mother's sister had died that night. 'Twas come to tell us.'[1]

Burgess the Miner

Burgess the miner was a widower, who lived with his little daughter in a cottage in White Water Combe. After a time he fell in love with a worthless woman, and as they found the child a nuisance he murdered it and threw the body down a mine-shaft. This proved no concealment, for a mysterious light shone above the shaft, so Burgess took up the body, buried it hastily in a bank side and left the moor. Two sheep-stealers saw a rag sticking out of some loose earth and thought a sheep had been hidden there, for this was the usual sign. When they began to scrape back the earth, however, they came on a child's hand. Burgess was pursued and caught. He was hanged at Taunton Gaol in 1858. There is still a ghostly light to be seen at the place of the murder but it is very unlucky to see it. If it is seen by a child it foretells death before twenty-one.[2]

According to Snell death comes within a year of seeing the light. This seems to be a common belief about seeing spunkies, for in 1909 a maid in our house who had been frightened by a turnip lantern came in crying out that she had seen a spunky and would be dead within the year.

There is said to be a light which appears occasionally at the scene of the Monksilver Murder. Again it is very unlucky to see it.[3] At Shapwick it is believed that a light is sometimes seen above the site

---

[1] Told by H. F., Hawkridge, gardener, Crowcombe, 1956.
[2] Simonsbath, 1920.   [3] Williton, 1954.

of the pit into which the bones of St. Indractus and his companions were thrown. It is always a sign of coming trouble. Lights, however, can be helpful and not dangerous, as the story of the Minehead Rood Light shows.

The Minehead Rood Light

Very early in the last century a terrible storm rose in the Bristol Channel, and the Minehead fishermen who were out at sea were given up for lost. But one by one the craft struggled into the safety of the little harbour. They had been guided, they said, by the light in the rood loft of St. Michael's Church, which had guided their forefathers for four hundred years. Only, in spite of the cloud and spray, they had never seen it shine so bright. The crowd who heard them knew that the light had been blown out by the storm. The old man who told this tale said that his grandfather and the other fishermen were convinced that the ghosts of drowned Minehead mariners had come to their aid. A carving on the outside wall over the east window of St. Michael's runs:

> 'We pray to Jesus and Mary
> Send our neighbours safety,'

and the sailors had come again in time of need.[1]

(b) *Dangerous Roads*

The Knight in Harptree Combe

A belated farm labourer passing late at night through Devil's Batch, and knowing it to have an uncanny reputation, saw a dark figure in front of him and anxiously asked the time.

'Past midnight, and time you left this place to Those to Whom it Belongs,' said a deep, cold voice. Then the vision clanked away, the starlight shining on his armour as he moved.[2]

The Smuggler's Road

A gentleman walking one moonlight winter night along the road from Chard to Crewkerne heard pistol shots, then a sweating, labouring horse galloped past him with a bleeding Preventive man swaying in the saddle. He was pursued by a lighter, faster animal

---

[1] From an elderly man who was told it as a boy (about 1890) by the eighty-year-old grandson of one of the survivors.
[2] East Harptree, 1940.

with a cruel-looking rascal atop. They took no notice of him. Down in the moonlit fields he saw a fierce fight between three or four men, and again saw and heard heavy pistols.[1]

There are several roads on the Blackdown Hills that have a sinister reputation. Among them is the road from Hillyhead which runs past a cemetery. It has been haunted time out of mind. From Cityford to Broadstreet along the Hemyock road a ghostly calf wanders, and the stones of this old Roman station are themselves uncanny.

West Somerset, too, has a good many haunted roads. At Merlands Corner near Churchstanton the traveller may be joined by a wisp of white mist which drifts along beside him with the sound of trotting hoofs. The less lucky travellers may actually see a headless man on a headless white horse, while at Duddlestone near Corfe on winter nights a very fine horse, whose hoofs make no sound, is sometimes seen, ridden by a headless rider with a long, flowing cloak.[2]

Surtees of Tainsfield

'At Tainsfield near Kingston St. Mary on Old Christmas Eve, old Mr. Surtees is supposed to ride a white horse down Tainsfield Drive. There's a rattling of chains and dreadful noises, then he disappears. We used to say:

> "Mr. Surtees
> He wobbled the knees
> All on a Saturday night." '[3]

From Hawkcombe to Chetsford Bridge the Exford Road has the name of being badly haunted at times. You will rarely find any hill ponies nearby after dusk, and horses are known to play up and break into a sweat and refuse to go forward along this road. A friend and I have heard hoofs clattering hollowly after dusk. Fortunately, as the farm people said, we were then riding across Lucott Moor and saw nothing. Our horses suddenly bolted for home. Another rider along that road once heard a most peculiar sound, 'neither neigh, whinny nor shriek,' coming from the road. He, again, was

---

[1] Chard, 1908.   [2] School-fellows, Corfe, 1907–12.
[3] Mrs. M., Nailsbourne, 1959.

down below by Chetsford Water, but he was unable to stop his pony till they reached the Wilmersham Common Gate.[1]

One portion of the old coach road over the Quantocks is a good deal troubled by the ghost of the Tinker Walford, who was hanged in chains on Walford Gibbet for the murder of his wife in 1761.

Between 1923 and 1955 I have collected scraps of tradition about the haunting. On winter nights one is supposed to hear the clank of the chains as the invisible body swings to and fro;[2] some even say that at the time of the murder you can see the gibbet and the body, and others say that at certain times there is a putrid smell, like a dead sheep, and a smell of tar. At Dead Woman's ditch, on the crest of the Quantocks, they say that the shrieks of Walford's victim can still be heard, though actually the murder took place about a mile away. Perhaps the tradition of another death clings to this place.

The Bridgwater coast road from At. Audries to Holford has a very uncanny reputation. The Black Dog has often been reported there, and a coffin has sometimes been seen lying in the middle of the road, and a white shapeless thing has been met by belated travellers. Though the road has been widened and the thick woods on the edge of it have been cut down, the road is still disliked by motorists.

Pinkworthy Pond

Pinkworthy Pond was haunted by the ghost of an old farmer who had drowned himself in it. It was said to be very unlucky to see him. In 1906 a Mr. Grey was walking over Exmoor near the Chains, back to the farm where he was staying. As he was unsure of his way he was very glad to see a figure standing by Pinkworthy, and he shouted out to ask which path he should take. He got no answer, and when he had shouted three times, the figure disappeared. He had to find his way home as he could, went astray into the bog and arrived back at the farm in a state of collapse, so thoroughly chilled that he fell dangerously ill of pneumonia. The farmer's old mother nursed him back to life, and her only comment was, 'Now 'ee do know who 'ee zeed up Pinkworthy.' In 1926 the tradition was still alive.

Brockley Combe

Brockley Combe, near Bristol, is a famous beauty spot, but is haunted by a terrifying trio of ghosts.

---

[1] Exmoor, 1948–50.   [2] Carew Arms, Crowcombe.

The first is a phantom coach, driven at a gallop, regardless of motorists, cyclists, or pedestrians. It is said to have caused otherwise unaccountable accidents, most of which have been fatal. It was seen fairly recently by a cyclist, a football team and a man who had been a complete sceptic.

The second is the Evil Clergyman, a Mr. Hibbetson, who rescued the injured Squire of Chelvey, nursed him, frightened him into changing his will, and then hastened his death. He was himself collected by the Foul Fiend during a great thunderstorm like a similar criminal on Exmoor.

The third ghost is The Old Woman. She is very rarely seen, some say once in twenty-six years, but is, curiously enough, the most dangerous of the three. Death or madness was thought to follow even a glimpse of her, as I was told by someone whose cousin had seen her in 1912.

Brockley Manor, nearby, is said to be very badly haunted, and I have obtained some accounts of the haunting from the Smyth-Piggott family who live in it, but they are rather vague, more about a presence that is felt rather than anything seen or heard.

Phantom hearses or coaches, like that on the Brockley road, are so common in Somerset that I have put a collection of references to them in the Appendix, to which I have also added a few references to the Wild Hunt, or Yeff Hounds, which are so widespread in West Country Folklore.

The New Year's Eve Hunt

A typical example of the Wild Hunt is to be found in the story of the Hunting Squire of Norton Fitzwarren. Folk fiction has been busy here, since there was presumably no one to overhear the squire's meeting with the Yeff Hounds.

One New Year's Eve the Squire of Norton Manor was drinking and roistering at Langford Budville, when he suddenly took the notion that he would go home. It was close on midnight, and they all warned him against moving, but he laughed and swore that he didn't care if he broke his neck, and he climbed on his horse with such a volley of oaths that they were glad to shut the iron bolts behind him and draw up close to the fire.

As for the Squire, he rode off merrily till he came to Young Oaks, where his horse swerved aside from a great pack of black hounds. If the Squire had been as sober as the horse he would have got to his prayers, but instead he told the Hounds to go to Hell (from which they had just come) and slashed at them with his whip. Green fire ran up the lash and scorched the rider and horse, which bolted in good earnest, and away the Squire went with the ghostly pack behind him. On the Common at French Nut Tree the horse stumbled, and it and the Squire both broke their necks.

Every New Year's Eve, and of late years on other stormy nights as well, the Drunken Squire rides his fated way towards Norton Fitzwarren. Sometimes the unfortunate may meet him galloping in terror over the Common from Carter's Gate to French Nut Tree. If such a traveller should hear other sounds let him not look, but cast himself down and cross his hands and feet for his soul's safety, — the Hounds of Hell are hunting their prey.

There are other nights when the unfortunate soul tries his best to return to his home at Norton Manor from Langford Budville, but he never gets there.

'The drive from Norton Fitzwarren Manor is haunted by the ghost of a hunting squire riding from Langford Budville to Norton Manor. He only appears on certain nights. We lived at the Lodge, but we never saw him.'[1]

(c) *Historical Ghosts*

The Danish Camp. Dowsborough, Quantock Hills

Dowsborough had been a Roman look-out or Summer camp, and tradition says that a band of the Danish sea-robbers made it their fort while they preyed on the villages. They were betrayed by the women they had kidnapped, attacked on a feast night and massacred. On wild autumn nights at midnight they say you can still hear the revelry, followed by the clash of arms.

Another tradition of the Dowsborough massacre is that one boy's life was saved by one of the kidnapped women. You can still hear the little exile singing sadly up on the height where all his kinsmen died. Wordsworth mentions him in one of his poems.

The Danes are still remembered in Somerset. I was told, 'The Danes were hurd-yeaded[2] men who did beat ours.'

The Island Ghost. Steepholm

On Steepholm there are the ruins of a thirteenth-century

---

[1] Mrs. A., Crowcombe, 1955. [2] Red-headed.

Priory, and on moonlight nights ghostly steps can be heard by the Battery. They are called St. Gildas' Tread.

Master Babb. Chard

Master Babb murdered a rich widow by stabbing her, after which he left the knife in her hand, robbed her, and made off quietly. It was supposed that she had committed suicide, and the luckless victim was buried at the cross-roads. However, a Justice of Taunton suspected foul play and ordered the corpse to be exhumed. He then summoned the already aghast inhabitants of Chard and ordered them to pass by the body and touch it — knowing the ingrained superstition in Somerset that 'a murdered body bleeds at a murderer's touch'.[1]

Master Babb was among the procession but as his turn grew nearer his nerve failed and he made a sudden betraying bolt for safety. He escaped the pursuit, however, but his own haunted conscience tormented by a persecuting ghost, with the dagger in the hand he had placed it in, forced him to give himself up later in the year. He was tried and hanged at Chard, 1614.[2]

The Duking Days

The Bussex Rhine and King's Sedgemoor

Believing that the Battlefield of Sedgemoor must be badly haunted an elderly gentleman in the last century began to make enquiries. He was met by stolid stares until at last a local farmer said: 'I been over they parts, man and boy. Never seed nothing, never heard nothing neither, but one foggy night, and then 'twas a drunken chap somewhere t'other side of the rhine shouting, "Come over and fight!" But there, I'd other things to mind.'

It will be remembered that 'Come over and fight!' was the despairing cry of Monmouth's Army.[3]

The Rider. Sedgemoor Levels

One of the cruellest tales of the Sedgemoor Rising is that of the captured countryman who was a noted runner. He was promised his life if, roped to a fast horse, he could keep up with it. He did so;

---

[1] Compare with 'Jack White's Gibbet'.
[2] Local traditions. See *Somersetshire*, C. R. B. Barrett, 1894, p. 218, with an account from Sir Symonds D'Ewes (17th-century Justice of the Peace).
[3] Told to Miss Phoebe Clatworthy in Taunton about 1890, and told to me by a friend of hers.

and, having won their bets, Kirke's Lambs hanged him. His sweet-heart drowned herself. At times she is seen as a White Lady, and at times the sound of running feet and galloping hooves are heard keeping step together.[1]

The Monmouth Officer. Taunton Castle

Taunton Castle is haunted by the tramp of soldiers bringing the Sedgemoor prisoners to the Bloody Assizes in 1685. The landing of Castle House is haunted by a man in riding dress and heavy boots. He is dark and wears a full Charles II wig. He has a sword, a sash, gauntlets, and a heavy pistol in his belt. He tramps up and down restlessly. I have heard and seen him as a child, and only realized in later years that he was a ghost.

Heddon Oak. Crowcombe

Tradition still says that half a dozen fugitives from Sedgemoor were hanged on Heddon Oak, and it has therefore an uncanny reputation. Chains can be heard clinking, and there are moans from choking men. Horses ridden hard come up from below at Lea Crossing, coming steadily nearer, but no horse or rider ever arrives. I had been told these traditions in 1908, and in 1935 I myself heard the sounds. I had difficulty in controlling my own pony. In 1953 two friends were walking along Heddon Browside when they became aware of a horse galloping so furiously from Lea Crossing that they stepped right off the road and well back against the hedge to get out of the way. They thought it was a runaway or someone hunting. Nothing arrived.

The Rebel and His Dog. Locking

There is a tragic tale at Locking of the rebel squire in the Duking Days who escaped from the Sedgemoor carnage and got home safely. His wife hid him, but alas, when soldiers came searching his faithful dog guarded his hiding place too fiercely and too well. The dog was killed and his master hanged, and ever since the unhappy pair wander around the home they both loved. Perhaps it is some comfort to them that they are together.

I know of two people who have seen them — both in their child-hood days when no one had told them the story.[2]

But according to a very old sexton in 1902 the Locking Ghost is

---

[1] Local traditions.   [2] Weston-super-Mare, 1900.

the Lady of the Manor. Sir John Plumley escaping from Sedgemoor, where his two sons died, hid in a coppice near the Manor,
was betrayed by his wife's pet dog, and hanged from an elm still
standing in 1900. The poor lady ran distracted and, with the dog in
her arms, plunged to her death in the well. Her ghost and the dog's
are seen between two yew trees at the end of the Manor Walk.
They disappear into a long disused well.[1]

Local Evil-Doers

Popham's Pit

Sir John Popham, the Hanging Judge, was riding above Wilscum
Bottom when his horse stumbled. Both horse and rider fell, and
were killed in the deep gulley below. In this lies a bottomless pool
called Popham's Pit. No one has cared to sound it, because it is
well known that it has an entrance straight into Hell. If any cattle
fall in they completely disappear. The Hanging Judge himself,
with his head awry from his broken neck, was seen by a cowman in
his own farmyard. Since then he has been banished to a copse on
Wilscum Hill.

Madam Walters. Harptree

There was a lime avenue at the foot of Smitham Hill where
Madam Walters was 'troublesome'. It led to Richmond Hall, her
old home, but since it was cut down she has not 'come again'.
According to local ancients she fell in love with a Captain, who
preferred her beautiful sister. As wicked as she was plain, she locked
the beauty in a cellar and starved her to death. She was a Litton
woman and owned mining rights in the calamine works, and on her
death a waggonload of gold and silver plate was sent up to London
to Chancery, guarded by Shepherd Hatch. Horses refused to drag
Madam Walters' hearse, so very unwilling men had to do it.[2]

Cannards Grave. Shepton Mallet and Frome

Giles Cannard owned a thriving inn and was a very prosperous
man.

Everyone knew him, most of them respected him, only a few did
not like him. They said, while the townsfolk laughed at them, that

[1] Local traditions, 1916. This is the version given in Knight, *Sea-Board of
Mendips*, 1902, pp. 398–400.
[2] Collected by Mendip friends about 1930.

young men gambled away their fortunes in his house and he stood and smiled. They said that swearing and vile speech were always to be heard there as soon as the Town Council or the Parson were absent. They said that he always had a·full cellar of choice wines when other inns had none, that he used silks and velvets no one else could buy, that there was always fresh meat roasting on his spits — in short, if some of his customers were not sheap-stealers, they were highway robbers or smugglers.

But Giles Cannard did not care for their tongues. He was rich and meant to be richer.

And then one day he found a way to sign a paper giving him a great estate — so he forged that, and grew so wealthy that the people of Shepton Mallet began to listen to the few merchants of Frome who were right.

They asked to see the papers and found his forgery upon them and a great crowd went out to the inn to hang him. When he saw them coming he killed himself, and they buried him at the cross-roads upon the hill where he and his footpads used to lurk.

It was useless!

In a little while all Shepton Mallet was in fear for he had 'come again' and was to be seen at his old inn, and on the hill above the town. The inn soon fell into ruin, but his ghost still swings from a gibbet near the cross-roads.

Jack White's Gibbet. Castle Cary

Another haunted gibbet story illustrates the belief in the bleeding of the corpse at the presence of its murderer. The story comes from the eighteenth century. A traveller had put up at an inn in Castle Cary, and had been unwise enough to boast of the money he carried in the hearing of some of the local roughs. One of these, Jack White, followed him and murdered him at the Wincanton cross-roads. The body was found and carried to the inn at Wincanton, where every-one for miles round came to look at it. Among them was Jack White, too self-conscious of his guilt to stay away. As he came up to the bier a thin trickle of blood ran down the face of the corpse. He turned to run, but it had been noticed, and he was caught and forced back to the bier again to touch the body. The blood gushed out, and the whole town was convinced of his guilt. He was hanged up at Wincanton cross, accused and proved guilty by his own victim.[1]

[1] Local traditions told to a friend at Bruton, 1920–35. See H. Irving.

(d) *Haunted Houses and Tales of Exorcism*

The Blue Lady

The Elizabethan part of the Rectory at Crowcombe is haunted by the Blue Lady. She appears at very rare intervals, and then only to children. The last time she was seen was in 1929 upon the landing of the old house. She was in silvery blue with blue shoes. It seems a common thing for children to see ghosts and to take them quite as a matter of course.[1]

The Person in Silk. Huish Barton

This good lady is to be heard at night at Huish Barton, her dress rustling as she moves about from ·room to room. She does not appear as an omen, but seems to have taken the family as her own. She might be taken for a variant of the Northern Silky but that she does nothing useful about the house. A pigeon is a death omen in this place, which suggests some connection with Northern tradition.

The Crescent Ghost. Taunton

A clergyman calling at a house in the Crescent at Taunton saw an old lady in black silk, wearing mittens, sitting quietly in the parlour. He thought she was a visitor like himself, and since she made no answer to his greeting he thought she must be deaf. He, therefore, stood looking out of the window until the maid came back to take him to the drawing room. When he turned round the old lady had gone, without a rustle of her stiff silk dress, nor did the maid, nor his host and hostess know anything about her. The ghost was, however, famous in the neighbourhood, and there was a vague tradition that she was Mrs. Fitzherbert.[2]

Tales of Exorcism

Master Lucott. Porlock

There is a pretty general agreement about the methods of ghost laying, and the tale of Master Lucott may be taken as a representative one. Master Lucott was a Porlock pirate, who made himself a general nuisance both at sea and on land, when he came into

---

[1] Mrs. B., Crowcombe, 1952. *Jack White's Gibbet*, for the true history of the murder.
[2] Taunton, 1907.

Porlock to spend his gold. At last a Bristol ship gave battle and it was Master Lucott's boat that was sunk. When his body was washed ashore it was given Christian burial because of his wealth, but for all that he could not lie still, and even appeared in Porlock Church at service time. So they sent for twelve priests to drive him out, but they were timid men, and when Lucott's ghost bore down on them they turned and ran. When he heard this the priest of Watchett offered to try. They sent him in first, and by the time they had plucked up courage to follow him, he had engaged the ghost in talk. If a ghost is spoken to it must answer, and ferocious as Master Lucott was he was no match for the Watchett priest, who soon trapped him into a question he could not answer. He was now in the priest's power, who made him mount a donkey and ride with him back to Watchett. The ghost could do nothing against the donkey because of the cross on his back, but by the time he got to Watchett he was in a furious temper. There was a fool in Watchett who had no more sense than to peer out at them, and to jeer at the ghost too. The ghost kicked out and put out his eye for that, but that was the last piece of evil he did, for the priest ordered him into an iron box, waded out and threw him far into the Severn Sea. Some people were afraid he might be dredged out again, but others remembered the quicksands just there, and praised the wisdom of their priest.

There are some differences of opinion about this tale. Most people say that the ghost's mount must have been a donkey because no horse would let a ghost ride it; but one old blacksmith said: 'If he were properly shod no ghost would fright'n.' The secret of protective shoeing is one widely known but strictly kept by the West Country smiths.[1]

The foolish watcher motif is one that occurs in several tales. I found a characteristic one in the Mendips.

There was a wicked old farmer who came again after his death. It became dangerous to cross his land and so twelve clergymen came together to lay him. They forced the ghost to appear to them and used all the right prayers, but it gave a burst of fiendish laughter and shot away. A foolish farm lad had crept up to the house to peep in at the window. This broke the power of the exorcism, and the ghost blasted the boy as he passed, so that he lost the few wits he had had. So the clergymen had to start all over again. This time

[1] See also F. J. Snell, *A Book of Exmoor*, pp. 228–9.

they locked all doors and covered all windows and put a pregnant woman in the midst of them. The sinlessness of the unborn child conquered the ghost, and they packed him off to the Red Sea, and he hasn't yet come back.

The Banker's House. Wellington

A less elaborate exorcism was performed in a house in Fore Street, Wellington, which had been the home and business place of a banker, who must have been a bad character, for he returned in a very malignant form. It took two clergymen to lay him, and they had to be of different denominations. So the Vicar and the Baptist Minister undertook the job, and they succeeded.[1]

Cock-stride Ghosts

The strength of an exorcism is believed to wane in time. In Somerset there are certain troublesome spectres who, despite repeated attempts to lay them, are known to be returning to their old haunts by one cock-stride every year. Two of these persistent ghosts are Judge Popham and Madam Joan Carne, the witch of Sandhill Manor.

Blue Burches, no longer friendly but bent on revenge, has left his duck-pond.[2]

Black Dogs

Halfway between the ghosts and fairy creatures are the Black Dogs which are widespread throughout England and Scotland, but which are especially common in Somerset. In Scotland the 'Muckle Black Tyke' is a form taken by the Devil, but in Somerset the Black Dog seems more generally to be thought of as a ghost, sometimes human and sometimes canine. The cross-road between Selworthy and Tivington, for instance, is haunted by a spectral dog. Some say this is the ghost of a suicide and others that a coffin fell and broke open, that the skull of the corpse was cracked and the ghost escaped — a primitive piece of belief — but both accounts agree in calling it a ghost. The Witch Tree near Stogursey has long been supposed to be haunted by a big, black dog which is the soul of Harriet the Witch. Tales of this creature have been recorded from 1890 to 1960. The latest was of a motorist who threatened to sue the owner of a big black dog which leapt out from behind a tree and

---

[1] A labourer, Wellington, 1947.   [2] See Part II, Section 2B.

went for him. One canine ghost is the Prior's Dog, who haunts a ruined monastery in North Somerset, and accompanies the ghostly Prior on his walk in the lane. The Black Dog of Huish Barton is described in a letter written in 1849 by the departing owner of the house, who had seen it. It was generally regarded as a family dog ghost, and was seen by the servants in the house, and once by the gardener, standing with the ghost of its master under a tree. It was most often seen lying across the threshold like a Barguest.

These dogs seem in some way to be allied with the Church Grim, the black dog who guarded the churchyard from the Devil. A dog was often killed and buried secretly in the north side of the churchyard so that its ghost could guard the dead. It was considered important that the dog should be pure black. The connection between the Black Dog and the Church Grim is clearest in the rather rare cases of the benevolent Black Dogs. In the 1930's there were cottage women living in one of the remote Quantock coombes, who used to allow their tiny children to wander off and play on the hillsides alone. When they were rebuked for letting the children run into danger they said, 'They'll be all right, the Gurt Dog up over, he'll take care of they.'

An old lady of eighty-five told me in 1960 of a Black Dog experience of hers in Canada. She had apparently carried the belief out with her from Somerset and brought it back again.

'When I was a young girl I was living outside Toronto in Canada and I had to go to a farm some miles away one evening. There were woods on the way and I was greatly afraid, but a large black dog came with me and saw me safely to the door. When I had to return he again appeared, and walked with me till I was nearly home. *Then he vanished.*'

A more indisputably Somerset story was told me by a very sweet and gentle cottager who had once had occasion to climb the Quantocks late one winter afternoon. When he had climed up Weacombe to the top the sea mist came down, and he felt he might be frozen to death before he got home. But as he was groping along he suddenly touched shaggy fur and thought that old Shep, his sheep-dog, had come out to look for him. 'Good dog, Shep. Whoame, boy!' he said. The dog turned and led him right to his cottage door, where he heard his own dog barking inside. He turned to look at the dog who had guided him, which grew gradually larger and then faded away. 'It was the Black Dog, God bless it!' he would always say. It is unusual for anybody to touch the Black Dog without coming to harm.

Other accounts of the Black Dog seem more as if it was the Bogey Beast of tradition.

'I hadn't left Budleigh Hill by two gunshots when there it was, the nasty thing, running by my side. 'Twas awful. It had four legs, and it was black, and had great fiery eyes as big as saucers, and it ran on until it came to where the water crosses under the road, and they things, of course, never can abide running water, so it just couldn't get across, and it went up in the air like a flash of fire.'[1]

The saucer eyes seem the most common feature in the description of the spectral hound, which may occasionally be white or grey instead of black. Another common feature is that the sight is generally a death portent. The Winsford Hill Dog is a representative type.

On Winsford Hill on autumn nights a traveller may be stopped by a black hound with glowing saucer eyes. If he tries to advance he will die, either at once or very soon, but if he stands still the dog will slowly vanish until only its eyes still glow. As soon as they disappear the traveller is free to move on, but some lesser ill-luck will follow. There was once a farmer whose frightened pony danced near to the spectre before he could stop it. The farmer did not die, it was the pony who collapsed half a mile from home.[2]

A large dog, 'bigger than a hound-dog,' which has eyes 'so big round as saucers', is sometimes seen in the lane near Stapley. It is always an omen of death. Some people say it is white and others grey, but all agree on its glowing saucer eyes.[3]

The sea-road from St. Audries to Perry Farm was said to be haunted by the Black Dog. As children we always called it 'Death Mile', for it was certain death to see the dog. The tradition is still alive, for in 1960 I was told by a member of Williton Women's Institute that a man had seen it recently and had died within the year. Another member said: 'Yes, I knew someone who saw the Black Dog along there. She was with her boy-friend and it came right up to them. No, I don't think he saw it, but *she* did, and she died within the year of T.B. The poor little dear didn't live to be twenty.'

Black Dogs are also seen near some of the barrows, such as

[1] Oral tradition, Selworthy, 1907.   [2] Mr. T., farmer on Exmoor, 1940.
[3] Oral tradition Water-Row.

Wambarrow near Dulverton. They are regarded as treasure guardians.

B. PIXIES AND FAIRIES

Fairies

The Fairy world, it is believed, impinges very closely on the every-day world and has a definite edge. In some places this world is so narrow that a hands-breadth spans it, in others it stretches away to infinity. This explains the many varying human experiences in fairy-land, and the perplexing time factors. A man may touch it in a stride over it, and see it in the twinkling of an eye, another may have one foot in it and one foot out, and be regarded as a monumental liar or a visionary, and yet another may step forward into it and be lost for centuries.

Fairy rings (gallitraps) are obvious entrances to the Edge of Beyond, so are cetain caves, wishing stones and wells, but no one can tell how long the stay may be if one enters.

Glastonbury's claim to be the Isle of Avalon was not made until medieval times in literature, although oral tradition must have been very strong. Such an island, glinting out among the shifting mists of the great marsh that stretched from Mendip to Quantock, must have appeared as being of another world. I have, however, in my childhood met with stubborn disagreement from this among the very old, who declared either by implication or definite statements: "Twere down Bristol Channel' (Weston-super-Mare), 'Down Severn Sea it do hidey' (Bridgewater), "Twere a island same's thiccy' (indicating the Holmes), 'but her do goo under-like zea if 'ee comes upzides with 'en.'

This is in direct agreement with the Green Meadows of Enchantment of the opposite Welsh coast. Sailors in the last century were said to have landed on these and spent a pleasant time, only to find as they re-embarked that the islands had disappeared. Fairy folk from there used to visit Laugharne Market, and the islands like the treasure of Cadbury are supposed to sink out of sight if the curious draw too near. The sea and lake maidens in this district are called Morgans as in Wales.

There is a cerain amount of confusion in this part of the world, as there is in the Danehills of Leicestershire, between the Danes of history and the Tuatha de Danaan.

'There be a bit of verse as do go

> "If Dolbury digged were
> Of gold should be the share",

but nobody hasn't found the treasure yet. And for why? Well, to start up with it don't belong to they, and so they won't never meet up with it. 'Twill go on sinking down below never mind how deep they do dig. I tell 'ee 'tis the gold of they Redshanks as used to be seed on Dolbury top. To be sure there's clever, book-read gentlemen as tell as they was Danes, and another say 'twere all on account of their bare legs being red with the wind, but don't mind they.

'My granny she did tell they was fairies, ah, and all dressed in red, and if so the treasure med be theirs. If they was Danes how do 'ee explain all they little clay pipes as 'ee can find on Dolbury Camp. They did call 'em "fairy pipes", old miners did. An' if there be fairy pipes then there was fairies, and nobody need doubt they was the Redshanks.'[1]

The Fairy Toot near Batcombe was an ancient barrow which was excavated in 1789. It was supposed to be a fairy-haunted spot, and the tradition of the desecration survived for many years, almost to the present day. There was also a Fairy Toot at Stoney Littleton near Wellow, which is now deserted by the Fairies. Cadbury Hill, too, was formerly a fairy resort. It is hollow, and they stored their gold in it. They were driven away by the church bells, but they left their gold behind them. It is not, however, to be found by mortal men, for it dives down into the earth when they dig for it.

When I was very small I used to help an old cottager in his garden (at least I thought I helped), but whatever else he might do I always made the charm sign for him in the new-turned soil. I don't know what the stick was, he always gave it me (hazel, I suspect), but no matter how erratic my efforts he was immensely pleased — a child had blessed his garden safe from the 'vairies'. The sign, which I have seen once or twice since, tucked away in some discreet corner of a farm or cottage garden, is a heart between two crosses. I knew one woman who used it on her pie-crusts, but only did it because her old mother always used to. Keightley mentions it as a pastry charm.

Buckland St. Mary is said to be the last place where the fairies were seen in Somerset. The Devon Border is a short half-mile

[1] Axbridge, 1907.

away. The Fairies no longer inhabit Somerset, for they were defeated in a pitched battle with the Pixies, and everywhere west of
the River Parrett is now Pixyland.[1] The tradition of the Fairy Fair,
reported by Richard Bovet in *Pandaemonium or the Devil's
Cloyster*[2] is still alive, but is now described as a Pixy Fair. I was
told at Staple Fitzpaine in 1926 that various travellers to Chard or
Pitminster had seen it, but no one dared to go near it. In 1930 I was
told at Stoke St. Gregory that my informant's grandfather had seen
it, but had kept well away. He was a gifted man, born in the chime
hours. This would be about 1856. Here is another version, which is
told along the Devon-Somerset border near Wellington. It was
taken down in the dialect as the tale-teller spoke.

"Ave 'ee yeard 'bout th'old man that come whoame vrum
Markut? He wuz comin' up road loike when 'er zaw the girt Pixy
Vair, an' on one o' the stawls thur he zaw a gold mug vull up top o'
gold pieces. Zo 'er thart to hisself, "Ef I d' grab 'ee I shall 'ave 'nuff
money vor rest of me loife." Zo, with no more ado he d' gallop
right on dru Pixy Vair, laying hold to mug as her went, an' went on
whoame as vast as pony's legs 'ood carry'n. Highly delighted with
proize he took 'n to bed vor zafe-keeping. Wull, next marnin' vust
thing he looks at what was 'is mug,— but 't 'ah gone! And what do
'ee think? Arl there was was a girt twoad-stool. And when 'ee goes
out to get pony 'ee finds 'tis scamble-footed, an' zo 'twas 'er was
like it the rest of 'er days.'[3]

There is another about a better-mannered man who received
better treatment.

'There were a Varmer over-right our place did zee the vairies to
their Market, and comed whoame zafe tew. Mind, he did'n never
vorget to leave hearth clean 'n a pail of well water vor'n at night, 'n
a girt dish of scalt cream tew. My granny did zay her'd get'n ready
vor'n many's the time. Zo when her rode up tew stall, zee, all
among the Vair, 'n axed mannerly vor a zider mug a-hanging up,
the vairies answers 'n zo purty as if they was to Taunton Market.
With that Varmer lugs out his money-bag 'n pays, 'n what do 'ee
believe! They gived 'n a heap of dead leaves vor his change, quite
serious like, Varmer he took 'n serious tew, then her wishes 'n
"Good-night, arl", 'n her ride whoame. He d' put zider mug on
table, 'n spread they dead leaves round 'n careful, then he d' zay,

[1] H. W. Kille, 1961.   [2] 1684, pp. 208–9.
[3] Mrs. B., Kingston St. Mary, 1960.

"Come morn they won't none o' they be yur, but 'twere worth it to zee the liddle dears' Market."

'Come morn, when Varmer went to get his dew-bit avore plough-ing what do 'ee zee on table but a vine zilver mug 'n lumps of gold all round 'n.'[1]

The Pixies

The Pixies are a more prosaic type of creatures than the fairies. Their physical characteristics are easily recognized. They are red-headed, with pointed ears, short faces and turned-up noses, often cross-eyed. The following account, given me in 1951 by a very old man at the cottage in the Brendon Hills, paints a vivid picture of the pixies.

The Red-Heads

'Old Billy he were coming to Washford Market, must ha' bin May time, an' he do meet Someone in under lane, and he'd a fine hurd-yed (red head) to him. Old Billy he d' take path over field, when he d' spy another hurd-yed, then he do croopy down like along hedge, an' try to go on down by covert, n', bless 'ee, there come along another hurd-yed, n' this one's got a North eye so well. So old Billy he did do what he should ha' done fust go. He d' shut his eyes, n' cross his two fingers, 'n go on sebem steps. That did it. Wadn't no hurd-yed nowhere when he d' look, and he come on down to Washford.'

Another noticeable thing in the pixies' appearance is that they wear green, while the fairies wear red, at least in Somerset.

The most famous activity of the pixies is to mislead travellers in the same way as Shakespeare's Puck. There are various safeguards against this, the two chief ones are to turn one's coat inside out or to carry a wicken cross. On the Hallow-e'en of 1943 I was sent by an old farmer's wife on Exmoor to fetch in her husband from the sheep lawn close to the house. She gave me a wicken cross to carry. I found him quite bewildered in the middle of his own field, though the gate was plain to see in the moonshine. I heard nothing, but he was plagued by the sound of pixy laughter. After I had given him the cross he recovered himself and came back quite readily.

[1] Compiled from fragments from Annie's granny, 1905; haymakers, Bishop's Hull, 1910, and a friend, Milverton.

When I was very small I used to go with the children from the Manor Farm at Brompton Ralph to visit a very old man and listen to his tales of the pixies. Here are two of them.

There was a farmer who sold his sheep at Raleigh's Cross and bought a bag of meal, and he left it late to come home to Brompton Ralph, so he took a short cut, and in the dusk he put his foot in a gallitrap. And then the pixies had him. They made a hole in the bag and the meal trickled away, they snagged his feet with brambles, and at last he fell down exhausted beneath a briar that grew in three parishes; and there he stayed, half dead with fear. When morning came the meal sack was nearly empty, so he turned back to gather up some of what he'd lost, and he had to go round by Elworthy Barrows. His poor wife was in a state when he got home. 'Gurt vule,' she cried, 'Why didn't 'ee turn thy coat and zave the meal!'

Bishop's Lydeard

There was a man on the Quantocks who picked up a pixy grindstone and put it in his pocket, though he knew the pixy wife had lost it.

The mist came down, and he tramped round and round Much-Care all night tripping over bramble loops until he fell flat.

'Gallitrap' is the local name for a pixy ring. It is made by the pixies riding the colts round and round the field. If you put both feet inside it you are in the power of the pixies, if only one you can see the pixies, but can still escape. If you have committed a crime the gallows grass is already woven for you and you will be hanged. Presumably this originally meant blood-guilt. A briar that grows in three parishes is magic.

The Pixy Field

'You know the field above Quantock Farm. Up by Butter Market Lane it is. I remember about thirty years ago 'twould be, there was a labourer from Little Quantock was pixy-led all round it one autumn night. He couldn't find his way out till next day. He went all round and about it, but the pixies had him. Albert Davis his name was. No, he couldn't get out.'[1]

Sometimes the misleading seems not to have been entirely idle, but to be a piece of fairy justice, as in the three following stories.

[1] Leslie J., shopkeeper, Crowcombe, 1956.

'There were a old farmer, a terrible near old toad as lived over Ley Hill, and he cheated at market something fearful. So the pixies they took and led'n home round by Horner Valley and Pool Bridge and left him up to the knees in the middle of the girt mud-zog[1] by Bucket Hole Gate.'[2]

'To Please the Pigsies'

There was a worthless, do-nothing old fellow, who was too lazy to give a hand even when everyone was pushed trying to save the harvest. He just went about in rags as dirty as a pig. So one night the Pigsies caught him crossing their field to steal the mushrooms and didn't they teach him. They led him all round and about through thorns and brambles all night till his rags couldn't be worn any more and they pushed him into the pond to clean him until he promised to mend his ways. He got home at last and borrowed his brother's breeches and went to work in the harvest field for a whole week without pay '*to please the pigsies*' or he would have been teased again.[3]

Old Farmer Mole

They'll tell 'ee three things 'bout an Exmoor Pony 'can climb a cleeve, carry a drunky, and zee a pixy'. And that's what old Varmer Mole's pony do.

Old Varmer Mole were a drunken old toad as lived out over to Hangley Cleave way and he gived his poor dear wife and liddle children a shocking life of it. He never come back from market till his pockets were empty and he was zo vull of zider he'd zit on pony 'hind-zide afore' a zingin' and zwearin' till her rolled into ditch and slept the night there — but if his poor missus didn't zit up all night vor 'n he'd baste her and the children wicked.

Now the pixies they did mind'n and they went to mend his ways.

'Twad'n no manner of use to try to frighten pony — he were that foot-sure and way-wise he'd brought Varmer safe whoame drunk or asleep vor years, wheresoever the vule tried to ride'n tew.

This foggy night the old veller were wicked drunk and a-waving his gad and reckoning how he'd drub his Missus when he gets to whoame when her zee a light in the mist. 'Whoa, tha vule!' says he,

[1] Large puddle.
[2] Told by John Ash, carter, as we drove home to Lucott from Porlock, 1941, past the 'zog'.
[3] Blagdon, Staplehay, Pitminister, Near Wellington.

'Us be to whoame. Dang'n vor lighting a girt candle like thic. I'll warm her zides for it!'

But pony he wouldn' stop. He could a-zee the pixy holdin' thic light and 'twere over the blackest, deepest bog this zide of the Chains — zuck a pony down in a minute 'twould, rider and all.

But the old man keeps on shouting, 'Whoa, fule, us be tew whoame!' And rode straight for the bog — but pony digged in his vour liddle veet 'n her stood!

Varmer gets off'n and catches'n a crack on the head and walks on to light. He hadn' goed two steps when the bog took and swallowed 'n!

Zo old pony trots whoame. And when they zee'd 'n come alone with peat-muck on his legs they knowed what did come to Varmer — and they did light every candle in house and *dancey*!

After that Missus left a pail of clean water out at night vor pixy babies to wash in, pretty dears, and swept hearth vor pixies to dancey on and varm prospered wondervul, and old pony grew zo fat as a pig.[1]

Not all pixies are dangerous or malicious, and they made good friends to those who treated them well.

There was an old man who lived down at Roebuck Gate, and when his wife died he stayed there all alone. One day Mrs. Trollope-Bellew said to him, 'Isn't it very quiet, Tom? You're all by yourself now. Aren't you ever lonely?'

'Oh no, ma'am. Yew zee, there's pixies in the garden.'[2]

The Broken Ped

A farm labourer whose way took him across Wick Moor, heard the sound of someone crying. It was someone small, and within a few steps he came across a child's ped (spade or shovel) broken in half. Being a kindly father himself he stopped and took a few moments to mend it neatly and strongly, never noticing that he was standing close to the barrow called 'Pixy Mound'.

Putting down the mended ped he called out, 'There 'tis then — never cry no more,' and went on his way.

On his return from work the ped was gone, and a fine new-baked cake lay in its place.

[1] I heard many versions of this tale as a child, but my favourite was this, told me by an old farm labourer at Kinsford in 1905.
[2] Crowcombe W.I., 1958.

Despite the warnings of his comrade the man ate it and found it 'proper good'. Saying so loudly, he called out, 'Goodnight to 'ee,' and prospered ever after.[1]

Withypool Ding-Dongs. Withypool; Knighton Farm, Exmoor; West Somerset

The farmer of Knighton was very friendly with the pixies. He used to leave a floorful of corn when he was short-handed, and the pixies would thresh it for him.

They did an immense amount of work for him until one night his wife peeped through the keyholé and saw them hard at it. She wasn't afraid of their squinny eyes and hairy bodies but she thought it a crying shame they should go naked and cold.

She set to work and made some warm clothes for them and left them on the threshing floor, and after that there was no more help from the pixies.

They did not forget the farmer, however, for one day, after Withypool church bells were hung, the pixy father met him on an upland field. 'Wilt gie us the lend of thy plough and tackle?'[2] he said.

The farmer was cautious — he'd heard how the pixies used horses.

'What vor do 'ee want'n?' he asked.

'I d'want to take my good wife and littlings out of the noise of they ding-dongs.' The farmer trusted the pixies and they moved lock, stock and barrel over to Winsford Hill, and when the old pack horses trotted home they looked like beautiful two-year olds.[3]

The Pixy Threshers

A farmer called Rawlins who lived near Stolford was awakened by the sound of flails coming from his barn in the dead of night, and despite his wife's entreaties got up to see who was threshing his corn without leave.

'No good'll come of it. Do 'ee bide,' begged the dame. ''Tis lucky to hear'n. Yew mid find 'tis all threshed for 'ee by mornin'. But They don't like to be seed.' But the farmer's curiosity overrode all thought of losing such luck, 'besides 'twad'n mannerly not

[1] Stogursey, Quantock coast.   [2] Pack horses and their crooks.
[3] Oral traditions: cottager's wife, Chibbets Cross; cottager's wife, Badgeworthy, 1940–55.

to say "Thank 'ee all" to the pixies when they was as welcome as flowers in May.'

At this time the dame was in despair at his thick head. "Tis the one thing as will send'n away so sure as God made liddle apples,' she cried, but the farmer stumped downstairs and out to the barn.

There was a strange light shining, the thud of the flails was deafening, and peering through the half-door he beheld half his corn already threshed and filling bulging sacks, while the other half lay on the floor being well and truly thumped by two sturdy little men in red caps. As he watched one mopped a steaming face. 'How I do tweet,' he said. The other, still swinging his flail, grumbled, 'So thee do tweet, do 'ee? Well then, I do tweet and double tweet, looky zee.'

Three days theshing completed before midnight and the rest half finished! It was too much for the farmer. 'Well done then, my little vellers!' he shouted. The light went out and all was silent. When at last he ventured into the barn half his corn was in the sacks, the other half was still stacked waiting in its 'stitches', and the threshing floor was as bare as a beaver's behind. They never came back.[1]

A fragmentary version of the fairy ointment story is *Minehead Market Pixies*, chiefly remarkable for the mention of the changeling, which is rare in Somerset folklore.

"Tis never wise to see pixies unless they wants 'ee tew. There were a Minehead woman, a clacketty giglet kind o' trapes, who zeed her uncle as was a pixy-child a-helping hisself in Minehead Market.

' "La, dear," say the gurt fule, "Fancy seeing you down yur. What be doing?"

' "Which eye can 'ee zee me with?" say the pixy man cunninglike.

' "Why, both on 'em," say the fule wench. Well, he blew in 'er vace and her had the dimpsies ever after.'[2]

To Prepare for the Pixies at Night

> Clean the Hearth,
> And sweep the floor.
> Then go out
> And shut the door.

---

[1] Kilve, 1908; Alfoxdon, 1905; Cannington, 1910.
[2] Told to a friend by an old market granny down at Quay Town, 1930.

A Pixy Invocation

> Pelm in ahind the door,
> Pail o' water on the floor,
> Go to bed and go to sleep;
> Us'll pinch 'ee if 'ee peep.
> Pelm in ahind the door,
> Pail o' water on floor;
> Go to bed and shut your eyes,
> Come mornin' ee'll get a nice surprise.

This is a children's game which I learned in a remote cottage near Simonsbath. The 'surprise', generally a bunch of flowers or a sweet placed on the child's boots, made the game a great favourite. If you looked everyone pinched you. It is interesting to find this late survival of Puck's ritual sweeping of the dust behind the door.

Other Fairy People

Apples left on the trees after the apple harvest are the property of the fairy folk. In West Somerset to gather these is to go 'pixying' or 'pisking'. On the Blackdowns it is called 'pixy-wording', that is 'pixy-hoarding'. In South Somerset it is called 'Cull-pixying', but in East Somerset it is just 'griggling'. It is a quite usual West Country description to say, 'He were so merry as a grig.' In the tale of Skillywidden the little fairy found by the hedger was called by him 'Bobby Griglans'.[1] It seems a reasonable inference that the grig is fairy of sorts, perhaps some connection of Lazy Lawrence, the guardian spirit of the orchard.

Lazy Lawrence appears to take a pony form at times, like the colt-pixy who attacked the boys who took the griggling apples. He was also known in Hampshire, where he takes the form of a forest pony. A Somerset proverb runs,

> 'Lazy Lawrence let me goo,
> Don't hold me Summer and Winter too.'

In 1930 I heard a Crowcombe mother call to a dawdling child,— 'Come on then! Have Lawrence got into your legs?' Apparently he

---

[1] Hunt, *Romances of the West of England*, p. 95.

could transfix orchard thieves. The Apple Tree Man (see Part IV, Section 1) may have been a variant of Lazy Lawrence.

Wayland Smith

A memory of Wayland Smith still hangs round Keenthorne Corner, near Fiddington, though in later years it was believed to belong to the blacksmith who shod the Devil's horse. This place has a very strange effect on horses passing by. Quite a number of them turn nappy, break into a sweat and try to bolt. Wayland Smith is now more definitely associated with Shervage Wood near Dowsboro. Wayland's Pool is here, where the smith would thrust his red-hot shoes to temper them. He was the blacksmith to the Wild Hunt, but if you had the courage to go away and leave your pony without looking back he might shoe it for nothing.

'It is a strange thing,' a hunting farmer said to me once, 'how still a horse will stand at Wayland's Pool. Why, you can dismount and walk away, and they won't move.'

White Ladies

I have come across three white ladies in Somerset, who seem to be more fairies than ghosts. One of them is the White Lady of Wellow, who haunts St. Julian's Well, now in a cottage garden. She played the part of a banshee to the lords of Hungerford, but she seems to have been rather a well spirit than a ghost. The Lake Lady of Orchardleigh is another white lady who is rather a fairy than a ghost, but the most definitely fairy-like of the three is the White Rider of Corfe, who on certain nights of the year gallops along the road on a white horse, turns aside clean through a field gate and into the middle of a meadow where she vanishes. I was told about her by some old-age pensioners in the Blackdown Hills in 1946. One of them said, 'She shone like a dewdrop,' and another, ''Twas like liddle bells all a-chime.' She seems like a stray member of the Fairy Rade.

The Woman of the Mist

On Bicknoller Hill, and above on Staple Plain, the Woman of the Mist can be seen. She has been seen within recent years, and like the Scottish Blue Hag she herds the red deer. Like her, too, she is sometimes reported as an old, frail crone and sometimes as a great, misty figure.

Uncanny People

'Ghoases, jackies, pixies and spurrits.'

Jackies are Jack o' Lanterns, Will o' the Wisps, Spunkies.

Unbaptized infants are believed to become spunkies until the Second Advent. Spurrits are Bogies, hobgoblins like Blue Burches, galley-beggars, bull-beggars, or even Bloody Bones.

Blue Burches

Old Blue Burches was a harmless 'spurrit' who lived in a shoe-maker's house on the Blackdown Hills. He was only once seen in his true shape and the little boy said he was an old man in baggy blue breeches.

On one occasion a farmer sitting talking to the cobbler heard heavy steps thudding down the stairs. The cobbler took no notice at all, then the stair-door opened and a wisp of blue smoke floated across the kitchen and out into the garden. The farmer rose hastily. 'Never 'ee mind old Blue Burches,' said his host. 'He never do no harm. Worst he've a-done was keep a-rapping when the bwoy was sick. I just throwed bed-stick across chimmer at'n and it do dis-appear. The missus her found'n next morn all a-stood neat'n nice down to kitchen. Full of mischief he is — he'll run droo house like a little black pig 'n pop into duck-pond without a drop of water splash. Comin' whoame market night he've a got the old cottage all aglow as if 'twere afire. 'Tis purty to zee.'

But the farmer had no admiration for such ways, he was a church warden. So off he went to the Parson and *he* got another Parson for moral support and they went to the cobbler's. An old white horse was quietly grazing by the duck-pond. They called the small boy and questioned him. Yes, that was old Blue Burches, said the child. Could he get a halter on him? The child meant no harm to the spirit, but was proud to show how well he could manage it. He threw the halter over the white horse's head, and at once both parsons cried, 'Depart from me, ye wicked!' Into the pond went Blue Burches, never to appear again in such a friendly form.[1]

The Creech Hill Bull-Beggar

At Creech Hill near Bruton two crossed bodies were found during quarrying in the 1880's. They crumbled to dust but were supposed to be Norman and Saxon. The waste land below the hill

[1] Collected from harvesters at Trull, 1907-9, and schoolfellows, 1909.

has a bad name and at one time was infested with badgers and hares. Late travellers hear following footsteps and a gruesome black shape suddenly leaps over the hedge.

A farmer returning from market saw something lying in the middle of the road and, fearing it was someone hurt, went to offer help. The figure in the road rose and, growing to an eerie height, let out an eldritch screech. The farmer took to his heels, his uncanny pursuer keeping easily beside him until he fell exhausted across his own fire-lit threshold. His family rushing from the lamp-lit rooms to help him saw a long black figure bounding back to Creech Hill and heard a shriek of laughter as it disappeared.[1]

Another very staid and sober Bruton gentleman had urgent occasion to cross Creech Hill late at night, and armed himself with a lanthorn and a stout hazel stick. Halfway across he became aware of deadly coldness and something tall and black rose out of the ground at his feet. He struck heavily at it with his staff — but the stick went through his tormentor and he found his feet were rooted to the ground. Peals of crazy laughter deafened him at every lusty stroke he made, nor could he free himself until a distant cock crew. At once he was alone on the hill with the first pale light of dawn. He took a couple of steps forward and fainted dead away. When he came to his senses the sun was shining brightly, and dragging himself from hedge to tree and stone wall and gate he somehow managed to get to a lane above farm land. Here his feeble call for help was heard by two ploughmen. Only staying, one to reach for his iron-tipped gad, the other to put a scarlet pimpernel in his hat, they bravely faced the haunted hill and carried the now fainting man to the safety of the farm. He was desperately ill for many weeks — but said my informant, 'Ef'n he hadn' took thic old lantern an' a hazel gad with 'ee he med ha' bin a dead corpus up along so her 'ood.'[2]

The Headless Galley-Beggar

At the cross-roads from Over Stowey downhill past Bincombe to Nether Stowey it is the amusement of a galley-beggar to appear suddenly on a dark night, and, shrieking with mirth, to seat himself on a hurdle, remove his head and place it firmly under one arm,

[1] Oral collection, Bruton, 1906.
[2] Oral collection, Bruton, a housemaid, 1906; an East Somerset gardner, 1925.

then push off on his toboggan downhill. The queer light around him and his yells of laughter continue right down to Castle Street.[1]

Bloody-Bones

This most unpleasant hobgoblin, as we were assured in my childhood, lived in a dark cupboard, usually under the stairs. If you were heroic enough to peep through a crack you would get a glimpse of the dreadful crouching creature, with blood running down his face, seated waiting on a pile of raw bones that had belonged to children who told lies or said bad words. If you peeped through the keyhole at him he got you anyway.[2]

C. THE DEVIL, GIANTS AND MONSTERS

The Devil played a very familiar part in Somerset folklore, and various tales about him will be found in Part IV. Like the Giants he was a great stone-thrower, he might be seen leading the Yeff Hounds in the tradition of Odin, or ambling alone on a black horse or a giant pig. He was always on temptation duty, and various precautions were taken against him. On Banwell Hill, for instance, a great cross of turf is built into the hill, two feet high and seventy feet long. I was told locally that the Devil would raise a wind to blow down an upright cross, but he could do nothing against this one. Some traces of Devil worship are occasionally uncovered. In a wood above Thurloxton a black leaden figure of the Devil is hidden. It is extremely difficult to find and it always brings bad luck on the finder.[3]

Standing stones or large rocks are humorously accounted for by the sport of the Devil or Giants, or a conflict between the two. 'The Devil threw Triscombe Stone at a man who cheated him, and it went so far into the hill that only a little bit of it shows'[4] is a typical example. A more elaborate one is the tale of how the Devil made Cheddar Gorge.

How the Devil made Cheddar Gorge

The Devil was wandering over Somerset one day and he spied the smooth green line of the Mendip Hills. Here was something he

---

[1] Collected by a friend, Kilve, 1920.   [2] Taunton, 1904–12.
[3] 1912 from an Ivyton labourer, and 1955 from William C., artisan, Crowcombe.   [4] Mrs. S., Crowcombe W.I., 1958.

could spoil! Taking a spade he dug a huge cleft out of the hills by Cheddar leaving the Gorge. Grinning with delight, he flung the first mighty spadeful out to sea, and it fell with a huge splash in Severn Channel making Steep Holme and Flat Holme. It was hard work or he was getting careless for when he tossed away the next load it didn't reach the sea at all but made Brent Knoll. This wasn't the mischief he had planned. They do say he meant to drop the rest of it on Watchet and Minehead, but he wasn't risking a bad throw. He loaded the rest of the Mendip rock into a basket on his back and set out westward — and there he found the River Parrett right across his way. He took such a mighty leap that he landed on all fours, and the rock was all flung out over his head. It made the hill at Combwich. The mark of his hoof can still be seen there, but where he put his hands down on the other side of it nobody remembers nowadays.[1]

The Devil is always appearing as a night rider, and in many of the tales he seems a descendant of Odin, though in two of them he is riding Frey's boar.

The Unholy Pig

The Squire of Sydenham was crossing his estate late one Autumn night when he met a black monkey astride of one of his pigs. The thing grinned at him, and said: 'How does your pig amble now, Squire?' But the Squire was one too many for him. 'In the name of the Lord she ambles well,' he said. At that the monkey vanished in a raging flame, leaving a smell of roast pork behind it.[2]

There is a Black Monkey Lane in the neighbourhood. Another version of the same tale is more rustic in tone.

Cannington Park is a place few country people will cross after dark. Witches haunt the old fort near Combwich, and between there and Dewsboro there is an ancient track where the Yeth Hounds run with horns on their heads and a horned rider behind them. And every night the Devil himself rides over Putsham Hill. Not many care to be out there after dark, but once an old man too feeble to make haste was overtaken by night, and heard clashing hoofs behind him. He was too crippled to fling himself face down and so save his soul, so he faltered on till the Fiend drew abreast of him, riding a monstrous boar. 'How does my mount amble, grandsire?' he said. 'The dear Lord knoweth her ambleth well,' said the

---

[1] Quarry men at 'Blue Ball', Triscombe.   [2] H. E. Killie, 26/3/61.

old fellow in terror. At that the wind died and the rider and steed vanished in a flash of fire, and left the old man to go home in safety.[1]

Often the Devil is seen carrying a soul to Hell.

The Black Rider

'Sam Thatcher was taking a bit of pudding and some teddies (potatoes) to Granny Thatcher down Combwich Track. His missus had just heard that the old lady was but poorly and a hotted-up pudding might cheer her up, and what was two-three teddies for a strong feller like Sam to carry to his mother. It was too late to send the children, so after his mug of tea, and bacon and cabbage, Sam set out again to walk back to Combwich. He slouched along the dark way wishing he had a match for his baccy, or a bit of company on the road. Then glancing up he saw a rider beside him. The track was pitch dark but he *saw* the huge black horse and its shrouded headless rider.[2] He heard no sound as they passed and vanished. Sam looked at the dark way and took a firm grip on the sack of teddies. 'Twould make a club of sorts and Granny Thatcher must have her pudding.

'When he got to her cottage she met him briskly. "Sammy," she cried joyfully, "I be so happy as a mouse in cheese. I bant over-looked (bewitched) no more. The old black witch down to Stert — have felled in rhine and drowned. The Black Man have took she, and I'll do justice to Susie's puddin'." '[3]

Again the Devil is on the look-out for any mention of his name, any infringement of taboo or unholy boasting. The following stories illustrate these three points.

The Croydon Devil Claims his Own

One evening at Rodhuish Forge a local bully — a red-haired butcher's boy — fell foul of a young plough-boy from Croydon and thought he would give him a scare. In the talk round the smithy fire he began to tell tales of the Croydon Hill Devil, who appeared on the lane with horns and tail, groaning. Everyone drew away

---

[1] Cannington, 1920.
[2] This 'hooded Odin' was seen by a man whose brother was living at Comb-wich in 1908.
[3] Combwich, oral tradition.

from him, for it was unlucky talk, and soon he went away to the butcher's, where a bullock had been lately flayed and he knew he could find horns and a tail to suit his purpose. The other lads were reluctant to go home in the dark after the name that had been spoken, but the Croydon lad had three miles to go, and he set out alone with the plough coulter, which he had brought to have mended, over his shoulder. The group had not yet broken up when he came running back like one mad, with a blood-stained plough coulter in his hands.

'I've a-killed the Devil!' he said. 'There he were on gate a-groaning at I, horns an' all. I asks 'n be he the Devil or no, 'cause I'd a-got to take plough coulter to farm. But he bellows that terrible afore I knows it I just up an' hits un with coulter so 'ards's I could, 'n her fell down dead. I've a-killed the Devil!'

The blacksmith had a good guess who the Devil had been, so he and a few more from the village went up the hill to look for the body. At the gate to Croydon Lane they found a bullock's hide with a great gash on its skull, but the butcher boy was never seen again. The Devil of Croydon Hill had taken his own. On stormy nights the butcher's boy can still be heard groaning and shrieking, and when the Devil rides over Croydon Hill the butcher's boy is among the souls that follow him.

This is said to have happened rather over a hundred years ago. I have met people who knew the old man 'who had killed the Devil' when he was a boy.

The Carter and The Devil

A carter at Combe Davey Farm was once ordered by the farmer to take a very heavy load over into Devon for a merchant. As it had to be delivered by a certain time, the man was ordered, to his great distrust, to put the team in and start overnight — *which was a Sunday*. He got the team to the top of the steep, dark hill and here they refused to budge. With a frightened curse the man jumped on to the wagon to lay the whip on to them, and at that very moment a distant church clock struck twelve and it was Monday! So out of the darkness stepped the Black Man himself and advanced to claim this sacrilegious team, driver, goods and horses. But the horses were good Christian beasts who knelt at Christmas and each had his stall decorated with a wicken cross. So off they went down hill within an inch of the Black Man's hooves, and maybe theirs trod on his for they left him far behind yelling in pain. At the last curves the carter left the wagon, out at one side, at the next the greedy farmer's goods were spilled, at the next the shafts broke and the wagon rolled off the road — but the Christian team were found grazing quietly at the bottom of the hill with not a scratch on them.[1]

The Devil and The Blacksmith

At Fiddington once lived a smith who was so proud of his craft that he very unwisely boasted he could shoe the Devil's own horse — 'Ah! An' shoe he to rights too.'

But one midnight he was called up by a traveller whose horse had cast a shoe, and when he looked at the rider of the great black horse, he found it was the Devil himself.

The terrified smith had the wit to pretend he had left a hammer at his cottage and ran for the parson. The parson, however, refused to return nearer than the roadside hedge where he remained to watch, having told the smith as he valued his soul to keep his word and shoe the horse —

But he must take no payment!

The smith set to work, and the Devil was so delighted with the result that he presented the man with a bag of gold, but was told politely, 'I never don't take nought vor work done at night.'

Baffled the Devil glanced round, and caught a glimpse of the lurking Parson.

'If it hadn' a-been vor that old blackbird in behind orchet,' he yelled, 'I'd a had 'ee vor zertain zure!'

With that both he and his horse 'vanished in a vlame o' vier'.[2]

The Giant Gorm. Maes Knoll

In the days when giants still roamed over England the Giant Gorm was one of the largest and stupidest. He was also as cowardly as he was clumsy — and that's saying a lot.

One day he was wandering across England carrying a nice sizable hill on his spade. Why he had dug it up he had forgotten, and what he meant to do with it or where he was taking it he didn't quite know.

At all events, he forgot he was coming to the end of the Cotswold Hills, and trod over the edge so unexpectedly that he dropped the hill slap in the Avon Valley, and that made Maes Knoll. Then he

---

[1] Pitminster, maid's mother.   [2] Oral collection, Aisholt, 1912.

leant on his spade to look at what he'd done, and his weight sunk it so far into the ground it made the Wansdyke.

Now, Vincent was Lord of Avon at that time, and he was very proud of his beautiful valley. He wasn't going to allow this monstrous chucklehead to spoil it any further. Mounting his war horse he rode out full tilt to challenge the intruder *and Gorm turned to run away!*

He took about five steps and fell over his own feet.

As his head splashed into the Bristol Channel and the water closed over it the Lord of Avon let him drown in peace and rode home again. His bones became the two islands, Steep Holme and Flatholme; but what happened to his spade no one remembers.

The Giants of Stowey

There was a time, long, long ago, when giants came to live close to Nether Stowey. They flung up a huge mound for their Castle, and lived under it.

Some of the people fled to Stogursey, others ran up hill for safety on Dowsboro' Camp, and others, poor things, just stayed where they were.

No one liked going past the Castle even if they had to, and most of those who *did* come back were pale and terrified. The Giants had a horrible way of putting their hands out of the hill and grabbing a sheep, or a cow, or a man.

Once the monsters had tasted men's flesh they grew ravenous. They made a raid on Stogursey Castle, and beat it down flat, and chased the Stogursey people till they caught them in handfuls. When this supply ran out they began again on the folk of Nether Stowey.

Most of them were very old (and tough) or very young (and tender) for all the able-bodied folk had run up the hills and were quite safe in Dowsboro' Camp and having a fine time. They didn't know what was going on so a poor old gaffer tried to tiptoe past the Castle and tell them, but an arm came out and got him.

Then a little lad got on one of his father's hill ponies along with a 'drift' of them, and went away past the Castle at a stretch gallop. A hand did come out, but it got such a kick it went in again mighty fast and there was a dreadful yell.

The folk on Dowsboro' heard that and got ready to fight — but when the little lad on his pony got to them they didn't wait to give battle up there. No. 'The men from Dowsboro' beat down Stowey Castle' and after that anyone could pass the hill again — they still don't like doing it at night.[1]

Quantock saying:

> 'Men from Dowsboro' beat down Stowey Castle,
> and men from Stowey beat down Stogursey Castle.'

The Quantock Dragons

According to eighteenth-century writers the Roman general, Ostorius, landed near the River Parrett and climbed over the Quantocks by Cothelstone to attack Norton Camp. The British were defeated, and so large a heap of bodies lay unburied that a huge serpent grew out of the corruption and ravaged the country-side. The Norton folk were in despair until their own Fulk Fitz-warine came to their aid. It was he who had killed the fiery Kings-ton dragon, and this monster he seems to have choked also, with a sword this time. The feat has been carved and painted in Quantock churches for centuries. The Norton carving shows the serpent busy on half a man while the other half prays Heaven for help. The local tradition mixes Roman and Norman as freely as that of the Brendon Hills, where an old man lumped together King Alfred and the Danes, the Duking Days and the Dissolution of the Monasteries as 'The War'.

The Dragon of Aller, who came out of Athelney Fens, was said to have been killed by an Aller man with a great nine-foot-long javelin, which is still to be seen at Low Ham.[2]

The Dragon of Kingston

'There was a terrible dragon to Kingston St. Mary, breathed out viery vlames he did, an' cooked his meat to a turn, looky zee. Well, no one couldn't get near to kill'n for vear of bein' roasted so brown's a partridge. Now, there were a bold veller as had a good head on him, and her climbed lane by Ivyton where there was a gurt rock those days. 'Tis a steep hill, look, and rock was right on brow, so he give a shout to dragon. Well then, dragon he d' look up and zees 'n. Then he opens his gurt mouth to roar vlames, and the veller gives

---

[1] Oral collection fragments, Over Stowey, Aisholt and Quantock broom squires (i.e. gipsies).

[2] Local tradition, Aller.

I

the rock a shove off. It rolled straight down hill into dragon's mouth and choked'n dead. Yes, it did.'[1]

The Gurt Vurm of Shervage Wood

'Now, look see, I wad'n there then so I couldn' swear 'twas the truth, could I now? But 'twas like this, see —

'There was a tremenjus gurt vurm up-over in Shervage Wood. Ah — all a-lyin' in and out the trees an' round about the Camp, so big and fat round as two-three girt oaks. When her felt hungry her just up'n swallow down 'bout six or sebm ponies or sheep and went to sleep comfortable.

'Well then, by 'n by, farmers do notice sheep idn' upalong an' there wadn' more'n a capful of skinny old ponies for Bridgewater Fair that year.

'Where was t'others gone to, then?

'Arter a shepherd an' a couple of Stowey broom-squires went upalong to look-see and didn' come back neither there wadn' nobody at all ready to go pickin' worts on the hill when Triscombe Revel time come around next year.

'The vurm he were gettin' a bit short on his meals like. The deer an' the rabbits they was all over to Hurley Beacon t'other side of the hills, and there wadn' a sheep left, and the ponies, I reckon, had run down over valley to Forty Acre.

'Now, I did hear there were a poor old soul who sold the worts for Triscombe Revel. Her made they tarts beautivull and filled'n up with a thick dap o' cream that made 'ee come back for more so fast as a dog'll eat whitpot. Well, look see, there wadn' likely to be no tarts for her to sell on account of no one going up over to see how worts was ripenin', n' if her didn' sell no tarts to Triscombe Revel her'd get no money for the rent. Poor old soul! Her was in a shrammle!

'Well then, there come a stranger to Crowcombe, all the way from Stogumber I expect, and he were a woodman looking for work. So her up'n tells'n, "Why don't 'ee try cuttin' in Shervage Wood upover, and look-see if worts is getting ripe?" Poor old soul were desperate, see. So her give'n a cider firkin and bread 'n cheese, and watches'n go off up combe.

---

[1] This tale was gathered in 1911 from harvesters and a maid-servant in Cothelstone and Ivyton. I was showed the very place in Ivyton Lane where the stone came from, but there are no real rock outcrops in the neighbourhood.

'Being a Stogumber stranger he wadn' used to Quantock hills and by the time he'd a-walked into Shervage Wood and seed a wonderful fine lot of worts on the way he were feeling 'twere quite time for his cider.

'So he looks round like and he seed a bit of a girt log in the fern. So down he quots an' takes a swig from the firkin an' gets out his bread 'n cheese. He'd just got nicely started on his nummet when the log begins to squirmy about under'n.

' "Hold a bit!" says he, picking up his axe, "Thee do movey do thee? Take that, then."

'And the axe came down so hard on the log he cutt'n in two — Mind, I'm only telling 'ee what 'tis said — and both the ends of• the log begun to bleed!

'Then the one end it up and run as hard as it could go to Bilbrook, and t'other end it runned to Kingston St. Mary, and since they two halves went the wrong way to meet, the gurt vurm couldn' nowise grow together again — so her died.

'Folks down to Bilbrook they call their place Dragon Cross, and folk to Kingston St. Mary they boasts about the same old tale of a fiery dragon — might be as they got the head end of our gurt vurm — but he were all Quantock to start with!

'Well then, the woodman he just sat and finished his nummet, and cut his faggot, and took the poor old soul a girt hatful of worts.

' "There were a dragon there fust go off," he tells her very thoughtful.

'But all her says is, "Didn' 'ee know? Didn' someone tell 'ee?"

'Her were a Crowcombe woman.'

I have written this from early recollections of a jovial Nether Stowey teller of the tale in my childhood and the recitals of local epics and libels by a thatcher of my acquaintance.

PART III

1

Superstitions and Customs

MARRIAGE

ENGAGED couples must never be asked to stand as joint godparents or their wedding will never come off. *Exmoor.*

Throw an onion after the bride. In the Brendons in my childhood it was the custom to throw an onion after the bride to bring a long family. *Brompton Ralph, 1903.*

No one must wear a bride's veil after her wedding or her husband will elope with the wearer. *Ethel Collins, dressmaker, Taunton, 1908.*

On Midsummer Eve tie a wedding ring to your hair and dangle it over a glass. As many times as it rings, so many years before you marry. *West Somerset.*

If you get married on Whit Monday all your children will go to Heaven when they die. *Jane Cobby, maid, Pitminster, 1908.*

In West Somerset the church path is still often chained against a newly wedded pair, with a rope of flowers, or in one instance with tin cans. Perhaps this couple was unpopular. *Minehead, Oxford; Brendon Hills; Broomfield, 1956; Over Stowey, 1960.*

BIRTH

Superstitions concerning a baby

Put a sixpence in its hand the first time you see it. *Porlock Weir, Withypool.*

Never praise it to its face or you will be thought to ill-wish it. Get behind it before you tell its parents what a delightful infant it is. *Crowcombe, 1958; Sandyway; Huish Champflower, 1961.*

Always carry salt in your pocket when you visit it until it is christened. *Blackdowns.*

Keep some primroses under its cradle or in its room, but always more than thirteen. *Wincanton.*

Never let it wear green. *Frome.*

If it is born at full tide it will die at ebb tide. *Porlock Weir, 1946; Kilve, 1939.*

If it is born with a caul it will always prosper, but it will always feel the cold. *Pitney Lortie, 1905–12; Ash Priors, 1908–12; Crowcombe, 1951.*

If you meet a widow when going to see a baby, turn back or you will 'take death to it'. *Annie Price, Taunton, 1906.*

'My brother was born with a caul and such people can never be drowned. He served on a minesweeper during the war and men were never afraid to go in his boat.' *Bruton W.I. 1961.*

There was a caul on sale in Poole Harbour about 1948. I saw it there, priced £5. It would grow damp if the owner were in danger. *Personal, 1948.*

A seventh child of a seventh child can cure the King's Evil on a Sunday, and say a charm over illnesses and sometimes see spirits. *West Somerset.*

DEATH

Touching a corpse prevents one from dreaming of it. *Brompton Ralph, 1908.*

Never cry over a child's corpse for it will have no one to change its damp shroud. *Exmoor, 1906.*

If a corpse remains supple it is waiting for the next member of the family to join it. *Washerwoman, Taunton, 1905–12.*

Dogs howling mean death to the sick. *North Petherton, 1912.*

Transplanting parsley will bring about the death of the gardener. *Schoolfellows, Wellington, 1906; cottager, Quantocks, 1950.*

A sufferer cannot die quietly if there are pigeon or partridge feathers in the pillow. Pull it away gently and he will pass on in peace. *Old lady, Norton Fitzwarren, 1902–12.*

There is a very ancient belief that the dead are blind at first and need guiding. This is a terrible danger to humans however devoted to their dead, so a dog is substituted, a Church dog.

A dead hand passed nine times over a swelling dispels it.

'An old man, whom I met with in visiting, informed me that as a boy he was taken to Ilchester "to be stroked" by a hanged man's hand.' *Excerpt from Poole, p. 52.*

I heard of a T.B. boy being taken to touch the hand of a dead aunt, and was told the cure followed. This was recently. *Porlock district, 1950.*

If an apple tree blooms twice in one year a death in the family will follow. *A farmer's daughter, Wiveliscombe, 1912.*

If you have both fruit and blossom on a tree, remove the buds or there will be a death. Bloom in December means one of the family dies in January. *Nettlecombe W.I., 1961.*

If a swarm of bees light on a 'diddiky branch' a death will follow. *South Somerset farmer's wife; Oare Exmoor.*

Anyone who reads a certain verse in the New Testament will fall down dead. It is not known which verse it is. In confirmation of this North Somerset superstition, I heard a friend of our maid discuss 'The Verse' in our kitchen at Taunton Castle about 1905.

AGE

Every time you tell your age you shorten your life by a year. *Crewkerne.*

Never tell your age or illness will follow. *Quantocks/Spaxton, 1925.*

THE BODY

If your head itches it is a sign of rain. *Quantock Hills.*

Red-haired people are always cruel and sly. *East Quantoxhead, 1907.*

'The sin eater who eats the bread and salt must be an outcast, if possible a convicted criminal, but he has got to have red hair.'

Put a first tooth under the pillow and you will find a present next day. *Taunton.*

Every time you tell a fib a pimple will come on your tongue tip. *School friends, Taunton, 1907, 1912.*

The nose, a sneezing rhyme

> Once your mother
> Twice your lover
> Three times a letter
> Four times you need the nurse
> So hurry up and get her.
>
> *Schoolfellows, Taunton.*

Say 'God bless you' if anyone sneezes or the Devil will catch his soul as it gets jerked out. *Charwoman, Taunton, 1905–12.*

If your finger nails are spotted you will die young. *Taunton, 1905.*

If they have no moons you are a miser. *Taunton, 1905.*

If a money spider runs along your right arm you will receive money, so if it has a web swing it widdershins round your head three times. If it runs on your left arm, you will have to pay out, but swing it sunwise round your head three times and it won't be much. *Quantock Hills, 1905–60.*

If your hand itches rub it on wood and you will receive money. *North Somerset.*

Left hand, pay out money, right hand, receive money.

> Rub it on wood
> Sure to be good
> Rub it on knee
> Sure to be.
> Rub it on a. . . .
> Come to pass (or Turn to brass).
> *Kingston St. Mary, 1960.*

The ring finger is the healing finger because it has been blessed. *Mid Somerset.*

The forefinger is poisonous. *Crowcombe School Children, 1957; Taunton, 1951; Kingston St. Mary, 1912.*

If your ears burn someone is spreading malice about you, so bite your little finger and they will bite their tongues. *Taunton Deane, 1905–60.*

A man with pointed ears was called a 'pixy man'. *West Somerset, 1905–12.*

Tingling ears: left, your lover; right, your mother.

Make a cross of spittle on the sole of your shoe if your feet go to sleep. *Carhampton, 1952.*

Never tickle a baby's feet. It will grow up with a stammer. *Taunton, 1905–58.*

If your feet itch someone is bringing you news.

Itching feet mean you are going on strange ground. Right foot, you will be welcome, left foot, you will have a cold reception. *Kingston St. Mary, 1960.*

TIME

Never ask your family the time, ask a stranger. *May Wyatt, near Crewkerne, 1909.*

(Apparently this means that you are anxiously hastening the lives of your elders in order that you may inherit.)

There is always one minute at noon when everything is silent and God walks the earth. *Glastonbury, 1905–12.*

There is one moment when dusk ends and evening begins when, if you make a wish, 'They' will grant it. *Quantocks, 1905–25.*

DAYS OF THE WEEK

Monday's curse wishes well
Tuesday's curse comes from Hell

(or, Rest of the week it come from Hell).

To curse on a Monday brings luck for the week by frightening away evil spirits and clearing the air. It must cease by noon as on Ashin' Day. Heard on the Gloucester borders: ''Twas only a bit of Monday cursing and the week went well.' *1940's.*

Spoken of a farmer whose cow had met with an accident: 'He'd a-carried his Monday cursing over to a Tuesday, and that was certain ill luck.' *West Somerset, 1950.*

Spoken in approval to a swearer: ''Tis a proper Monday you've seen about.' *Taunton Market, 1955.*

Spoken of an excellent farm worker: 'He were a true Monday-man, swear 'ee black in the vace a' 'ood, and zo quiet as a sheep come twelve o'clock.' *Exmoor, 1949.*

Along the western hills there is also a belief that the more cattle are sworn at and belittled the better the price they make at market.

Monday:	Curtsey to the moon and wish. *Alfoxden, 1911.*
Tuesday:	Get your boots mended on a Tuesday and they'll last twice as long. *Frome.*
Wednesday:	Never tell a secret on a Wednesday. It is sure to be found out. *Wincanton.*
Thursday:	Never picnic under an oak tree on a Thursday. *A school friend, Taunton Deane, 1906–12.*
Friday:	Never start a journey, plant onions or start to make a dress on a Friday. *Quantock, 1906–22.*
	Never marry on a Friday or start any important work. *Taunton Deane, 1904–56.*
	Never put to sea on a Friday. *Minehead, 1904–57.*

A Friday night's dream on a Saturday told
Is sure to come true 'ere 'tis nine days old.

A maid, Pitminster, 1907.

Saturday:　A Saturday new moon is unlucky. *West Somerset.*
Sunday:　　Those born on a Sunday are free from evil spirits.

SUN, MOON AND STARS

The sun and stars dance on Christmas Day and Easter Day. *An old man, Ilminster, 1910.*

If the stars seem very near and the Milky Way is very clear, there will be a children's epidemic with several fatalities. *A Shepherd, Western Hills, 1908.*

A falling star is an angel come to fetch the newly dead. *Miss Ostler, Taunton, 1905–12.*

If on Christmas Eve you can see the Star of Bethlehem you will be lucky all your life. *Kate Littlejohn, maid, Taunton, 1904.*

First new moon of the year

New moon, New moon,
First time I've seed 'ee
Hope avore the year's out
Shall I have summat gied me.

Quantock, 1903–57.

A new moon on its back means a month's rain.

Always curtsey to the new moon and turn your money. *Michael Webber, Crowcombe, 1957.*

Never kill a pig when the moon is on the wane. *Mrs. Keal, farmer's wife, East Lucott, 1946.*

Pick apples when the moon is waning. *Langport, 1956.*

The weather at full moon is fine for a week unless the moon was 'ringed'.

Never sow seeds or beans or peas, cut your hair or kill pork, or make any important change at the dark of the moon. *A gardener, Triscombe, 1956; Exmoor, 1949.*

Never point at the moon, it is dreadfully unlucky. *Quantocks, 1956.*

WEATHER

Never point at a rainbow. *1956.*

If you ever see three rainbows, you will be rich and lucky late in life. *Bagborough, 1925.*

Never whistle on a hot day or you will call up a storm. *Farm labourer, Norton Fitzwarren, 1905.*

If it thunders between November and April it will be followed in three weeks by severe frost. *A farmer, Stogumber, 1958.*

DOMESTIC

Get a clergyman to bless a new house before anyone lives in it. Anything evil will go away. *North Somerset, 1934.*

If a house does not like new tenants they won't be able to stay long.

Houses are lucky to some people.

Always send a cat in first into a new house. If the house is unlucky the cat won't stay. *1905–12.*

Always hang a bunch of fennel over the house door. *Mrs. Govier, Bathpool, 1906.*

If you nail a horseshoe over your house door you will never be troubled by pixies. *Old labourer, Kinsford, 1907.*

Never go out by the front door and come in again by it at once. Use the back door, or you will bring death into the house, but if you sit down and say a prayer all will be well. *From a friend from Glastonbury, 1924.*

A door opening by itself should be closed carefully in case you pinch the ghost who opened it. Never say 'come in' or 'They' will. *Comeytrowe, 1905–12.*

Never start a journey from the back door, or your journey will not prosper. *Farmer's wife, Rowden, 1932; Personally heard at Lawford, 1957.*

A secret of vital importance is always told under the ceiling 'egg'. *Dodington, 1911.* (Many West Somerset plaster ceilings contain ovals).

Never open an umbrella in the house, it brings a shower of bad luck.

A spark in the candle wick is a 'letter from God'. *North Petherton, 1912.*

A coffin handle in tallow, when it runs down and forms a loop, is a sign of death to the person in whose direction it points. *Taunton, 1904–12.*

A winding sheet in tallow, if it runs heavily, betokens ill news. *Broomfield, 1911*.

Draw a cross on your new hearthstone before you light your first fire. Never use an elder stick. *Mrs. Venn, washerwoman, Bishops Hull*.

If the fire will not burn up, sign the cross above it with the poker. *Kate Littlejohn, maid, Taunton, 1904–7*.

Make a cross in salt on your hearth or oven if the chimney smokes and the fire won't burn. If possible, do this with iron.

Blue flames betoken a death. *Minehead, 1938*.

Leaping flames talk. If you are lucky enough to be listening there is one moment when they will tell your future. *Exmoor Gipsy, 1937*.

A tall smoking flame means bad news. *Alice Marchant, maid, North Petherton, 1911*.

Never include elder in your faggot.

Always bind more than thirteen branches together. *Quantocks*.

Never let a clock face the fire. It will surely put it out. *Charwoman, Langport, 1956*.

A harmless old fellow, who had suffered for years with his chest, died. 'He did get the brown-kitties that bad you could hear'n crackly all down the lane.' But old Mrs. Govier was quite fierce in her condemnation of him. . . . 'The wicked old witch, he did spit all over the hearth stone.' It wasn't the insanitary habit that affronted her, it was a far worse danger. Both she and Annie's granny kept their hearths spotless — 'Anyone could use them for a dancing floor.' Annie's granny's uncle had a loose hearth-stone. 'And we know where his savings was tew. No one daren't take they from there.' *Personal memory, Taunton Deane, 1905–10*.

Never spit on the hearthstone, it will bring you seven years' bad luck. *Axbridge*.

Breaking a clock must be paid for in silver. My charwoman accidentally cracked my clock's face and stopped it, and in much distress she at once paid me sixpence. This was not for its value, but because 'you must pay silver for 'un'. As she had unwittingly condemned my soul to cross the dark river she must pay my ferryman's fee. *Drayton, 1956*.

A clock stopping is a sign of death.

If a picture falls down for no reason the Devil is coming after you. *Pickney, 1935*.

Never stand behind anyone to look in a mirror. It brings bad luck. *Kingston St. Mary, 1960*.

If among your household ornaments is an elephant (white or black), it must always stand facing the door. *Mrs. Milner, Nailsbourne, 1940.*

Never step over a broom if you are unmarried. You will bear a bastard child. *Quantocks.*

If two people use a towel together it makes a quarrel. *Middlebrook, 1940.*

Never put new shoes on a table, it is unlucky.

Never put your feet on a table, or there will be quarrels.

If an unmarried girl sits on a table she must marry quickly. *Taunton Deane, 1905–60.*

If knives are crossed on a table, they must be uncrossed by the person who crossed them. *Hinton Blewitt, 1925.*

If knives are given away they must be accompanied by a halfpenny in payment. *Quantocks, 1960.*

It is unlucky to drop a knife, less so if it falls flat.

> 'Stir with a knife
> Stir up strife.'
>
> *Kingston St. Mary, 1960.*

If you leave the teapot lid off, you will have to call the doctor before the day is out. *Quantocks, 1960.*

Throw a pinch of salt over your left shoulder and hit the Devil in the eye. *Taunton, 1905; Kingston St. Mary, 1960.*

> Eat a bit,
> Burn a bit,
> Throw a bit over your left shoulder.
>
> *Exmoor, 1935.*

Stir your pastry clockwise or it won't rise. *Woman cottager, Lydeard St. Lawrence, 1953.*

Jam will shrink if you don't sign a cross over each jar. Use a hazel or rowan twig to stir it, then the 'varies' won't steal it. *From friends, Exmoor and North Somerset, about 1920–30.*

DRESS

Always leave a pin in a baby's frock until it is safely christened. *Informant near Bath, 1920.*

If you stick a crooked pin in the lining of your coat, all the girls will have to follow you. *Exmoor gipsy, 1946.*

Wear a pair of crossed pins under your lapel on market day and you will get the better of every bargain. *Martock, 1907.*

On wearing a new dress, the first person you meet should wish you —

> 'Health to wear it,
> Strength to bear it,
> And money in both pockets,'

then they should spit. *May Wyatt, Chard, 1909.*

FLANNEL

'My mother used to tell all sorts of tales about ghosts and such like and she was afraid of them, so she used to make us all wear red flannel.' *From an informant, a Countryman, Brendons, about 1920.*

FARM

Burn all hedge brushings in thirteen heaps and make sure the most ill-smelling is for Judas. *West Somerset.*

Never leave a rake lying prongs upwards, it will bring rain. If you want to correct this you must pick it up and curtsey to the sun. *Maid's mother, Staplehay, 1909.*

A virgin or a little child can manage a bull or a stallion when no one else can. *Farmer, Martock, 1907.*

An ugly horse is often the best worker. *Farmer, Williton Horse Show, 1955.*

Ugliness is often regarded as a sign of supernatural strength. *Taunton Deane, 1905–12.*

A sow that farrows in May is liable to eat her litter. *An informant.*

To put your hand in dung by accident is lucky.

Bird droppings bring luck.

'Muck luck, good luck.' *Quantocks, 1960.*

The water diviners on the Polden Hills use willow twigs. *Glastonbury, 1946.*

In some parts of Somerset dowsers use hazel twigs placed in a bag. *Street, 1946.*

Dowsers, or Jowsers, are still used in the Mendips and the Brendons. Local dowsers are seldom wrong. Women can be dowsers; Elworthy mentions two, and I know three. *Somerset, 1925–59.*

Never set an even number of eggs or the hen will kick one out. *Quantocks, 1957.*

A double yolked egg is very bad luck to the one who cracks it. *Schoolfellows, Wellington, 1905–12.*

A double yolked egg means a wedding in a hurry. *Corfe, 1911.*

CHURCHES AND CHURCHYARDS

It is very unlucky to get the left hand of the Bishop in Confirmation. *Mid Somerset.*

If a surplice is laundered by anyone of ill repute there will be a stain across it. *South Somerset.*

'Like parson's sermon that ended at four o'clock,[1] there's bound to be another burying in the week.' *Mrs. Keal, East Lucott.*

Never meet a nun face to face; step to the right and the bad luck will pass on the left. *Alice Haggarty, washerwoman, Taunton, 1905.*

The lych gate is the only fairly safe place for a church spy on St. John's Eve, and even then it may mean that he'll be the next corpse through the gate. *Exmoor, 1941.*

Never sit on a lych gate or you will get 'sexton's bones' (rheumatism). *Old sexton, East Somerset, 1912.*

A child's funeral should have girls as pall bearers dressed in white and carrying the coffin slung from white handkerchiefs. *Miss Anne Clatworthy, Taunton, 1902.*

Never have an odd number of mourners on the procession. The lone walker will be the next one to go. *West Somerset.*

Never have a funeral on a Friday.

All flowers used at a funeral must be sweet scented. *Kate Littlejohn, maid, Taunton, 1905.*

Plant a red rose tree on the grave of any good and generous person.

Never disturb the flowers on a grave.

All flowers grown on a grave must be sweet scented.

The grave of an unbeliever will crack open and try to throw out the coffin. *East Somerset.*

Note: This is still believed in a Kentish village, where a dying woman refused to believe in God, and said that if she were wrong seven trees would grow on her grave. The seven trees have grown at separate times, the last one pushing up twenty years ago. The

---

[1] I.e. as sure as sure.

K

iron railing round the grave has had to be moved outwards a second time. *Told to Mrs. Fisher of the Carew Arms, Crowcombe, by a commercial traveller, in 1957.*

'The north graveyard is too cold for a loved corpse. *Taunton Deane.*

The north graveyard is used for suicides, tramps and unbaptized babies. These unfortunates will haunt the locality unless a dog or cat is buried there first. *An informant, Mid Somerset, 1920.*

It is sometimes thought that burial in the churchyard will save unchristened children from being spunkies. 'There's a bit of the churchyard we d' call Chrysamer, where us d' put the poor liddle dears as weren't christened, so 's to save 'n from being spunkies.' *Old Exmoor woman, 1930.* (It has been suggested that Chrysamer may mean 'Christ have mercy'.)

A shroud must be warm, for the grave is very cold. *Mrs. Perry, Stoke St. Mary, 1911.*

Never speak of a shroud or you'll see one too soon. *Mrs. Williamson, Blagdon, 1932.*

The dog's side

An old uncle of an informant came on a visit and on returning from Sunday service was noticed to look very worried. 'They've got their Church Door on the Dog's Side,' he explained, 'whoever heard tell of such!' This particular Church's main door was on the north. The North, as the ancient seat of evil, appears to be accepted as the unlucky side. The sun cannot linger on the graves and warm the occupants. Very possibly the 'Dog's Side' has a deeper meaning than 'unfortunate side' and the church dogs were buried there. *From an informant, 1959, South Somerset.*

Clipping the Church

The old custom of 'clipping the church', that is, dancing round it in a circle with shouts and bell ringing, was observed in several of the Somerset churches on their Revel Days. It continued in Wellington until 1948 and in Staplegrove till 1954. The story told to account for the ritual is of an attempt of the Devil to possess himself of the unfinished church which was foiled by the use of a weathercock, gargoyles and church bells. Finally, he was caught by the dancers and chased away. In Wellington they say he went down

Bug Lane, over Bug Hole Field and on over Bogey Hill till he fell splash into the River Tone.

Sextons' Lore

Those born after midnight on a Friday and before cockcrow on a Saturday can see ghosts and spirits and talk to them without coming to harm. They can cure illnesses and handle animals. As one of these people I was, even as a child, made free of many closely guarded secrets. As a chimes child I was collected into a clan of sextons and listened to many gruesome and frankly heathen rites carried out by various members of this far flung family, which I am quite certain would never have been discussed so openly before any but an initiate.

It seemed to be an approved act that one of them, who was also the village carpenter, secretly reversed the corpses of those of ill repute before nailing on the coffin lid so that they were buried face downwards. 'Showed 'en which way they was bound vor,' said the clan grimly.

Another member had buried a sinner, who had died in a very questionable odour of sanctity, 'on top of the dog'. The belief that a black dog was buried in the churchyard 'to keep the Old Un out' was an article of faith with them all. 'A church do want a galley-cock to crow to the four winds on tower to warn 'en off, and they liddle, wicked vaces all around the church in and out, see, to vright 'ee, and a gurt old black dog to church yard to take a good nip out of Old Nick's back-side if he venture where he idn't wanted.' I was told the reason no dogs' skeletons were ever accidentally excavated was because unpopular souls were laid on top, 'so's they was both kept awake', the dog to do his duty, and the late sinner to repent in endless leisure.

There was always difficulty if a new cemetery were to be opened as no one wanted their dear one to become the 'church walker', and the sexton was secretly appealed to behind the parson's back. I knew one knowledgeable clergyman who expected trouble, but found the first funeral went off most decorously. But I also knew that the large black dog of a local farmer had disappeared mysteriously just before. 'He runned back to his old whoame out over,' said the village, to a man. The Sexton had known what to do. *Personal Collection, 1905–9, West Somerset.*

The ghost of a dearly loved old vicar was seen by his parishoners several times, looking most unhappy. 'They must ha' buried he facing East,' said the village, but no one dared dig up the coffin and set the poor ghost's body the correct way for parsons. *A North Somerset friend, about 1930.*

'Have you heard the superstition about burying a clergyman? All the others are buried facing east ready for Resurrection Day, but a priest should face west in order to be facing his congregation when they rise, and lead them to heaven. I've often wished I could see inside their coffins to see if it is true.' *Member of Stogumber W.I., 1960.*

Bury a corpse where it is sunny.

The last corpse buried must guard the graveyard, unless it is buried face downwards. *Farmer's wife, Exmoor, 1941.*

A suspected criminal is sometimes buried face down. *South-west Somerset.*

Bury a seventh child with a stake through it or it will turn into a dangerous ghost. *A Schoolfellow, Stogursey, 1909.*

In Germany also the seventh child is either a werewolf or a nightmare.

The illegitimate child of an illegitimate child becomes a blood-sucking ghost. *East Somerset, 1940.*

Stick pins in the churchyard wall and you will be safe from evil spirits ever after. *Quantocks.*

Bastards (the Legalizing of)

This was told to me by a bed-ridden old granny somewhere near Goathurst on the Quantocks. She was repeating the tale told by her mother who, as a girl of fourteen, was a witness of this service. I do not know where the mother's family came from — it may have been another western county, but for its interest I have included it. It is a verbatim report except where the dialect was so archaic that an interpreter was needed. Even so, I have tried to use phrases still to be heard in casual speech. The names and locality are slightly altered in order to protect any relatives.

'There was a farmer *Hewlett* up around as were highly thought of by all. When his time came he were terrible worrited 'bout Mr. *George* as he'd done wrong by. Oh dear, 'twas a gurt shock 'twas! Mr. George he'd a-handled varm and stock vor his vather come twenty year and there wadn't none as folks didn't set by like Mr. George, Squire and all. Well, it did sim like he were going to lose all his labour and farm would go to a cousin over to *Taunton*. But varmer he set his mind to do right by un, and his wold Missus as had been the friend to the whole parish she come out brave and she said she'd do as he wished. So poor Mr. George he just done what his dad want. I see them come to church and me but a maid then. And Mr. George he had a loving arm to his dear mother. Then she did up and say in front of all as her and Farmer wasn't a-wed when this dear son come along. Poor old soul! She called him her dear and there wadn't a dry eye to hear her old voice. And that gurt beardy man he do croopy on hands and knees and she do pull hem of her Sunday black over'n and Parson do say the words to right'n so he should a-get farm. Parson he was so quiet as death, but his looks they proper daunted any to miscall 'en, but there wadn' no rabblement, they was too well liked. Farmer died happy — but 'ee see, my dear — old sins do come up again like weeds after a shower.'

SEAFARING

At Worle, when the fishermen go down to sea, they each put a white stone on the cairn or 'fairy mound' on the hillside and say,

> Ina pic winna
> Send me a good dinner.

And more times than not they come with a load of fish. Now in the old days, there was a clever Dick of a fellow who said he didn't believe in luck. He wasn't going to put a stone on the fairy mound, not he. And his catch would be as good as theirs. They'd all see! They did! First go off, *he went to sea on a Friday*, yes, he did. And he'd hardly gone a quarter mile when blest if his old woman didn't come *running after him* in her white apron *calling his name*. You'd think that would have been enough to bring the fool up short. But he wouldn't go home, not he! On he goes and his addlehead of a wife *watches him out of sight*, and *he doesn't put any stone on the cairn*, and he doesn't even say the rhyme, so it just serves him right when he comes *face to face with Parson*, and what's more, *Parson says, 'Good day' to him*. But he still wouldn't go home. Down by the harbour what should run across the road but a *black pig*, and you should have heard the fool swear, but still he went on down to the boats, and as he sailed out he heard a voice from the cliffs shouting, '*Good dog, after that rabbit now.*' But even then he wouldn't turn back.

Out he went and down channel and whether he was wrecked or picked up by a Bristol slaver and sold in the West Indies nobody knows. He never came back to Worle, and nobody cared!

Note: This is compiled from a Weston-super-Mare fisherman, the cairn story only. The rest of the tale came from such people as a maid-servant with sailor brothers, the driver of a tourist waggonette, a retired sea captain, a weaver of lobster pots and a carter of kelp for farm manure. The versions were often fragmentary — this is the best, but many of the superstitions are still alive from Clevedon to the Exmoor sea-board. Phrases in italics are bad luck omens.

Never say the word 'rabbit' to a sailor. *Shopkeeper, Watchet, 1955.*

'I can't go on the water, you bin talking of rabbits, nor can I go shootin' since I'd a-met a woman in the lane.' *Conversation overheard on Somerset coast, 1948.*

COLOURS

White should never be worn by any of ill repute. *South Somerset.*

Dress a child in white on a Sunday. *East Somerset.*

An Easter Egg must never be green. *Schoolfellows, Taunton Deane, 1905–12.*

Never dress a child in green.

Never wear green in May. *An old woman, Ashbrittle, 1920.*

I am told that houses with green tiles are regarded askance by the elderly. 'I wouldn't want to live in one of they, not for no price.' *Scoutmaster, Minehead, 1956.*

A woman should never wear a red handkerchief. *Cottager, Castle Cary, 1925.*

CROSS-ROADS

Cross-roads are dangerous after sunset until cock-crow.

Suicides were buried at the cross-roads with the stake of the sign-post through them to prevent their return in vampire form.

A cross-road is a place of sanctuary if you are a truly good person. *East Somerset.*

FEATHERS

Do not bring a jay's feathers into the house or you will never get a moment's peace from noise. *Gamekeeper, Bagborough, 1906.*

A kingfisher's feathers will drown your beasts if you keep it. *A cowman, Otterspool, 1920.*

A kingfisher's feather will keep you from drowning. *Taunton schoolboys, 1906–12.*

Peacock's feathers are unlucky unless they are a gift. *Wellington, Taunton, 1904–50.*

If you collect hen's feathers from a nest, your voice will go cackly evermore. *Cottage woman, Bathpool, 1907.*

MISCELLANEOUS

Gold that is found is unlucky. *Jane Cobby, maid, Pitminster, 1909.*

Never kick an empty tin, you are taking away someone's life. *Taunton, 1945.*

Never carry a farthing in your purse, if you do you will always lack a pound.

Cross your fingers if you hear a witch or ghost. *South-west Somerset; Exmoor.*

'Drake's Cannonball' always rolls up and down if a national disaster is coming. *Coombe Sydenham; Mrs. Trollope-Bellew; Crowcombe W.I., 1958.*

2

Calendar Customs

JANUARY

Ask a man or boy to be the first to step over your threshold on New Year's Day. *Mrs. Herneman, Crowcombe W.I., 1957.*

Never allow a red-headed man, or worse, a red-headed woman, to enter your front door or wish you a Happy New Year first of all. *Mrs. Jordan, Crowcombe W.I., 1957.*

If you cannot get a dark man to enter your house and bring in the year's luck, you may save it by first entering the house yourself 'back avore' by the back door. *Mrs. Keal, East Lucott, 1946.*

Carry a horseshoe into the house on first entering, but be sure to carry it pointing upwards. *Mrs. March, Kinsford, 1907.*

Watch the sunrise from a hilltop and you will have a good year. *Innkeeper, Triscombe, 1923; R. M. Heanley, 1902.*

Never wash anything. If you do you will wash away one of the family. *West Somerset.*

Open the Bible to see what the year foretells for you. *Nether Stowey, 1908; Quantocks, 1952; Taunton and Rowbarton, 1905–9.*

Put a key in the Bible, then open it and read the verse below the key for guidance through the year. *Exmoor, 1905–50.*

The first three days of the year foretell the next three months. They are noted down for future use. *Mid Somerset.*

Old Christmas Day

January 6th is Old Christmas Day. It is the working beast's holiday on a farm. If you use them you will have an accident or ill luck will follow. I have known farmers who would not go hunting on this date, and several bad accidents are accounted for by this belief today.

There is a local tradition on Exmoor of a farmer's wife who, in spite of warnings, drove her pony to market on Old Christmas Day. She sold her wares at a good profit, but on the way home the pony bolted and tipped the cart into a ditch and the farmer's wife had her leg broken.

January 6th

Burning the Ashen Faggot. This is done before the Wassailers go out to the orchards to 'apple-howl' them.

Wassailing the apple trees in West Somerset is celebrated from January 6th to 17th. *Dunster, West Somerset, 1955.*

Twelfth Night (*January 6th or 17th*)

Every time a willow band burns through drink a toast to the day for luck. *Farmer, near Vexford, 1953.*

Burn all your Christmas Evergreens. If you do not they will turn into pixies and plague you for a year. *Wilton, 1949.*

St. Distaff's Day (Saturday after Twelfth Night)

The women should all return to work after twelve days of Christmas. This is a good day for turning out chests and cupboards. You will get no moth if you do. *North Somerset, 1920; Ruishton, Mid Somerset, 1952.*

Plough Sunday (First Sunday after Twelfth Night)

The plough is brought into the church and blessed. This seems to have become the rule at the end of the eighteenth century. *West Somerset, 1956.*

Plough Monday (First Monday after Twelfth Night)

Any man not at work again is chased round the village. *Exmoor, 1890–1914.*

St. Agnes Eve (January 29th)

You must go to bed in silence and turn your stockings inside out. If you don't you will never marry. *A maid, North Petherton, 1911.*

FEBRUARY

St. Bridget's Eve (February 1st)

The Festival of St. Bridget was revived in Glastonbury in 1923. Her bell was found in a farmhouse nearby. Tradition says that when she left for Ireland she left her missal, her sleeves and her bell.

Some of the St. Bridget's Day Celebrations were held on May Day and related to flowers. 'Biddy's Bed' of mountain pansies (Viola Lutens) was made in Brendon hill farms. On May Eve a doll was laid in this and covered with periwinkle petals. *Skilgate, 1900; Periton, 1916.*

A very hesitant version of the verse sung by children was given to me, something like this:

> Ring the bell Biddy's dead
> Please give us a flower (or penny) for Biddy's bed.
> *Crowcombe, 1956.*

In West Somerset, particularly the remote hills, pansies are called 'Biddy's eyes'. *Personal recollection, 1909–56.*

'There was an old woman down to Skilgate, and I remember as a child she had a round bed of vi-olas, they were dark blue and light blue ones — the two sorts, 'n she did put a doll in the middle, different times of the year. The two blues the vi-olas was, and she did dress the doll in the two blues. 'Twas a wax doll. My sister, she's three years younger'n me, but she'd remember the doll 'n how 'twas dressed. 'Twas light blue skirt and a dark blue top.

(Was it a blouse or a cloak, I asked? No, not a blouse. The word cloak brought perplexity until I amended it to mantle. This with its memories of braid and bugles was highly satisfactory.)

Yes, that's right, 'twas a dark blue mantle 'n the little doll was wax'n it sat in the middle where Ole Lizzie did put it to. I did write to my people to see if any of hers was yet living 'n could tell 'ee more about it, but they've all a-passed on.' *Mrs. Badcock, Triscombe; Mrs. White (sister), Upminster, 1956.*

There is a St. Bride's field at Cannington and in old days a church of St. Brigid in Bridgewater.

Candlemas Day (February 2nd)

> If Candlemas Day be fine and clear
> Winter will have another year.
> *Frome.*

This is the day to make a bonfire of all the Christmas evergreens. There are the wreaths that have been hanging up all Christmastide from November 24th onwards. The fire should be lit by a Christmas candle stored away for the purpose. It must burn as long as the bonfire and then must be quenched and carefully stored till next year. *From a South Somerset friend, 1906.*

No light must be used. Rise at daybreak and go to bed at sunset. *Mr. Chidley, farmer, near Godney.*

FEBRUARY–MARCH (Shrove-Tide)

Burning Judas. Somewhere in the early months of the year a farmer went round his fields to make sure the rubbish was burned. He found several signs of bonfires, but at the bottom of the field a large, ill-smelling one was still smouldering. It was loaded with weeds. Upon his remonstrating with his old labourer he got the reply, 'That be Judas, zur. Let 'un burn slow.' *A farmer, 1945.*

Shrove Tuesday Eve

The Rector of Hawkridge, Exmoor, says in 1888: The custom of throwing old cloam (pottery) on the Monday night before Shrove Tuesday is still continued in our village. Why it is done I cannot find out. The words they say when it is thrown at the door or inside the house are —

> 'Tipety, tipety tin, give me a pan cake
> And I will come in.
> Tipety, tipety toe, give me a pan cake
> And I will go.'

The young men in the house rush out and try to collar the invaders, and, if successful, bring them inside and black their faces with soot. After that they are given pancakes.

This is still continued in the neighbourhood of Stogumber. *Taxi-driver, 1961.*

Old Mrs. Badcock remembers doing this in her childhood at Winsford and at Skilgate. On one occasion she tripped when running away and was caught. She had her face blackened, but as it was a poor cottage she got no pancake. Mr. Badcock remembers as a boy hanging stones to the latches of unpopular people's doors so that they clattered against them. *Minehead, 1890.*

> Flitter me, flatter me floor,
> If you don't give me a pancake
> I'll beat down your door.

The boys run round the village throwing stones and brick ends into doorways.

Pan Shard Night they collect pots and pans to bombard the doors. *Milbourne Port, 1950.*

Throwing stones was practised on Shrove Tuesday Eve in Taunton right through my childhood. I heard of it again in the 1920's. You must not be seen either throwing or running away.

A handful of small stones (which rattle like hail) is still thrown in Quantock hamlets and farms. *Kingswood, 1951.*

Shrove Tuesday

At mid-day the church bells rang and all the women ran out of their cottages clattering pots and pans and calling 'Pan, Pan, Pan'. The school-children had a half holiday and paraded the village street singing a Shrove Tuesday rhyme (see Folk Music). *Polden Hills, Mid Somerset, 1948.*

> Shrove Tuesday, Shrove Tuesday,
> When Jack went to plough
> His mother made pancakes, she did not know how.
> She tissed them, she tossed them,
> She made them so black
> She put so much pepper
> She poisoned poor Jack. Hooray.
>
> *Chilton Polden, 1917.*

> Shrove Tuesday! (prolonged shout)
> Jack's mother made a puddin'
> 'Twas done in an hour
> She hadn' no eggs and she hadn' no flour
> She hadn' no figs and she hadn' no fat
> She slapped down the plate
> And she says, 'Jack, eat that.'
>
> *Taunton version, 1903 – 11.*

Dimmering

At mid-day the school children to the number of forty paraded to the 'gentleman farmer's', and were given a box of apples. They visited other farms and houses, receiving pennies or cakes. They sang this verse:

'Dimmery, dimmery dinky do
Give me a pancake and then I'll go
Off with the kettle, and on with the pan
Please to put a pancake in my hand.'

Mrs. Owen, Cothelstone, 1916.

At Bagborough sometimes faces were blackened and pancakes given out. *Bagborough W.I., 1957.*

Cock-shy

Eight or nine clay cocks used for Shrove Tuesday cock-shying (Aunt Sally) and dated 1791 were found in a Minehead house in 1936.

Clipping the Church

Until recently at mid-day on Shrove Tuesday the villagers 'threaded the needle' up the main street, and forming a circle round the church 'clipped' it three times. *South Petherton, 1930.*

At Wellington they 'clipped' the church up to 1850, and also hung stones on door latches.

Egg-Rolling

Hard boiled eggs were rolled down a slope, the least cracked to reach the bottom being the winner. *Blue Ball Inn, Triscombe, 1930.*

Shackle-Egging

At Martock children brought eggs to school. These were put in a sieve and gently swung round. The owner of the egg which did not crack was the winner, and took all the cracked eggs as a prize.

At Langport 'egg-shackling' took place up to 1870. In this case the broken eggs went to the school master, and the winner had a prize and wore a crazy patchwork fool's cap, the victor's cap. The winner headed a procession of school-children who paraded the parish collecting money.

Both these customs were also used at Exeter.

Daffodils

Daffodils are still called Lide Lillies on Exmoor. *1950.*

In South Somerset daffodils are called Leny cocks by old folk. They were used instead of cock shies. *1840–1900.*

Ash Wednesday. Cursing Day

I was told as a child of someone's granny who carefully sifted all her winter wood ash into a heap in the outhouse and used it on Ash Wednesday to cover the kitchen floor instead of sand. She probably came from a more northerly county than Somerset. Old Mrs. Govier emptied the ashes on her doorstep once. *Mr. Govier, Near Bathpool, 1905.*

Up to mid-day on Ash Wednesday the farm men could swear unreproved as it was Cursing Day. *Mr. Quick, farmer, Wiveliscombe, 1953.*

On Ash Wednesday every child wore a sprig of ash or was chased and pinched or pushed into nettles. *Farmer's daughter, Kingston St. Mary, 1939.*

APRIL

April 1st

Make a fool of somebody before noon, then shout,

> 'April fool, April fool.
> Send your mother back to school.'

Send the fool further — give someone a pretended message to take on a false errand. Old Mr. Govier once trudged three miles with a cart horse to the smithy to be greeted with grins from the blacksmith. He lost half a day's pay too. 'But I had 'em come Allern' he said with a chuckle. I imagine his practical jokers met with a particularly horrid turnip spunky when they were not expecting it. *Mr. Govier, Near Bathpool, 1905.*

Ask riddles. If a peacock laid an egg in your garden whose would the egg be?

Answer: Peahens lay eggs.

School friend, Taunton, 1909.

Send a child on a nonsense errand. 'Go to the pigsty and see if the old cart 'oss have had kittens.' *Farm children, Brompton Ralph, 1904.*

Sing nonsense songs of the red herring variety. 'The Derby Ram', 'As I was going to Banbury', etc. These all belong to other counties. *Taunton Market, 1907.*

Be very guarded in answering questions. I heard this between two boys in a village street one April.

'Hey, Jan, where be goin'?'
'I baint gooin', I be coming back.'
'Where be coming back from then?'
'Where I went tew.'

Porlock Weir, 1940.

At mid-day songs and jokes cease. If anyone overlooks the time limit he is greeted with:

April Fool time's gone and past
Thee'st the biggest fool last
When April Fool time comes again
Thee'll be the biggest fool then.

Eli Vellacott, Brendons, 1952.

Other names for an April Fool are April gowk, April gawby, April gobby or April gob.

Cuckoo Day. April 15th

This is the day the cuckoo should arrive. If he comes earlier frost will destroy the blowth in the orchards. It is also called Cuckoo Fair Day, but no fair has been held within memory. *Crewkerne, 1925.*

When you first hear him you must be standing on grass, then your hay crop will be assured. *Bath, 1916.*

Palm Sunday

Black the dunk's hoofs and put a posy of Easter lillies on either side of his ears, and give him a good feed. 'He did carry our dear Lord.' *Exmoor gipsy, Larkbarrow, 1937.*

Decorate the clavel-tack with twigs of palm. *Brendon Hills, 1904–12.*

Wear a spray of Calvary Clover. This, I think, my old informant had muddled with Good Friday. She gave me a root. *A friend's grandmother, Bradford on Tone, 1908.*

Good Friday

You must plant your beans on Good Friday so that they will come up on Easter Day. *Bagborough, Bicknoller, Holford, 1956.*

Parsley is a dangerous plant to move, but on Good Friday it is safe to do so. If it is transplanted on any other day it brings death. *Wellington, 1906; Quantock Hills, 1950.*

Until the 1920's men and boys went hunting Judas in Shervage Wood. Their substitute for the betrayer was the red squirrel, on account of its chestnut fur, for Judas was a red-haired man. *Nether Stowey, 1906–20.*

On Good Friday it was the custom to cook a dish of furmity. *Minehead, 1954.*

Cook a dish of whitpot for dinner.

Easter Sunday

Climb to the top of Dunkery Beacon to see the sun rise for good luck. *Porlock, 1944.*

Climb Will's Neck before dawn on Easter Day and watch the sun do a dance. *Cothelstone, 1911; Stairfoot, 1925.*

Put out a pail of water before dawn. If the sun dances in it you will have a good life and a peaceful end. *Bishop's Hull, 1904–11.*

Egg shackling took place at Langport and Martock.

In the nineteenth century the parish clerk went round the district giving everyone Easter cakes. These were flat, sweet spiced biscuits. One old man said they were flavoured with saffron. Another said in his parish the clerk climbed the church tower and threw them for the lads to catch. I have never been able to trace this. *Taunton Market, 1905–6.*

Easter Garlands

Decorate the house with Easter flowers and stick a branch of greenery (never elder or whitethorn) before the front door. Flowers used are: Easter lilies (daffodils), Easter Roses (double sweet-scented jonquils), primroses, none-so pretty (polyanthus, white or yellow), sweet violets (white), ivy and catstails (hazel), but no late snowdrops. *Mrs. Vinney, Porlock Weir, 1941.*

Carry a 'tutti' of primroses, catkins and violets to church on Easter Day. You must include violets as the other two are unlucky if there are only a few of them. *Mrs. Westmacott, Near Cutcombe, 1944.*

Easter Eggs

Hard-boiled eggs dyed with onion skin and a leaf or pattern stuck on before boiling, afterwards peeled off to leave the design white, the egg then taken to church. *West Somerset, 1952.*

Hard-boiled eggs held in the hand and used as 'conkers'. The least cracked egg wins an Easter cake. *Taunton Deane, 1905–12.*

St. Mark's Eve. April 24th

This is one of the 'Wisht' nights when conjurors watch the church porch for the wraiths of the year's coming dead to remain in the church at midnight while other 'night walkers' go home after the ghostly service. *North and West Somerset.*

If you are anxious to see your future wife or husband, open the barn doors and sit in the dark in silence. At midnight he or she will pass through the barn, but if an owl cries while you wait you will die single. If the dunk (donkey) brays a man will die before his wife. *Churchstanton farm labourer, 1905; Taunton Deane, maid-servant, 1911; Exmoor gipsy, 1936.*

May Eve. April 30th

Minehead hobby horse parades the town. *1956.*

Put primroses in the cow stalls and hang bunches over the beasts' doors. *Exmoor farm above Porlock.*

Hang branches of greenery over the threshold last thing at night. *West Somerset W.I. Member.*

MAY

May 1st to 12th

A relic of the hobby horse still exists at Dunster and many conjectures as to its origin have been given, one asserting that the famous hobby horse was the ancient King of May, and another that it was a religious fracas long ago in which one party trounced the other. Even recently it seems to have been not unusual for those connected with the hobby horse to catch some luckless man and give him a good drubbing.

Booing the Victim. 'Oh one, Oh two, Oh three,' up to ten. The hobby horse bows at each 'booing'.

During the war years the fishermen's boys took on the custom of the hobby horse. He is the property of the Fisherman's Guild and all donations go to seafarers charities. Of later years he has been repainted and rosetted, and still drags his famous cow's tail. It has been shortened and he has lost his terrifying masked 'Gullivers'.[1]

[1] See Glossary.

L

During the nineteenth century their horseplay and enforced demands ended in a fatal accident and now the hobby horse parades alone. Even now his cow's tail is long enough and hard enough to bestow a sharp slash on the unwary. The tune which he is known to prefer is 'Soldier's Joy'. He comes as far as Elliscombe Lane and goes out to the Porlock road beyond the parks.

An excellent pamphlet by a Minehead folklorist can be got at the West Somerset Free Press giving vivid photographs of the early twentieth-century hobby horse. Many of my elderly Minehead friends have danced behind him and got a slash from the cow's tail. They also set their doors wide to allow him or his 'Gullivers' to go right through the house, which of course he is too bulky to do — but it was bad luck not to have the doors open. The fatal accident arose over the obstinacy of a sceptic in the face of town superstition.

The cow's tail is said to be in memory of a shipwreck off Dunster's marshes when the only thing washed ashore was a dead cow.

There is a curious dispute between Minehead and Padstow as to which place is the original home of the hobby horse. In Minehead it is said that some Padstow sailors, reaching Minehead during the revels, stole the horse and took it to Padstow, while in Padstow a similar accusation is made against Minehead.

May Day Customs

Hang a primrose ball over the 'drasshle' (threshold) on May Day. *Quantock Vale, 1952.*

Make a cross in the ashes with a hazel twig, and set a branch of hazel outside your door.

In every village school in my childhood a May Queen was chosen and there was a procession in which everyone wore spring flowers, and while wealthier schools danced round a Maypole, others, nearer to the old days, danced in a ring. One informant says she thinks in her village they danced round a thorn tree. *Taunton Deane, 1903–12.*

You must have whitethorn in your May tutti. *Brendon Hills, 1904–08.*

In direct contradiction, in Taunton Deane it is said that if you wear whitethorn on May Day or carry it in your posy, or take it indoors, you will bring death to the family. It is the 'varies', flower and they don't like it touched.

I have come across faint memories of a 'Jack in the Green' on the Somerset-Dorset border, but so far have not really traced it.

Plant branches of greenery in front of your farm house.

Carry a May basket with a May Lady in it round the village and show it for pence. *Mid Somerset, 1904–12.*

If you meet a red-haired man on May Day you will be unlucky, but if he squints as well then you will meet with disaster in the coming year. *Quantock seaboard, 1951.*

Oak Apple Day. May 29th

This is known in the south of Somerset as Shik-Shak Day. Up to the twentieth century it was the custom to adorn the horses' bridles with oak apples. The carters themselves wore a spray of oak leaves in their button-holes, in fact, everyone wore these otherwise they were chased and pinched.

Wearers of oak leaves chanted —

> Royal Oak
> The Whigs to provoke,

and wearers of plane leaves —

> Plane tree leaves
> The church folk are thieves.

A fierce fight ensued, non-oak wearers were flogged with nettles, they in their turn endeavoured to snatch the oak leaves in order that the robbed lad should himself get a taste of a nettle whip. At mid-day this ceased. *Chard, 1910; Taunton, 1904.*

Oak boughs were set in front of the cottages. *Crewkerne.*

On Exmoor the school children wore oak leaves to school and demanded their holiday.

> It's the 29th of May
> It's Oak Apple Day
> If you don't gie us a holiday
> We'll all run away.

They got a holiday and any child who had no oak was pushed into nettles. *Winsford, 1888; Porlock Weir, 1890.*

It was considered an excellent joke to hide your own oak leaf and answer the challenge with 'Thee's shik-shak theezelf then', after which you were free to pinch him as often as you could before he got out of reach. *Blackdown Hills.*

As on All Fools Day anyone trying to penalize another after mid-day was greeted with —

> Shik-shaks gone and past
> Thee's the biggest fool last
> When Shik-shak comes again
> Thee 'st be biggest fool then.
>
> *Crewkerne, Chard, 1909.*

Men would go round the town with boughs of trees with oak apples on to decorate the houses. They would knock at the doors and offer you a bough, and if you gave them sixpence they would give you one to put up over your door. If you gave them a shilling they would not forget, and next year they would bring you two boughs. *Langport W.I.*

Whitsuntide

Whitsunday

Eat gooseberry pie and cream. *West Somerset.*

Wear something white, preferably a white buttonhole. Daisies were popular, and the pink tipped ones particularly correct. *Galmington, 1904.*

Eat roast duck and green peas. *Crowcombe, 1956.*

Whitmonday

Friendly Walks. Up to a few years ago West Somerset villages still held their club walks carrying 'tuttis' or flower poles. Everyone had to wear something white if "twas only Dad's hankercher'. *A maid, Exton, 1920.*

There was always a village tea after the service at church and then a procession and sports.

The Kingston St. Mary walk started at the Farmers Arms and finished at Bishop's Lydeard, about five miles. They had a band, with paper streamers and carried staffs and wore blue sashes. This was continued between the wars. *Mrs. Milner, 1920; Mrs. Tucker, Cannington, 1910.*

In many villages it was Revel Day, and is the traditional day for the cart horse show, and nowadays for the early gymkhanas. *Ted Hunt, carter, Lawford, 1955.*

Ascension Day

Robin Hood plays at Yeovil. The dramatization of the ballads was played at the church ales until the Reformation and revived during Queen Elizabeth's reign. The last record is in 1577, 'the sayd John Dyer (Churchwarden) being Robyn Hood this yere doth yeld uppe to the pishe madye by keeping of the church Ale the somme of XXIII£ IIIs Xd' (i.e. doth yield up to the parish, made by keeping of the Church Ale, the sum of . . .).

If the plays were revived to help the Church Ale moneys after this they are discreetly noted as 'reparacyon' of the church. The play was that of Robyn Hoode and hys Merry Men.

There were performances of Robin Hood plays at Wells according to their records. In both places details of costumes are noted, such as a 'grene silke rebyn for the Sheriffe'.

This used to be a great day for church bell ringing, parish against parish.

Rogation tide

One old man told my informant that as a boy when they beat the parish bounds, he was thrown into a stream and later soused in a duck-pond. *Mid Somerset.*

Another old man described how his brother was 'bumped' to make him remember the parish bounds, but in his grandfather's day boys did not get off so easily, being well switched to 'make 'un mind'. *South-west Somerset.*

School children processed carrying posies, up to 1920. *Quantocks, 1960.*

May Superstitions

Never 'tuck' a baby in May. 'If you tuck him in May you will drive him away.'

Never wear green in May, it is the pixies' colour and they are powerful this month. *Ash Priors.*

If you have to wear green in May make sure you have a spray of late primroses or forgetmenots (magic spring-wort) to protect you from bad luck (fairy stroke). *Tolland, Exmoor.*

People born in May are either saintly or 'turrible wicked bad'. *Frome; East Somerset.*

JUNE

Midsummer Eve

Find the biggest stone in the farm and put a bunch of flowers on it for luck. *Taunton Deane, 1920.*

Climb a hill, make a pile of stones on top and put a bunch of flowers on it for luck. *Quantock Hills.*

Charming the Cattle against fairies and pixies

Tie a piece of wicken (quicken or quick beam) to the tails of your cows with a red thread. *Exmoor, 1907.*

If you go on a journey be sure to put a piece of wicken in your pony's head band. *West Somerset, 1908.*

Midsummer Day

Pluck a full blown white rose blindfold as the clock strikes noon, and wrap it in white paper. Put it in your bosom on Christmas Day and your future husband will snatch it away. *North Somerset.*

At Langford Budville on Midsummer Night the church bells are rung to drive the Devil over to Thorn St. Margaret.

An old farmer used to pass a lighted branch over and under all our cows and horses, and singed the calves and foals. He refused to tell us why. *Farmer's daughter, Holford, 1915.*

At Langford Budville the parish 'clipped the tower' and shouted. This is done up to this century.

JULY

Old Midsummer Day. July 3rd

Find an even ash leaf and repeat this charm:

> This even-ash I double in three
> The first one I meet my true love shall be.
> If he be married let'n pass by,
> But if he be single let'n draw nigh.

Throw the leaf in the face of the person first met. *West Luccombe, 1939.*

Drop a pin in Queen Anne's Well before sunrise. If it sinks beside another you will soon marry. Some people throw in two pins to see if they separate. *South Cadbury, 1944.*

Dance round a white-thorn tree with bare feet before sunrise to charm your lover to wed this year. *South Somerset, 1912.*

St. Becket's Day. July 7th

The church bells at Thorn St. Margaret are rung to drive the Devil back to Langford Budville.

AUGUST

Lammas-Tide and Harvest

Triscombe Revel

This was held on the last Sunday in August when 'whortleberry pickers' foregathered at the 'Blue Ball'. You then ate your first 'wort-pie' of the season with cream. *Mrs. Lock, Carew Arms, Crowcombe, 1935.*

If you could eat your pie without smiling or speaking, no matter how you were teased, you would have a lucky fruit season. *Quarryman, Triscombe, 1952.*

The traditional fare at Triscombe Revel was 'wort-tart' and cream. You were supposed to eat one between every dance and song. *Mrs. Ames, Lea Crossing, Yeawe, 1953.*

Traditional songs at Triscombe Revel were 'The Old Grey Mare' and 'Farewell, Farewell, my own dear Love'. *Mr. Rich, Triscombe Farm.*

Priddy Fair, August 21st

This is the day they say winter begins. Prize fighting and cheese rolling were the most popular amusements. No one was ever supposed to go to Priddy Fair without receiving a buffet. One man on his way home is reported to have said to himself 'Theest been to Priddy Fair and not had thee buffet, thee must go back'. Back he went to pick a fight and get well trounced, returning home happy.

Norton Dog Fair, August 28th and 29th

A fair was held up till 1890 for the sale of cloth and linen. It is suggested it got its title from the 'dog days'. *Norton St. Philip.*

Harvest

A corn dolly was woven into the corner of the stack to bring luck. Some stacks in West Somerset still show a miniature stook at either end of the ridge. Also you can still see a peaked projection to some thatched cottages which very old folk call 'the dolly' or 'the cock'. *West Somerset.*

Some upland farms leave the last stook in the field to stand till it disintegrates, others hang it on a barn wall or a pole in the yard. Nowadays if you are curious you might be told "twas vor they birds'. *Western Hills.*

Crying the Neck

An ancient custom of reapers when they have cut the last of the corn on the farm. A bunch of ears tied together is called the neck.

'When yew did get tew last two-three oats yew did ztand back aways and drow at'n till her were a-cut right dro', then if 'ee were sprack 'ee did up'n bicky off tew varm an' all runned after tew catch 'ee. Maid were awaitin' vor 'ee back door with a gurt bowl o' water 'n her tried all to souse 'ee avore 'ee carried un into back place. Proper drownded I been. More'n likely they did catch 'ee 'n drow 'ee in duckpond. Oh aye, neck as well. Then us had a drop of zider'n cakes.' *An old farm labourer, Near Horner, 1941.*

The Corn Dolly

In some West Somerset churches the corn dolly is permitted as a decoration for Harvest services, but in others it is refused admission. The corn dolly, or 'baby', is still made in West Somerset.

The last sheaf was garlanded and decorated with ribbons, and brought home alone. *Bagborough W.I., 1957.*

Apple harvest which goes on until November in Somerset has one traditional point met with in most areas. The little apples are left on the trees. This, old folk will tell you, is the pixies' harvest. To steal these, as lads do, is called pisking, col-pixying, griggling, pixy-hunting and pixy-wording, all words connected with the fairies.

In one village of a flax-growing district, the first day of harvesting everyone had to wear a bit of blue to ensure a good harvest in the next year. *A maid, South Somerset.*

The rush harvest took place in the early autumn and had its own procession and customs, and it is thought that at times rush brooms were carried. *Mrs. Hill, Ilton W.I.*

Michaelmas Day. September 29th

Apple Grabbing

This is the day to gather crab apples to store till Old Michaelmas Day (October 11th).

Blackberries must not be picked after Michaelmas Day as the Devil has spoiled them.

OCTOBER

Old Michaelmas Day. October 11th

Collect the crab apples stored on Michaelmas Day and form them into the initials of your sweethearts. Those in the best condition will make the best husbands.

Hallowe'en

'There was a young girl, my mother used to tell, and she was very pretty, and on November Eve she went to look in the glass to see who she should marry, and she saw a coffin with that date on it. She was so scared she died on the spot.' *Mrs. Hill, Crowcombe W.I., 1958.*

Write your name on paper, throw it over your left shoulder into a bowl of water and stir 'widdershins' with the left hand, and then turn your back and leave it till midnight after wishing. If the paper still floats your wish will come true, if partly submerged half true, but if it has sunk, it will not come true at all. *Crowcombe W.I.*

Never stand your doors open on All Hallowe'en, you don't know what uninvited guest may enter and stay with you for ever. *West Somerset.*

Peel an apple, throw the peel over your left shoulder, then look in a mirror to see what letter the peel has made. If it makes a letter your husband's name will begin with it. *D. Quick, Wiveliscombe, 1925.*

Look in a mirror at midnight if you dare, and see your lover look over your shoulder. If no one comes, you will not marry this year. If you see a white cloth, that will be your shroud, but if you see the Devil then you will be his for ever.

Around Hallowe'en, the children of the hill farms used to scoop out turnips and carve faces on them, putting a candle inside. They would sing outside farms and cottages:

> It's Spunky Night, it's Spunky Night,
> Gie's a candle, Gie's a light,
> If 'ee don't, 'ee'll have a fright.

Unpopular people were deliberately scared by them as a death warning. These spunkies were stood on gateposts at Hallowe'en. *Brendon Hills, 1958.*

Hang a lighted lantern in the stable all night.

'Punkie' Night merry-making is held during this week at various South Somerset villages. Processions of dressed up children carry hollowed out carved mangolds with lights inside. Prizes are given for the most grotesque.

At Langport the boys used to beg mangolds for Punkies and the largest won. The girls painted faces on jam jars and put candles inside for their 'punkies'.

All Souls Eve Rhyme

> A soul, a soul for a soul cake
> One for Jack Smith
> And one for Tom White
> And one for myself and I'll bid you goodnight
> My clothes are very ragged
> My shoes are very thin
> I've got a little pocket
> To put three halfpence in
> And I'll never come a-souling
> Till another year.

There are one or more remote Exmoor churches where the curious or evil-minded have come to watch on Midsummer or Hallowe'en for the sight of the coming year's dead going to their funeral service. One church had its doors covered with nails, points outwards, to keep away the conjurors, so it is said. *Culbone, 1940. Porlock, 1925.*

A local braggart, overfull of cider, took on a bet he'd sit in Crowcombe church porch till midnight to see whose wraith went into church and never came out. He never spoke of what he saw, but went so 'white as a sheet'. *Quantock Hills.*

In the seventies of the last century, a widower watched in Crow-combe church porch in the hope of seeing his wife's ghost, although he must have known of the terrible danger. No one knows if he did see her, but I was told, 'He didn't live after zo long as a bird's twitter, he were drawed away to a shred, and his life was a-took.' Note that the usual 'Heaven have a-tooked 'n' is ominously silent. The sacrilege had to be paid for. *A roadman, Bicknoller, 1938.*

If you watch by the gate at midnight on All Hallow's Night to see who will die within the coming year you are in danger of being the first comer yourself and you will become the 'churchyard walker' and the guardian of the graveyard until another foolhardy and impious person disturbs the Service of the Dead on this most powerful night of the year. The man or woman who is stealthily touched by the Church-Yard Walker (even his icy breath is fatal) dies then and there or only lives long enough to curse his sacrilegious curiosity. An old woman died in this way at a remote church and my informant told me 'no one wadn' gwaine to churchyard walk in place of thic wicked old twoad'. So apparently her evil spirit still acts as watch-dog there to check impiety. *John Ash, carter, East Lucott, 1945.*

Warnings to travellers

Never start a journey on All Souls Eve but, if you must, end it before sunset. *Porlock, 1942.*

If you are on a journey carry a bit of bread crossed with salt in your pocket. *Brendons, 1903–9.*

Always carry a wicken cross on All Hallows Eve, and smoke a pipe over the cows' backs. *Exmoor, 1906.*

If you go on a journey put a piece of wicken in your pony's head-band. *West Somerset, 1908.*

In remote hill farms this is the night for lifting gates off hinges and laying them in the hedge. This is never done where there is stock in the field, but otherwise all obstacles to invaders (who are generally red deer) are removed. On this night at least you 'lett'n droo'.

If you can find a four-leaved clover on this day you will prosper all your life. *Martock, 1907.*

Allerntide Apples

Allern apples were stored with nuts for All Hallow's E'en

specially for the children to see whose Allern apple was the finest. The winner was given a handful of nuts. *Mrs. Lathom, ex-post-mistress, Crowcombe, 1956.*

Allern apples were begged for by Exmoor children, sometimes with blacked faces. There was no rhyme or song. *Mrs. Badcock, Winsford, 1887.*

NOVEMBER

St. Catherine's Eve, or Cattern's Eve. November 24th

This, though a Christian saint's day wisely incorporated by the early church, is the traditional day which ushers in the winter.

> Cattern's Eve
> Yew 'oodn' b'lieve
> 'Tis but a month
> Tew Kirsmas Eve.

Cattern Cakes made like Catherine Wheels of viggy pastry flavoured with spice are eaten hot with a drink of mulled ale, while an ashen faggot with eleven withy bands burns. As in the later ceremony each time a withy burns through cider is drunk.

Cattern pies are also made, with a filling of mincemeat or treacle, honey and crumbs, and shaped like a waggon wheel. To eat a spoke ensures a safe winter season on the farm.

This Carol is sung, to the tune of 'A dis, a dis a green grass':

> Now welcome, welcome Winter with a right good cheer
> Away dumps, away dumps, nor come you not here.
> So welcome noble Winter and a joyous New Year.
> I wish 'ee a Merry Christmas.

The Christian version of this is also used by the Mummers who often introduce their play with this song.

A Cattern-tide Feast is held with apple rings and pork collops or bacon to embellish the Cattern Pies and Cakes, and decorated with ivy or winter sweet. No holly — 'Holly be a man.' *Mrs. Lock, Stogumber W.I., Mrs. Lock, Crowcombe W.I.; Mrs. Herniman, Crowcombe, 1900–60 — who also said the cattle knelt at midnight, as on Christmas Eve.*

Stogursey Mummers, 1900–1910

'I can remember the Mummers to Stogursey when I was only small. They had black faces and they had a banjo and concertina and the bones, and they danced in the village. Yes, there was King George and Father Christmas, and one of them dies and I remember they sang "This poor old soul is dead". No, they didn' have any horse. It was going out in my time. I don't remember much about it.' *A gardener, Crowcombe, 1956.*

Mummers Verse

> This poor old soul is dead and gone
> We'll never see he no more.
> He went to bed with his trousers on
> And left his hat on the floor.

Quantocks, 1900–12.

The Holly Riders

In very remote districts the holly riders went from farm to farm on pony back carrying lanterns. They wore a sprig of holly and a wreath of holly round their hats. They sang carols and received cakes and cider or pennies. *Brendons and Exmoor, 1905–56.*

Boxing Day, St. Stephen's Day. December 26th

Stag hunting on Exmoor and Quantocks. *West Somerset.*

Fox hunting on Exmoor, Quantocks and in general over Somerset.

This is a great day for rough-shooting on farms, and snaring of wild fowl, rabbits and hares. *West Somerset.*

Rabbiting parties were always held on this day. *Wiveliscombe, 1954.*

One North Somerset family I knew always had jugged hare for Boxing Day dinner and assured me it was the custom in their district. *North Somerset.*

Pull all the berries off the mistletoe without being seen. If you are seen you may be chased and kissed as many times as there were berries. *Somerset-Dorset borders.*

New Year's Eve

Townspeople met at the centre of Weston-super-Mare on what

had been the village green, to dance the old year out to the music of the town band.

A village party was held until midnight. *Farmer's wife, Lea Mills, 1957.*

A red-haired woman is unlucky to anyone coming face to face with her. In one village red-heads were more or less shut up in their cottages from December 30th to January 2nd. This would be about 1880. Cross your fingers if you meet a red-head on New Year's Eve. *Crowcombe, Norton Fitzwarren, Chipstable, 1936–57.*

Wassailing on New Year's Eve

South and Mid Somerset, unlike the West, keep to the new calendar, and December 31st is well within their twelve days of Christmas. The wassailers travelled to outlying areas on different nights. *Langport.*

Wassailing the apple trees (also January)

'No, they didn't wassail the apples out over (Stogursey and Bridgewater coast), I never heard of them doing so. 'Twas all on this side.' *A gardener, Crowcombe, 1956.*

'Oh, yes, we did go round all the farms on Old Twelfth Night 'n fire our guns into they trees. Yes, we'd give cider to nearest tree and we'd sing. I can't call to mind they old words 'bout hatsfull, capsfull, and a two-tree liddle heaps under the stairs. We did go to all the farms round Crowcombe on Kirs'mas.' *Ted Hunt, carter, Crowcombe, 1900–10.*

The Yule Log

This large log of apple-wood or oak is dragged from its orchard or field with a rider on top. He provides the fun, and my informant had an idea he was called King (the King of Yule?). The idea was to buck or roll him off, but if he reached the farm kitchen in safety he brought good luck with him and was rewarded with lamb's wool and cakes. Lamb's wool was the name for a mixture of mulled ale and roast apples. The log, which must burn the twelve days of Christmas, or in West Somerset the whole six weeks of Yule tide, was lit from a carefully saved brand of last year's yule log. *East Somerset, 1920.*

The Yule log is still burnt on farms which retain the old open fireplace. It is usually of oak or apple. Oak, so it is said, was for 'strength in the maister and safety from thunder'. Apple brings good luck. *From an informant, 1940; Personal collection.*

December traditional food

Christmas Eve. Lamb's wool (mulled ale and spiced roast apples) and nuts and hot cakes.

Christmas Day. Roast Goose and stuffing and mince pies. Roast beef and crab-apple jelly, and plum pudding. Roast chicken or turkey with sausages, stuffing and bread sauce, apple sauce, mince pies and/or apple dumplings.

Boxing Day. Cold Christmas dinner with hot plum pudding. Jugged hare and red currant jelly, and mince pies.

2

Local Customs

Tatworth Candle Auction

Here in this Somerset village of Tatworth the ancient custom of 'bidding by candle' is still in use for one piece of land on one day of the year, Old Lady Day, April 6th. A meeting is held at the Pop Inn of the members of Stowell Court, Stowell being a field which is put up for letting every year among them. An inch of candle is lighted and the highest bidder as the candle goes out obtains the field for the year.

A similar method of sale is said to prevail at Fivehead, Curry Rivel and at Chedzoy, where a piece of land was left to be put up for sale by candle auction every twenty-one years, for repairs to the church.

Auction of Toll Bridges

It is recorded that in 1939 the auction of the tolls of Somerset's last toll bridge took place at Burrowbridge. Bidding took place while the sand ran through a wooden-framed hour glass, a condition laid down by the act under which the bridge was built. A Mr. F. Dyer paid £1,725 for the right to collect tolls for twelve months from all the traffic using the bridge.

No Man's Land

'In Tatworth there is a meadow called No Man's Land with the best watercress bed in the district. Every year it comes up for sale to the farmers who lay claim to it. Now, one old farmer had fallen on poor times and if he could get the watercress bed it would just about put him on his feet. Everyone wanted him to have it, so when the day came only two farmers turned up to bid against him. The inch of candle was lit and farmer No. 1 made his bid quickly. It was a kindly thought, but to everyone's horror the candle began to splutter. His son gave the old man such a tremendous dig in the ribs that he nearly choked as he got his bid out; if he had coughed it wouldn't have counted and he would have been fined.

The candle recovered and burned brightly on, and everyone looked sadly at the poor old man, now in deep despair. It was no use Farmer No. 2 trying to cough before he spoke, for even the auctioneer would have known what was up (he probably did) but no one had tried to *sneeze*. Farmer No. 2 winked at Farmer No. 1 then his nose began to wrinkle up. Very slowly and surreptitiously out came a red handkerchief. "You can't sneeze in here while the candle is lit," said the auctioneer, looking hopefully at it — it was down to a quarter-inch now, and the flame as steady as a rock. Farmer No. 2 rose gingerly and tiptoed to the door with the red handkerchief to his nose. The candle flickered and recovered, but he was a man of resource. Unseen by the auctioneer he flicked his finger to his sheep dog waiting outside. Barking with joy that the long wait was over it leapt up at him, wagging its tail — and the candle went out. The auctioneer solemnly explained that a poor dumb beast could not be held to blame, and amid great good humour the old man was given the field for the year. Then everyone went cheerfully off for the yearly feast with watercress. The old fellow never guessed.' *A local tradition, from an informant.*

The Dolemoors

On the Saturday after Midsummer Day an ancient and remarkable custom was formerly observed at Puxton village, concerning the allotment of two large pieces of common land, called East and West Dolemoors, which lie in the parishes of Congresbury, Wick St. Lawrence and Puxton.

The several proprietors of the estates having any right to those moors, or their tenants, were summoned at a certain hour on the morning by the ringing of one of the bells of Puxton Church, to repair to the sacred edifice in order to see the chain kept for the purpose of measuring Dolemoors. The proper length of the chain was ascertained by fixing one end of it at the foot of the chancel arch, and extending it through the middle of the nave to the foot of the arch under the tower, at each end of which places marks were cut in the stones for that purpose. The chain was only 18 yards in length, 21 yards shorter than the regular land measuring chain. After the ceremony had been properly performed, the parties went to the commons. Twenty-four apples were previously prepared bearing the following marks:

5 pole axes, 4 crosses, 2 Dung pikes, 4 Oxen and a Mare, 2 Pits,

3 Pits, 4 Pits, 5 Pits, 7 Pits, Horn, Hare's tail, Duck's nest, Oven, Shell, Evil, Handreel.

It is necessary to observe that each of these moors was divided into several portions called furlongs, which were marked out by strong oak posts placed at regular distances from one another. After the apples were properly prepared they were put into a hat or bag and certain persons began to measure with the chain until one acre of ground was marked out.

The boy who carried the hat or bag took out one of the apples, and the mark which it bore was cut into the turf with a large knife kept for the purpose. As this process was completed each proprietor, knowing the marks and the furlong which belonged to his estate, took possession of his allotments for the ensuing year. After this everyone went to the overseer's house for the candle auction of certain acres let to meet expenses. These were called the out-let, or out-drift, and were bid for while an inch of candle burned. During the time of letting the whole party was to keep silence, except the bidder, on penalty of one shilling. When a bidder named his price he put a shilling beside the candle; the next bidder did the same and the first bidder took up his shilling. The bidder whose shilling was on the table when the candle burned out became the tenant of the out-drift for the year. There were two overseers, and the auction was followed by drinking. The moors were enclosed in 1811. *Excerpt from eye-witness account, 1770.*

The Frying Pan

This small amphitheatre on Ham Hill is one of the places in which every visiting girl or woman must sit down and slide from top to bottom of the bowl. 'It's lucky.' Surely here is a relic of pagan rites such as those embodied in the game of Trundles, and others. *Stoke under Ham, 1908.*

Pack-horse Bridges

There are about ten of these still existing in West Somerset, all leading to ancient chapel paths. On Exmoor they are to be found at Horner, Burrowhayes Farm, Allerford, Winsford, Weir Valley, Malmsmead and Dunster. The bridge at Kentsford, near Watchet, gives added protection to the benighted runaway from witch and evil spirits, for although the sea-gods have washed away its chapel of St. Mary le Cliff, it has a cross carved on one of its buttresses.

Auster

A method of allotting and dividing land. *Worle, North Somerset; North Curry.*

Rough Music

The only instance of this I know of was when I was a child, and occurred, I think, on the Somerset-Devon border. The married man who had led a 'maid' astray was serenaded with tin cans, saucepan lids, whistles and sustained shouted scurrility, after which a bowl of blood was poured out on his threshold. *Personal, 1905.*

'There was an old girl, a wicked bad 'un she was, and they put her on a sheep hurdle and hanged tin cans round her neck and ran her out of town. Oh yes, there was a band and all sorts. Us wouldn't let she be.' *Old East Somerset man, 1937.*

Riding Skimmetty

This curious custom was, it is said, intended to ridicule a man who has been beaten by his wife.

Skimmerton

The effigy of a man or woman unfaithful to marriage vows was carried about on a pole accompanied by rough music from cows-horns, frying pans, etc. Formerly it consisted of two persons riding back to back on a horse with ladles and marrow bones in hand, and was intended to ridicule a hen-pecked husband.

Tarring and Feathering

'He ought to be tarred and feathered' is said very promptly over any extra-marital culprit, particularly in the case of a married man and an unmarried girl. There is a tradition here that this form of village justice was used in nearby hill communities. *Mrs. Bryant, Kingston St. Mary, 1960.*

At Cannington (about 1908-14) the villagers seized the secretary of the Agapemone in mistake for the messiah of this Abode of Love. They rolled him in tar and feathers. He had seduced a 'maid'. *Mrs. J. Tucker, 1960.*

It seems from fragmentary indications that the East Quantock hamlets dealt in this form of retribution to the immoral married man.

Mommicks

The burning of Mommets ridiculed the unfaithful husband or wife.

PART IV

Narratives and Traditions

A CERTAIN number of the International Folk-Tale Types and their variants are still to be found in Somerset, but for these I must refer the reader to *The Folk-Tales of England* shortly to be published in an international series by the Chicago University Press under the editorship of R. M. Dorson. The following tales embody local rather than international traditions. In some of the historical tales I have drawn on printed sources, but I have never included these unless they have been corroborated by a living tradition, though sometimes this may have been fragmentary.

1

Saints and Worthies

St. Congar's Walking Stick

One day word was brought to King Ina of Somerset that a strange prince from the East had landed in Weston Bay and come up country to camp. In fact, the messengers said he was building there. Who was he? And what was he building? The King himself decided to find out. And there on the banks of the River Yeo he found a Byzantine Prince and a tiny wattled church sheltered by a magnificent yew tree. It had been the Saint's staff until he set it in the ground where he hoped to found his monastery. After such a miracle it is not surprising that St. Congar got his town and church from the King. A stump of the 'walking stick' is still there, but St. Congar's church is at Badgeworth.

It is possible, however, that St. Congar's was the original church at Congresbury. There is a vague tradition that on May Day, or Midsummer Day, which is the festival, the Congresbury women used to process round the well at Southwells Farm barking like dogs. The conger eels of the nearby Severn Sea are credited with barking, and there may be a trace here of a fisherman's cult. On the other hand, such a dance may be one of the Cadbury Hill witch rites still remembered. Apparently Black Magic was practised there on May Eve and Midsummer less than a hundred years ago. *Mrs. Clifton, Crowcombe, November 1959; The Rev. W. Griffin, Angersleigh, January, 1960.*

St. Dubricius of Dunkery. Porlock, Horner and Luscombe; West Somerset; Exmoor; Dunkery Beacon

Nobody knows very much about the life of St. Dubricius, but he is still remembered for three things.

(*a*) It was he who officiated at the ill-starred wedding of King Arthur and Queen Guinevere.

(*b*) He was a Celtic Saint who settled down in Porlock where the climate so suited him that he lived to the age of 150 years.

(c) While he was at Porlock he built a wayside chapel, St. Saviour's, between Horner and Luscombe at the foot of the terrible mountain track across Dunkery Beacon. At the sound of its bell the hideous forest fiends and dragons went deeper into the moor, even the Devil on his mountain top had to go away. And under its altar St. Dubricius buried a chest full of gold, to be spent on keeping the bells in order, and giving in charity to all who dared to cross the dreaded waste alone to earn their market monies.

The site of the ruined Chapel can be seen today beside the coach road 'but nobody can find the gold'. *Told to me in 1950 by Jane Rudd, aged 11, whose parents came from Wootton Courteney.*

The Murder of St. Indractus. Shapwick, Polden Hills

St. Indractus and his sister Drusa had been on a pilgrimage from Ireland to Rome and on their homeward journey stopped to visit St. Patrick's tomb at Glastonbury. All the pilgrims carried bags filled with millet and other seeds which they hoped to grow in Ireland to help the poor, and they leant on staves tipped with brass.

Some of King Ina's servants, seeing the sun shining on the brass, thought it was gold. They looked at the bulging wallets and believed they were stuffed with money. They followed the pilgrims through the dusk to Shapwick, and when night fell entered the house and massacred them all. Finding their terrible mistake they threw the bodies into a pit on the Polden Hills, and trusted that everyone would believe the pilgrims had gone back to Ireland.

For three days and nights a pillar of light from Heaven shone over the pit and all was discovered. King Ina had the bodies buried in Glastonbury Abbey, though some say it was at Shepton Mallet.

The murderers who dare not be absent from the burial were there and then so tormented by devils that they tore their flesh in their teeth and died horribly.

There is a tradition that the light still shines if a crime is committed.[1] *Oral collection, Chedzoy, 1945, labouring man at smithy.*

Our Lord in Somerset. Priddy, The Mendip Hills

Somerset has long boasted that its first church was founded by St. Joseph of Arimathea only thirty years after Calvary, but an even

---

[1] See Poole, *Customs, Superstitions and Legends of the County of Somerset. William of Worcester, 1847. Malmesbury*, p. 25.

more lovely tradition persists on the Quantocks and the Mendips.

Our Lord when a boy came voyaging with a sailor uncle to Britain. Their trading ship put in at Watchet, and from there He walked across the Quantocks to Bridgewater where He boarded a punt and crossed the lakes and marshes to the foot of Mendip, ending his journey high up at Priddy.

Here, say the miners, He walked and talked and worked with them a happy while, and then, loaded with Somerset gear, He went back to Nazareth. *Oral tradition and collection, Crowcombe and Holford, 1901–55.*

As a tiny girl I heard the very old grandfather of a visitor direct my brothers how to find 'Our Lord's Path' — at least, I think he called it that — but he was toothless and indistinct and my brothers careless. That was in 1901. When in 1908 we explored the Quantocks for it, we could neither find trace of it, nor recall the exact details. I am still hoping to meet some other guide to it if the tradition still lives.[1]

The Holy Thorn (A.D. 35). Glastonbury

One of the versions of the story of Glastonbury is to the effect that:

(*a*) It was a walnut staff upon which St. Joseph of Arimathea leaned as he climbed Weary-all Hill, and he planted it there. It took root miraculously and always flowers on St. Barnabas Day, June 11th.

(*b*) St. Joseph brought with him two precious relics, both of which he buried in Glastonbury soil for safety. The first was a single spike from the actual Crown of Thorns, the second the very cup of Our Lord at the Last Supper. The single thorn grew into a tree visited by hundreds of pilgrims for hundreds of years. It bloomed for a short while on Old Christmas Eve, January 5th, in memory of Our Lord.

(*c*) The precious cup or chalice was hidden below Glastonbury Tor, and with that at its foot and St. Michael's Church on its crest, all the fenland evil spirits were driven far away. It became famous through the centuries as the Holy Grail. If you drink of the Chalice Well water today you will find it stained in memory of the Crucifixion.[2]

Oral traditions. Somerset (general).

[1] See *Somerset Year Book, 1933*, p. 20.   [2] See Boger, p. 29. Poole, p. 83.

The Snakes of St. Keyna (A.D. 500). Keynsham

St. Keyna was the daughter of Braglan, Prince of Brecknock. She became famous for her holiness and desired to leave the world and become a hermit. To this end she left Wales, and came to the West of England where she asked permission of a local prince to build her cell in a desert spot. He, either disliking the lady's religion or hoping to make use of it, directed her to a valley near Bath that was shunned on account of the size and venom of its snakes. Undeterred St. Keyna went boldly among them and turned them all into stone.[1] Some escaped to Exmoor and the Quantocks, but the laggards on Mendip were overtaken by the Saint at Banwell. *Oral tradition.*

St. Wulfric and the Devil. Hazelbury Plucknett

St. Wulfric had his cell in this village and folk came from far and near to talk to him and tell him their troubles.

He had been a hunting squire until he turned priest and he always wore a suit of mail because of a vow he made. When it came over his knees and stopped his kneeling to pray he told a young knight to cut it shorter for him — and the sword went through the links of iron like butter.

A wretched creature, who had sold himself to the Devil and repented, fled to St. Wulfric for protection. He got as far as the ford, the Devil close on his horse's heels, when the Old One seized him — keeping one foot on the dry bank — no devil can cross running water — with the other he pushed horse and man into the stream and held them down, nearly drowning both.

St. Wulfric, in a vision, beheld this struggle and at once despatched one of his own company to the rescue. As the disciple approached, armed with the holy cross, the Devil let go hastily and as the holy water was sprinkled over the mounted man he made off with a screech.

The poor wretch was brought safely to St. Wulfric who listened to his confession, and sent him away in peace and free from his terrible bargain. *Oral collection, a maid-servant, Bruton, 1905.*

St. Wulfric and the Mouse

St. Wulfric, like all the Somerset saints, was very gentle to small creatures.

---

[1] Ammonites.

A stumpy (wren) made her nest above his fern couch and scolded him terribly for disturbing her eggs by coming so near. He moved his couch into a draughtier spot where he could not lie down properly.

A squirrel kept his hoard in the Saint's wooden cup, so he carved himself another. . . .

But there was one self-willed little mouse who insisted on nibbling pieces off the Saint's shortened tunic to make her fleece-lined nest finer, and worst of all she went on doing it during his prayers. . . .

At last the good Saint looked down and quietly rebuked her and the silly vain little mouse died of shame.[1] *Oral collection, A maidservant, Bruton, 1905.*

The Silver Horseshoe. West Camel and Queen Camel; Cadbury Castle

Cadbury Castle be King Arthur's Camelot! Never mind what other folk say! — The river near it be the Cam and they two villages is Queen Camel and West Camel. There's King Arthur's Well, so fine a wishing well as you could ask your heart's dear thought at; there's King Arthur's Palace, or the grass grown mounds of it, and down below there's a drove that goes all the way to Glastonbury and 'tis called King Arthur's Hunting Causeway — so what more do 'ee want?

There's gentlemen say Glastonbury be Avalon where the great King goed when he got his death-stroke and the barge come for him, and Glastonbury men do boast as he and his bewtifull Queen, poor fulish dear, was burred there —

Then why deny as Cadbury be Camelot? Surely *us* knows best!

Would you believe it, they didn't listen when us told 'en how every seven year on Midsummer Eve the door in the hill do open. And then King Arthur and all the Knights of the Round Table do come riding along the Causeway with lights to their spears, and their horses shod with silver shoes.

No, they wouldn't hear on it — and then one of the gurt fules went a-digging for to find the Round Table — not likely! It just went a-sinking down away out of reach, so it did — but he found a silver horse-shoe! That showed 'en! *Oral tradition, 1906–29; Oral collection, Rev. E. Skelton and a gardener, Stoke under Ham, 1907.*

[1] See Poole, pp. 94–8.

Cadbury Hill. Nailsea

The folk of North Somerset call it Camelot, and here they say if you could only find the magic door and enter you would find King Arthur and his Knights of the Round Table mounted and armed, but fast asleep — Then if you had the courage to shout for help, men and war horses would thunder out into the world again to face the enemies of England. *Oral collection.*

Here up to sixty years ago Black Magic was practised on May Eve and Midsummer Eve; dances around a thorn tree were remembered. *Letter from Clevedon, 12/59.*

2

Historical Traditions

HISTORICAL TRADITIONS AND MEMORIES

THERE is a strong sense of the past in Somerset, and folk memory goes back to the Danish invasions. In medieval times, the death of William Rufus, the murder of Becket and favourable memories of King John are most notable, various sixteenth century notables are kept in mind, but the deepest impression was made by the Monmouth Rebellion and the Bloody Assizes. Local crimes and tragedies also made their mark, and are chiefly remembered by ghost stories.

Fire Beacon Hill. Crowcombe

Tradition has it that from this point Alfred lit his beacon light to summon the men of the Western Hills to gather for the final attack on the Danes, which resulted in their defeat at Aethandune. It is a fact that such a light cannot be seen from the Polden heights, whereas both Will's Neck or Bagborough fires can.

There is a definite dislike of red-heads in the Quantocks. They have been called 'Dene's bastards' through the centuries. Even now a red-headed boy may be called 'a proper little Dene' by the very old. *Local traditions.*

Tuckfield of Crowcombe

There is a tradition that when the Danes landed at Bridport in Dorset they marched across England by way of Crewkerne and the Smugglers Track. A Tuckfield of Crowcombe was set on guard at the Beacon Hill to keep the beacon alight to give warning if the Danes approached. But he fell asleep, and the Danes passed down the valley below and attacked Watchet from the rear. This may have been the battle that took place at Battlegore near Williton.

There are Tuckfields at Crowcombe and Stogumber to this day. *Oral collection in 1955. Told by Mr. Young, the Rector for forty years, to William Chidley in 1940.*

William Rufus — What Happened to the Messenger

One of the Hippesleys of Ston Easton was the first to bring the
news of the murder of William Rufus, whereupon he was promptly
taken out and beheaded. *Collected by an informant from a local
version.*

Thomas à Becket

The murder of Thomas à Becket is still remembered strongly in
parts of Somerset, for his murderers were said to be Somerset men.
They all had to flee for their lives, and later on pay the Church very
dearly for their penance.

The Priory of Woodspring in North Somerset was founded to
pay for their sacrilege, and other churches in West Somerset
benefited from their remorse. One of the four was the Lord
of Sampford Brett, and within living memory the people of
Stogumber (three miles away) always planted their beans on St.
Thomas's Day. The four murderers were de Brett, Tracy, de
Morville and Fitz Urse, all claimed by West Somerset. *Local
traditions in Sampford Brett and Worspring.*

Sir John de Courcey. Stogursey, The Quantocks

Sir John de Courcey was a gigantic warrior to whom King John
gave the village of Stoke. In those days for safety from the robber-
baron of Nether Stowey it was built on the top of Farringdon Hill.

Sir John, however, raised himself a stronghold which was named
Courcey Castle and the villagers made their homes close to it. No
one could harm them with a lord whose 'breakfast mug' held over
a quart of cider at a time.

Fulke de Breauté was the lord of Nether Stowey Castle, and he
had no wish for a neighbour. So he set out one day to ambush the
Lord of Stoke Courcey, as he rode back down hill from making a
truce with the outlaws of Danesboro'.

Now, Sir Fulke had not yet seen Sir John and he had laughed at
all the tales that his men brought in. . . .

So the Lord of Stoke Courcey was King John's champion, was
he? The King must be hard put to it to make such a choice. . . .

And what was this tale of his meeting the French King's
champion in combat? Now, was that likely? Everyone knew he was
a giant of a man. Nobody lived who dare challenge him!

And now these fools of his insisted that when he caught sight of

Sir John de Courcey the terrible French champion turned and ran away.

Here, through the distant trees, Sir Fulke caught his very first glimpse of Sir John — And did the very same thing![1] *Oral tradition.*

'Sir John Curcy's breakfast mug' was an eighteenth-century ale-taster's quart mug. He was believed to empty it at one swallow.

Sir George Sydenham. Combe Sydenham

Country memories are extraordinary in the tenacity with which they retain seemingly trivial details, which are enlightening to the seeker after old tales. When I was talking to an old farmer about Combe Sydenham and the ghost of Sir George who rides a galloping horse towards Monksilver, shouting wildly, I said I supposed he must have been a wicked man to 'come again' in so terrifying a way. The farmer agreed — after all he had 'gone against' Drake (I wanted to ask if he thought the haunting was part of Drake's revenge) — but he went on to say he took *what he never should* like the Hanging Judge over to Wellington — *He* let off a murderer for money — and they had the *same trouble* with him.

The interest in this folk memory lies in the fact that Sir John Popham let off Wild Darrell of Littlecote Manor, when accused of an atrocious murder, but took the Manor as a fee. Sir George Sydenham's sins were less obvious but probably some countryman will be found yet to cite chapter and verse as if speaking of last year. *Oral collection 1946, Brendon Hill Farmer.*

Sir George rides a headless horse and is all in white. *Stogumber 12/1/60.*

Drake's Cannon-Ball. Combe Sydenham

Sir Francis Drake was betrothed to one of the Sydenham girls, but before they could be married he had to go away on a voyage. How long it would be before he came back no one knew and he did not trust his betrothed's father. The lovers exchanged very solemn vows to be true to their troth-plight and Drake sailed away.

He sailed away for three years and Sir George Sydenham found a rich suitor for his daughter. In spite of all her pleadings the marriage was announced, and, still half afraid of her absent love, but more afraid of her father, she gave in. She was more right to be

[1] See Whistler, *Quantock Folk Lore*, 1907, p. 54.

afraid of Drake than anyone realized. He could do very strange
things. Didn't he sit on Plymouth Hoe whittling a stick? And all
the chips that fell in the sea turned into ships to fight the Spanish
Armada. Although he had been gone three years *he* knew what was
happening. At the very door of the church he dropped a red-hot
'cannon-ball'[1] in front of the bridal party which so frightened them
all that, when he did come home at last, it was to find his bride and
her father waiting for him with smiles. As for the other bridegroom,
he had taken himself across the breadth of England — but I expect
Drake knew where he was.[2] *Local traditions.*

Paying the Scot-Ale. Skilgate (Brendon Hills)

In the old days the Lord of the Forest and the Ranger could hold
a Forest Court to try deer stealers, and people who cut down trees
or let their beasts stray beyond the king's boundary: they could
fine people for very small offences (and often for nothing at all) and
they could hold Scot-Ales to which everyone must come to buy the
ale whether they wanted to or no. Altogether in remote places like
the Brendons and Exmoor they could do very much as they pleased
to raise money for themselves as well as the King. It was very easy
to accuse a man of hunting the deer, and then fine him or threaten
him with prison until he parted with all his wealth. But one day
they caught a tartar — the Ranger accused a train-band Captain, a
jovial rascal, leader of sturdy rogues, and the Lord of the Forest as
usual sent out a charge for him to appear. But the Captain and his
merry men had other notions. They sent in turn all the way to
Taunton and got a charge laid against the Ranger. To pay for this
they let it be known in all the Churches round that they would hold
a Scot-Ale in Skilgate Church, and hold it they did. By the time the
Church ale men arrived, the ale was already sold, and the sermon
was half-preached. Everyone was in a merry humour and the
Captain had collected £60 to pay his lawyer.

When the case did come up at Taunton it seems to have been dis-
missed. Taunton was used to lawful ways and it probably decided
it was a healthy thing for Exmoor folk to see 'the biters
bit'.[3]

---

[1] 'Cannon-ball' = meteorite.
[2] See A. E. Bray, *The Borders of Tamar and Tavy*, Vol. II, pp. 29–42.
[3] See Greswell, *Forests and Deer Parks of Somerset*, 1905, p. 208; *Star Chamber
Proceedings*, 1592.

The Hanging Field at Shute Shelve. Worle

The Hanging Field lies above the Bridgwater Road on Shute Shelve. In 1609 two men and a woman were executed and hung in irons here for murdering the woman's husband.

Excerpt from Burial Register. Worle 1609

'Edward Bustle cruelly murthered by consent of his owne wyfe, who with one Humfray Hawkins, and one other of theyre associates, were executed for the same murther and hanged in Irons at a place called Shutt Shelfe neare Axbridge — a good president for wicked people.'

A North Somerset informant was warned by an old man not to travel the road after dark for horrible sounds were sometimes heard, a woman's scream of despair, choking breaths and the clank of chains. He was most insistent about it. As he was a shepherd it is possible he had suffered himself. *Collected by friend, Axbridge, 1925.*

Haydon's Gully. Hinton Blewitt, The Mendip Hills

Colonel Haydon was a fugitive in one of 'they old wars' (probably from Sedgemoor). By night he hid in Hinton Blewitt and by day he kept himself and his horse concealed in a wooded gully nearby.

When we lost anything as children, or anyone hid from us, we were told to 'look in Haydon's Gully'.[1] *Personal memory.*

The Legend of the Sword (Monmouth Rebellion). Western Zoyland near Sedgemoor

Turrible times the war was! Ah! turrible doings. They d' zay from yur to Burgewalter was all a-ztink with the dead corpuses hanging every step of the way. But there was brave deeds tew, oh yes. Have 'ee ever heard tell how Squire were tew Bristol and they blood-thirsty sojers do come up to Hall? Proper wicked drunk they was, and they offered disrespect to Madam, poor dear zoul, and her near her time. Well then, Miss Mary, and her but a maid in her twelves, she outs the villains zword and runs he droo the heart so clean's a whistle. No one never blamed her. Proper brave maid her was. *Collected from fragments round Bridgwater and the lower Quantocks, 1912–30's.*

[1] See Poole, p. 99.

Note. I was told the actual sword was in Taunton Museum. The incident is quite true. 'The war' may mean any battle from Roman days on. Usually the very old call the Monmouth Rebellion 'The Duking Days' in memory of Monmouth.[1]

Blood Field. Crowcombe and Stogumber

The Monmouth men had a terrible battle there, s'pose to. 'Twas said they hanged the Monmouth men on Heddon Oak, and they fought so hard the field was full of blood, and it ran out over the gate bars. There was a pine tree on Quark Hill. It was standing twenty years ago, but it had the iron spikes in it. *From William Chidley, artisan, Crowcombe, 25/2/57.*

Blood Field, or the Field of Blood, is the high field above Heddon Oak. It was the scene of a British-Saxon battle, but legend insists that it is where six West Somerset men were tarred and quartered after hanging. The pine may have been another, later, gallows. Heddon Oak has an uncanny reputation.

Owen Parfitt. Shepton Mallet

The memory of this historical mystery still survives in Shepton Mallet. Owen Parfitt was an elderly seafaring man who returned to Shepton Mallet from no one knew where. He was supposed to be wealthy, and rumour went round that he had been a pirate. He and his sister lived together for many years until he became paralysed, and a younger relation came to look after them both. One summer day old Parfitt had been settled outside in his chair, to which he could just shuffle, when a passing neighbour told him that a seafaring man had been enquiring about an old sailor. Old Parfitt turned white, but he said nothing. Next day he was settled as usual, and his cousin went out to do her shopping. When she got back his chair and rug and cushion were there, but there was no sign of Parfitt himself. The haymakers were working in the field near, and had heard or seen nothing, but he was never found again. The local explanation is that he was not so lame as he pretended, and that he had made off with his hoard when he heard of someone who had a right to share it. If so he had gone off just as he was, without even changing his slippers.[2] *Local traditions.*

[1] See A. L. Humphrey's *History of Wellington*, pp. 100–1.
[2] See Andrew Lang, *Historical Mysteries*.

The Ploughman's Treasure. Aisholt

Old Mrs. Caddick used to go hoving, or 'uvving' as she called it. She put a knife blade on her hoe, and she'd pick her bit of field to do, didn't matter where the farmer was working, and she'd do it lovely. She lived in the little chapel up Buncombe, and she kept it clean for her rent. She'd pluck a chicken for you for the entrails and work extra to earn a bit of meat for her Sunday dinner. She used to tell me when she and her brother went to school they were so hungry they'd dig up pignuts in the fields. Ever so sweet she said they were, and so round as a hazel nut.

There was one of the Caddicks used to go ploughing with oxen. Six of them there was, and he had a pointed stick to keep them straight in the furrors. Times they'd go on quiet and he'd go back for a word with the ploughman. And they turned up a heap of money at the old Castle near Three Horse-shoes Hill above Aisholt — And when he went to the States he sold the coins there for a dollar each! *William Chidley, artisan, Crowcombe, 25/2/57.*

The Farmer and the Footpads. Buncombe Hill, Quantock Hills

The farmer from Bullers Farm[1] went to Taunton Market one wintry day. He returned late with his market-money in his breeches pocket not in his saddle-bags as was customary.

At the foot of Buncombe Hill he came up with a well-dressed foot-passenger who asked him for a lift behind on the horse. The night was getting dark and the way among the trees even darker, but the farmer dare not refuse. There might be more of the gang ahead. There was only one thing to do. He pretended to be still cider-hazy. He told the man to mount behind and hold on to his belt, warning him that the horse might not 'stand' for him. Then he slyly spurred his old horse into a most uneven and spirited gait, and the fellow clinging behind got the benefit of all the buck-jumps and had rather a rough passage. He did gasp out as warning to the farmer who was singing drunkenly as the old horse jinked and propped along, 'Don't 'ee whistle on no account.' Hearing this the farmer knew a gang lay in wait ahead, so stealthily drawing a pocket knife, he sliced through his belt and spurred the horse frantically to the top of the hill. His unwelcome passenger landed so heavily he could not get his breath to whistle until the flying pair had passed

[1] Bullace = wild plum (farm now ruined).

the Traveller's Rest. At the signal four mounted men rode out of the wood and galloped after their terrified prey, who fled down Broomfield Road and along by Ruborough Camp. Just ahead of the pursuit the farmer finally rode the old horse into the middle of a gorsey field and ran to the ditch to hide. The pursuers came up with the horse and emptied the saddle bags, but finding nothing rode off cursing. The farmer crept home along the hedges and so saved the market money. *Oral collection 1955. Told to William Chidley by Mr. Sanders, carter, aged 70, who was told the story when a boy by the farmer himself.*

I am told that according to the Sessions Papers in Taunton Museum this gang was tried and sentenced in 1830.

3

Local Legends

'The Healing Springs of Prince Bladud' (900 B.C.). Bath and
Swainswick

Prince Bladud was the eldest son of King Lud of Britain. He was
greatly beloved and so wise that all men looked to him to reign
gloriously when his turn came. Wishing to gain greater knowledge
he travelled to Greece and spent many years there.

The day came when he returned from Athens to Britain and was
welcomed joyfully — When alas! a fearful tragedy occurred. He
found he was a *leper*!

With all haste he journeyed away from men and their kindness
— only living on such food as was left by the wayside for such as
he. At last he came to Swainswick, where a farmer allowed him to
herd his hogs and live afield with them.

Bladud was thankful to feel that there was still something a poor
outcast could do and under his care the swine began to thrive. But
when the winter came some of them became restless and sick, their
skins cracked and chapped and Bladud could find no herbs to ease
them. Suddenly the herd began to move purposefully down the
hillside to the marsh where faint steam arose, and by the time
Bladud had caught up with them they were wallowing happily in
slime and *warm* mud.

Yes, it was warm — for Bladud waded into it to drive out the
herd.

The next day they came back again; the coats of the sick pigs
shone with health, and Bladud looking upon his own feet and hands
found them healed. Filled with joy he too bathed in the hot springs
and was cured of his leprosy.

He returned, a healthy man, to his father's court amid great
jubilations, and when he became King of Britain he built a city by
the springs that cured him. It was a sign of his gratitude and his
thought for the sick among his people.[1] *Oral tradition, 1912.*

[1] See Collinson, Poole, etc.

Hogs Norton. Norton Malreward

When Prince Bladud became King of Britain he sent for a Somerset farmer. This was the old man who in charity had given him charge over his swine when all men shunned him because he was a leper. Now that Bladud had built the city of Bath to cure the sick, meat and fruit were wanted from the countryside daily. In gratitude King Bladud made the old farmer lord of a village, which the country people promptly called Hogs Norton.

Later on when the Normans came everyone was still agreed that a whole village wasn't a bad reward — and since that time it has been called Norton Malreward.[1] *Oral tradition, Bath and Clifton.*

Norton Malreward should be Malregard from the Norman lord who had an 'evil eye'.

Simon's Bath. Simonsbath, Exmoor

Old Simon was a wild robber who roamed all over Exmoor, and people in the farms and villages were afraid for their dear lives of what he would be after next. So they sent the dodman[2] to bring them back a saint to go and talk to Simon.

The dodman came back with a Cornish saint who was on the look-out for sinners, and as for being afraid of Simon, he was just aching to meet him. So he went out over the moor alone and there he met the robber, but he was so friendly and unafraid that Simon began to listen, and in the end he wanted to be a Christian. 'Then I'll baptize you,' said the Saint, 'There's a nice deep pool in the Barle over there.' 'Wouldn' somewhere a bit shallower do?' says Simon, "Tisn' the right time o' year for bathing, there's a "lazy wind"[3] and 'twas a "coat colder" this morning when I woke.'

But no, the Saint was adamant. 'Deep water for sins as deep as yours,' says he, so in Simon went, and it was icy. 'Will one bath be enough, zur?' he says with his teeth chattering like cankervells.[4] But the Saint was a cunning man, and he looked at the poor fields and wretched neglected farms around and answered thoughtfully, 'One will do for here now; but it will take another two to get your soul clean. We'll both go and try Cornwall — *it's warmer!*' *Oral tradition, Simonsbath, Sandyway, Withypool; Oral collection, Mr. March, farmer, Kinsford, 1906.*

[1] See Boger, p. 23.
[2] Packman, pedlar.
[3] One that goes through you not round.
[4] Icicles.

The Hermit. Blackwell

Next to the chapel window towards the altar is a peep-hole in a stone quatrefoil, and here, immured for life, lived a hermit. Tradition says that the eremite was a lady who repented her sins too late, for her beauty was gone from her and her face was 'fearful to see'. She had herself walled into this tiny cell, and spent the rest of her life in holy contemplation.[1] *Local version from a North Somerset friend.*

The Barefoot Pilgrimage

There was once a Lord of Dunster who was hard on his people and hated all churchmen. He had a lady who was as gentle as he was rough, and who was much beloved by the people. It happened one time that the Lord had the notion of enclosing Dunster Common for his own use. The poor of Dunster went to the monks about it and they went to the Lady. She was ill of fever at the time, but she got up and went to ask the Lord to change his mind. He was obdurate, but at last he said as a kind of joke that she could have as much of the Common for the poor as she could walk round barefoot on a winter's night. Ill as she was the Lady set out that evening. The poor people, who loved her, begged her to stop and go home, but she limped on. At length they went to fetch the Lord, and he came to stop his Lady, but it was not yet dawn and the circle was not finished, so she went on until she fell fainting. The Lord carried her home in his arms, and the men of Dunster kept their Common.

The Prior and the Nun. Muchelney

This is the heart-breaking tale of ill-starred lovers that still lingers near Langport and the Levels.

He was the youngest son of an impoverished house and she was the daughter of a wealthy knight, and so their wedding was not to be thought of. She was sent away, and he was told that she had been married to the rich nobleman of her parents' choice. In his despair he entered a monastery — some say it was Glastonbury Abbey — and because he needed to direct his sorrow he worked so well for the Church that he became the Prior of Westover. And here, after years of struggle, Fate again took a hand; for among the nuns in his charge was none other than his lost love. She had refused to marry

[1] See Knight, *Heart of Mendip*, p. 19.

and had preferred to become a nun for his memory's sake. And now they met face to face, and both found their love was a stronger thing than vows made in unhappiness to the Church. There was an underground passage or cellar-way where they met in stealth and planned their escape. Alas, they were spied upon and reported. On the very night that the Prior was preparing to escape he was removed to a far-off monastery without a word of explanation or time to get a warning to the unfortunate nun. She, waiting in the cellar-way for her lover's arrival, was seized there and bricked up in it. Whether the Prior ever learned what had happened to his true love is not on record.[1] *Local traditions reported by a Bruton friend, 1922–30.*

A similar tale is told of the Old Abbey House, Barnwell, Cambridge.

The Primrose Peerless. Churchill

In a field near the church grows or grew a colony of these lovely flowers — nor were any others to be found on Mendip.

The tale is a sad one.

A Crusader came home to Churchill after years of the heat and bloodshed in the Holy Land. He had gone away rich — he came home poor, but he had brought his beloved wife a carefully cherished present — two bulbs of the Primrose Peerless. She had always loved rare flowers.

Alas, when he reached Churchill the primroses on her grave were blooming for the fourth time. In his despair he flung the precious bulbs over the churchyard wall and, falling beside his lady's grave, died of a broken heart.

Throughout the centuries the bulbs have grown and flourished and kept his memory alive.

Another version of the story is to be found at Churchill.

Sir Thomas Latch returned from journeyings abroad in the Civil War on the very day that his dear wife died of the plague — as he gazed upon her his own heart broke and he also died where he stood.

There is a most dramatic painted tomb in the church and the

[1] See E. Boger, *Myths, Scenes & Worthies of Somerset*, pp. 182–5.

whole tale is set out in local verse, but, as the villagers still say, 'It don't explain they bewtivull vlowers.'[1]

Church Treasure. Street

In the dark days when Glastonbury Abbey was dissolved one of her priests hid a quantity of Church Treasure at Ivythorn, uttering a terrible curse on any sacrilegious man who should find and raise it. The priest died or was executed, and centuries later a farmer of Ivythorn dug up the treasure. Laughing at all the old wives' tales he proceeded to spend it wildly. He got neither pleasure nor peace from it for the curse rested upon him until he lost farm, family and his own wits and died raving. *Local traditions.*

Moles Chamber. Kinsford

This version was heard by my father on one of his walks from Kinsford to Watchet to preach on the Sunday. It was told him by a moorman near the Chains 1904.

1. In the old days there was an inn called the Acland Arms on the drove road from Sandyway to Lynmouth. It stood not far from the much-feared bog. One evening after a day's hunting a young squire named Mole took on a drunken bet that he could ride across it. Before anyone could stop him he spurred his hunter straight for the dreadful quagmire. The horse swerved aside, and the drunken man was slung from the saddle straight into its depths and was sucked under at once.

2. *Exmoor.* A farmer went to Lynmouth with his pack-horse for a load of lime to put heart in his poor fields. Returning in the mist he lost the way to Kinsford, and man and horse were swallowed in the quagmire. When it was drained years later, man and horse were found preserved by the lime. *This, probably the true version, was told to my eldest brother by the farmer at Kinsford, Nr. March, 1906.*

The Seven Sisters. The Polden Hills

There are seven villages upon the Polden Hills — Chilton, Catcott, Greinton, Edington, Moorlinch, Sutton and Stawell — and so they are called the Seven Sisters. It appears however that there was great rivalry among them as to which should become the Mother Church until the Bishop decreed that the largest entries

[1] See Knight, *Heart of Mendip*, p. 230.

for one year in the Church Registers should decide the matter. I was told darkly that Stawell was in the lead with 3 births and 1 death, when just at the very last Moorlinch came racing home to win with *4 more deaths* than Stawell. So Moorlinch became Mother Church, but Stawell still has grim ideas. *Oral collection, Poldens, 1947.*

The Pilots of Pill. Cróckerne, Pill and Portishead

There was great rivalry between the pilots of Pill and the pilots of Portishead. Severn Channel is one of the most dangerous in the world with its ever shifting quicksands and its tide, which rises at times to 45 feet at Portishead. Merchantmen bound for the Port of Bristol some miles inland were glad enough to hail a pilot from either village, but their sailors homeward bound after years at sea were becoming wary of being paid off at Pill with its street of taverns, to wake up outward bound again and penniless. 'Pill sharks' was the name Portishead used about them, but Pill answered with the one word 'Wreckers', and as one of the clergy had, in far off days, been as guilty as his parish Portishead had no answer for it. Now it chanced that there was a shortage of food one year, meat was unheard of in either village, and when two merchantmen were due the two rival pilots raced down Channel as far as Lundy to get their prize and payment. To the surprise of Portishead the Pill pilot reached the greater prize first, seemed to hang behind it uncertainly, and then went on to fumble around the smaller vessel before boarding it. The Portishead pilots brought their large West Indiaman safely to Pill where the horse teams towed it on to Bristol quays. Having jeered at the clumsy seamanship of the Pill men they went home well paid, but to face still empty larders. The next day they were assailed by their own furious women folk. It seemed that Pill was dining on roask pork — great slabs of it. To be sure it was a bit salt, for it had been towed behind both merchantmen as shark bait, but it was none the worse for that, and if the 'Pill Sharks' had earned the smaller pilot's fee they had secured the bait from both ships. *From Maurice Adams, lighthouseman, born in Gordano; his father and ancestors were Channel pilots; 1956.*

PART V

Songs and Sayings

1

Rhymes and Songs

Judas was a Red-Headed Man

There were twelve bonfires burning in a field;
(Judas, Judas)
There was one for Peter, there was one for John,
And every disciple he had one.
(Judas, Judas)
There was one for James that died by the sword,
But the biggest and best was for our dear Lord.

Burn, burn, Judas, burn slow.
Bright, bright, bright for our dear Lord's sake;
Burn slow for Judas.
Judas was a red-headed man.

There was one for Judas and it stood all alone
(Judas, Judas)
Down by the marish and it smoked away,
It smoked all night and it smoked all day.
(Judas, Judas)
'Twas a proper green smother for all to see,
But the fire burned sweet for our Lord on the tree.

Burn, burn, Judas, burn slow.
Bright, bright, bright for our dear Lord's sake;
Burn slow for Judas.
Judas was a red-headed man.

The Garland of Clay

O my love wore a garland of may,
O my love wore a garland of may,
And she looked so nice and neat
To her pretty little feet
When she met her false lover in the dew.

O my love wore a garland of red,
O my love wore a garland of red,
For he left her all alone
Her sad fate to bemoan
When she met her false lover in the dew.

O my love wore a garland of rue,
O my love wore a garland of rue,
There's a baby to sing
But there's no wedding ring,
For she met her false lover in the dew.

Now my love wears a garland of clay,
Now my love wears a garland of clay.
She was ruined in her prime
And she died before her time
For she met her false lover in the dew.

Early 1900's. The false lover in the song was supposed, by those who taught me, to be a fairy, like the Love-Talker of Ireland.

Harvest Song

We've adone, and well adone
Hip hip hip hooray.
And all our corn be in the barn
Hip hip hip hooray.

Churchill (Mendip Hills).

An Ancient Carol, or Round

At Chrissimass, at Chrissimass
Long time ago
The shepherd lads they runned and runned
All in the snow.

At Chrissimass, at Chrissimass
Long time ago
Ox and ass they curchied down
All in the snow.

At Chrissimass, at Chrissimass
Long time ago
Brave St. George he singed aloud
All in the snow.
*From the bed-ridden grandmother of a friend's maid-servant,
about 1940.*

Another Carol Tag. Mummer's Song

Now welcome, welcome Christmass
With a right good cheer
Away dumps, away dumps
Nor come you not here
And I wish you a merry Christmass
And a Happy New Year.

Holly Boy and Ivy Girl. Green Ivy O. (Traces of procession and
dances)

O the ivy O, she'd grow, she'd grow
And the holly he is white
And the little birds sing because it is spring
And the plough boys follow the plough.
O 'tis ivy O, green ivy O
O the ivy she do grow.

O the ivy O, she do twine all about
And the holly he is green
And they tosses the hay in the field all day
And the sun he do shine out
O the ivy O, green ivy O
O the ivy she do twine all about.

O the ivy O, at the Allern tide
And the holly he is yellow
There be apples fell adown and they picks 'n from the ground
And they lays 'n in the tallat side to side
O 'tis ivy O, green ivy O
O the ivy at Allern tide.

o

O the ivy O, she is Queen of old
And the holly he is red
Hang'n high on the farm and us wont come to no harm
Till the Chrissimass Days be told
O 'tis ivy O, green ivy O
O the ivy she is Queen of old.

This carol I was taught by an old man in 1906–7 at Taunton
Market. It possibly embodies the Carol of the Holly Boy and the
Ivy Girl, of whom there are faint traces on Blackdown. It may have
been the processional dance as the tune is of a pipe and tabor
variety. I have only just recovered it entirely. *Taunton, 1906;
Crowcombe, 1959.*

The Holy Thorn

O the beastes all heard the angel call
When the cock sang 'Christ is born'
And they all kneeled to pray down upon the hay
When the cock sang 'Christ is born'.

(*Chorus*)
And the ruddick sang, O the little ruddick sang
So sweetly sanged he
On Chrissimass Morn on the Blessed Thorn
On a twig of the Holy Tree.

Then the oxen they did low and the ponies they did bow
When the cock sang 'Christ is born'
And the dunk he roared 'Praise our sweet Lord'
When the cock sang 'Christ is born'.

(*Chorus*)

Let us kneel in the hay for 'tis Chrissimass Day
When the cock sings 'Christ is born'.
And there's blooth on the twig and the little lambs do jig,
When the cock sings 'Christ is born'.

(*Chorus*)

This was taught me by the widow of a cowman when I was

small. It should only be passed on from cowman to successor as it is their mystery. However, the old man would not transmit it to a new man who was unfitted, and on dying passed it on to his widow in order that she would hand it on to a 'right person'. Apparently a Chime child, even a girl, was considered correct. *Nailsbourne, 1906–10.*

The Cold Cold Sea

A ship went a-sailing up into the North
A ship went a-sailing the cold cold sea
She sailed forth
All into the North
And took my lover away from me
Away from me, away from me.

I sat by the side of the flowing tide
But never a ship nor a sail to see
Then into my sight
A sea-gull so white
Came flying out of the North to me
Came flying — came flying.

It came to rest within my sad breast
'My love I'll bid fare well to thee
For never no more
Will I come on shore
I'm drowned in the cold cold sea
The cold, cold sea, the cold cold sea.'
(Chappell)
Taunton Market, Porlock and Kilve, 1905–9.

Over Quantock

As I went up they Quantocks
As I went up they Quantocks
As I went up they Quantocks
When I were very small
I couldn't get up they Quantocks
I couldn't get up they Quantocks
I couldn't get up at all.

When I went over Quantocks
When I went over Quantocks
When I went over Quantocks
And took my love with me
We danced along they Quantocks
We danced along they Quantocks
From Buncombe to the sea.

Now I want to get up they Quantocks
Now I want to get up they Quantocks
Now I want to get up they Quantocks
Along of my girt old stick
But I can't get up they Quantocks
But I can't get up they Quantocks
But I comes down very quick.

The Deadly Sand (Wreckers' Song: Somerset)

The tide runs up, the tide runs down;
'Tis forty-five feet at Possett Town   (Portishead)
The tide do ebb and the tide do flow
And the deadly sand it do lie below.
The deadly sand it do crawl around,
And there's many a tall ship cast aground,
And there's many a craft in sight of land
That is swallowed up by the deadly sand.
Down a-down, down a-down,
The deadly sand do drag them down.

We lighted a fire on the cliff so high
And a merchantman came sailing by;
She turned our way and afore our eyes
The deadly sand did swallow our prize.
There was never a barrel nor a bale of lace
And of goodly silk we saw no trace;
And kegs of spice and passels of tea
She dragged all down in the Severn Sea.
Down a-down, down a-down,
The deadly sand do drag them down.

A revenue cutter gave us hail
A-hoping to bring us to Bristol Jail;
She turn—ed swift to cross our way
And the deadly sand beneath her lay.
The pilot he cried, 'Farewell dear wife,
There's never a man shall save his life!'
And some they did pray and some took oar,
But none of the crew did come ashore.
Down a-down, down a-down,
The deadly sand do drag them down.

But we do row when the moon is low
And follow the tides and the sand below,
We do land our prizes in Watchet Bay
And the pack-horse train is away, away.
We shall all be hanged on Severn shore;
With our chains and our rope we shall wreck no more;
And every ship a-sailing by
Will be over our heads when the tide runs high.
Down a-down, down a-down,
The deadly sand will drag us down.

2

Proverbs and Proverbial Sayings

SAYINGS ABOUT PLACES

1. Rode Revel, Beckinton Rout
   The Devil's in Frome and cannot get out.
2. There was an old cobbler lived in Frome
   And all he wanted was elbow room.
3. Exmoor, where they as can't live, dies.
4. Withypool, where they has vower harvests a year, snow, frost, rain and muck.
5. Norton were a Market town
   When Taunton were a vuzzy down.
6. Watchet true, Watchet blue.
7. If you look at Martin's Ape
   Martin's Ape will look at *you*.
8. Exmoor, where they have nine months' winter, and three months' hard work. *Mr. Coleman, gardener, Crowcombe.*

PROVERBIAL SAYINGS

'They say so is half a liar.' *West Somerset, 1959.*
'Better do a thing than wish it done.' *Crowcombe, 1955.*
'Nurse a trouble, make it double.' *Skilgate, 1940; Exmoor, 1950.*
'Yew can't have no Pilgrim's Progress wi'out bunions.' *Exmoor, 1940.*

'A Friday's holiday be always sad,
But a Wednesday's holiday brings summat bad.'

'Calls he a gentleman? I calls 'n a gentleman wi' dree 'thouts—'thout wit, money nor manners.' *West Somerset.*
'The pride of the poor stinks worse than a badger.' *Mr. Milner, Nailsbourne, 1939.*
'To say "Yes" three times means that you will say "No" in the end.' *Wedmore, farmer's wife.*

INN VERSES

1.
Call frequently
Drink moderately
Pay honourably
Be good company
Part friendly
Go home quietly
Let these words be no man's sorrow
Pay today and trust tomorrow.

2.
Since man to man is so unjust,
I am determined not to trust
I've trusted many to me sorrow
So pay today and trust tomorrow.

Brendon Hills, 1925.

3.
Kind gentlemen, I you entreat
While you are here to keep your seat.
Sit and drink to your desire
And do not sit before the fire.

4.
My liquor is good, my measure is just,
Believe me, sir, learn not to trust.
I have trusted many to my sorrow
So pay today and trust tomorrow.

Rising Sun Inn, Blackdown Hills.

WEATHER LORE

Cloud in the valley
Hot on the hill
Will 'ee take shelter?
Yes, if yew will.

Hot in the valley
Cloud on the hill
Will 'ee go a-walking?
Yes, if yew will.

Taunton Market, 1905

Mist

> When it run vrom hill tew sea
> There 'ont be enough tew drowned a vlea.
> But when her run vrom sea tew hill
> 'Twil be enough tew turn the mill.
>
> *Crowcombe, 1958.*

> When the mist be on the hill
> There runneth water tew the mill.
>
> *Flatpool, 1951. Mr. Webber, roadman.*

April is a 'catcheldy' month. *Saltford, 1950.*

> When Dunkery's top cannot be seen
> Horner will have a flooded stream.
>
> *East Lucott, 1949.*

Cloud

> Mares tails, ponies tails,
> All the boats have set their sails.
>
> *Porlock.*

Rain

> One day's thunder, two days rain
> Three days hot and thunder again.
>
> *School friends, Trull, 1908.*

> Mackerel sky, mackerel sky,
> 'Tisn't long wet and 'tisn't long dry.
>
> *Porlock, 1945.*

If the sun sets in the wind's eye there will be rain. *Watchet.*

Yellow and grey, rain all day. *West Somerset.*

Winter

> A mild November, a black March.
> Green winter makes a black Spring.

White riders on black horses (blackthorn). *Crowcombe, 1960.*

If Michaelmas ice can bear a duck,
Winter will be rain and muck.

As Friday, so Sunday.

Friday in the week is seldom alike.

March
March dust a guinea an ounce. *H. Bole, carter, Crowcombe, 1960.*

Lady Day (March 25th)
Whatever quarter the wind is, it will continue for the next three months.

When Our Lord's Day falls in Our Lady's lap
England will meet with a sad mishap.

Wiveliscombe, 1955.

Appendix I

HERE is a list of ailments which particular wells were supposed to cure.

Consumption

North.   Bishop's Well, Yatton.

Epilepsy

East.   St. Dunstan's, Witham Friary. 'Because he did drive off the devil.'

Eye Troubles

North.   Bully Well, Chew Magna.

East.   St. Anthony's Well, Bathford, was used to clear eye troubles in 1681. It certainly clears up some cases.

Puck's Well, Rode.

Stowey Blind Well.

St. Andrew's, Ansford.

Mid.   Sunset Well, Ansford.

Holy Well, Chilton Polden.

South.   Holy Well, East Coker.

West.   Holy Well, Quantock Barn.

St. Leonard's, Dunster.

St. Sidwell, Wick Moor.

Bath Water, Dulverton, was credited with only healing the good.

General Tonic and Curative Purposes

North.   St. Catherine's, Bath.

St. Chad's Well, Midsomer Norton.

East.   Combe Hill Well, Bruton.

Jaundice

Alford Well in 1800 was believed to contain a curative quality for jaundice, obstructions and scurvy.

Leprosy

Harry Hill's Well, Stogumber, was for a short time in the early nineteenth century regarded as a curative spring for leprosy.

Rheumatism

Bathealton Well is a warm spring used by rheumatic labourers for years.

Scurvy

St. Sidwell's, Wick, and St. Decuman's, Watchet, were used by sailors after long sea voyages.

Sprains and broken bones

St. Agnes' Well, Whitestaunton, was famous locally for its ability to cure sprains and knit broken bones, and was used by the Taunton schoolboys after playing-field injuries.

Skin troubles

Edington was a sulphur spring much used up to 1900.

Veterinary Wells

St. Adhelm's Well, Doulting, for ailing beasts or those that have been 'overlooked'.

St. Agnes' Fountain, Doulting, for the Quarter-ail (cattle paralysis). It never healed stolen cattle.

Pilgrim's Wells

Chalice Well, Glastonbury, is still in occasional use, and St. Jacob's Well and Holywell at Pilton, all on the road to Glastonbury.

Fons George, Wilton, near Taunton, on the south side of St. George's Church is reputed to be another Pilgrim's well.

Dangerous Wells

South. Holywell at Watchett petrifies objects and is considered uncanny. St. Nipperton's (Cyprianus), Ashill. The ebb and flow of this is supposed to foretell national disaster.

East. St. Dunstan's Well, Stoke St. Michael. This spring is from an underground river large enough to turn a mill. It disappears in a slocken hole, and comes out near Stoke House. It is regarded as uncanny.

West. The Devil's Whispering Well, near Bishop's Lydeard Church. Here curses can be whispered.

The Witches' Pool, Sandhill. The ghost of Madam Joan Carne, a notorious witch, was laid in it. 'When we were children we never gathered blackberries by the "Witch Pool".' Farm labourers used to be most reluctant to work near it.

Furber's Well, Milverton. ''Tis one of they where 'ee do wish a wish.'

Saints' Wells and Holy Wells

North.   Holy Well at Yatton.
South.   St. Mary's at Chaffcombe.
Mid.   St. Rumbold's at Bishop's Hull.
    St. Ursula's at Trull.
    Holy Well at Taunton.
    St. Mary's in the crypt at Glastonbury.
    St. Catherine's, Swell, a wishing well. You must go round it
      three times at sunrise, but if it was crawled round counter-
      clockwise it brought an ill wish.
    St. Winifred's Well, Chew Magna, a mother's well.
East.   Lady Well and St. Patrick's Well, both at Bruton.
West.   Holy Well and St. Pancras' Well at Roadwater.
    Holy Well at Halse.
    Holywell Lake at Rockwell Green.
    St. Luke's Well at Cutcombe.
    St. Michael's Well at Minehead.
    St. Peter's Well at Over Stowey.
    St. David's in Seven Wells Combe on the Quantocks.
    St. Agnes at Cothelstone was resorted to by the love-sick.

Wishing Wells and Pixy Wells. St. Agnes, Cothelstone

'We used to wonder why 'twas called St. Agnes Well, but we never dared wish there because of the pixies and there's a Pixy Well down near the farm somewhere.' *Roebuck Farm, Crowcombe W.I., 1958.*

'There was a Wishing Well somewhere down Roebuck. I can't remember about it but 'twas something to do about pins, and pixies.' *Carpenter's wife, Crowcombe W.I., 1958.*

Cadbury Castle

Extract from a letter from Clevedon & Congresbury 3/12/59.

'No one knows about a Holy Well (at Congresbury) but at Cadbury Camp one mile from Congresbury they carried out Black Magic and Beltane rites to within a hundred years (or less)'.

(b) TREES

Apple

> Eat an apple going to bed,
> Knock the doctor on the head.

West Somerset.

Ash

(a) Stick a pin in an ash tree and your warts will go away.

(*b*) An even ash and a four-leaved clover
Sure to see my true love before the day is over.

Ash Tree

(*a*) Split a sapling ash and pass an ailing child through the gap, *passing sunwise* three times. Bind up with a hay band.[1] *West Somerset.*

(*b*) Split an ash and bury a shrew mouse in the living tree to cure your cattle of quarter-ail.

When I was a child I was secretly shown a shrew-ash tree on Cothelstone Beacons. Shrews are accused of bringing palsy to the stock. *Personal, Cothelstone, 1905–11.*

(*c*) Split an ash and two women pass a child with hernia through the gap seven times, sunwise before sunrise. Bind up split with hazel bands — as tree knits so child will thrive, *but* if tree is injured in after years the patient will also pine away. *Old Woman, Exmoor, 1938; Ashbrittle; Langford Budville.*

Note: There are in Taunton Museum two of these trees.

Note (c): I saw one of these trees in Horner Valley about seventeen years ago but must not tell where. There were threatening letters and village trouble when some trees elsewhere were cut down and lifelines threatened.

Aspen

The Cross was made of Aspen Wood and the Tree shivers incessantly in its grief.

Blackthorn

A Blackthorn winter means a spoiled summer.

If brought indoors it means you will hear of a death. *Mrs. Pope, Langport, 1956.*

Chestnut

Chestnuts make good flour if baked and crumbled.

Plenty of nuts, plenty of cratches (cradles).

Elder

A witch may transform herself into one. Never break it or bring it indoors.

Dwarf elder always grows where blood has been spilled.

[1] See Humphreys, *History of Wellington*, 1889, p. 245; Thorne, *Antiquities of Wellington*, p. 7, 1940.

Elm

> 'Ellum when cometh a blow
> Up with her roots and down do go.'

The Bleeding Elm. Radstock, North Somerset

Woodborough, Rowbarrow, or Round Hill Barrow. Cromwell fought on Round Hill Barrow and there is a tradition that the barrow is the grave of a Saxon chieftain who was killed in a very sanguinary battle. There is an elm growing on this barrow which has an uncanny reputation. If it is cut with a knife it bleeds, but if you are so reckless as to touch it with anything but iron or steel you will sooner or later die very bloodily.

Hawthorn

Never cut down hawthorn trees to build your house, you and yours will never live long.

Holly

Many berries, much snow. *Taunton.*
'A gurt holly tree was down to Oare.' *Triscombe.*

Hydrangea

If you plant a hydrangea close to your house your daughter will never marry.

Ivy

Put a trail of ivy across a drunkard's path and he will become a sober citizen. *Mendip Hills.*

Juniper

Never tell a secret by a Juniper tree. Everyone will know it in a week.

May (Whitethorn)

If brought in the house brings death. *Mrs. McDowall, Huish Episcopi, 1956.*

Nut trees

Hazel gads fatten your beasts.
Horse chestnuts are used for conkers and if you carry one in your pocket you will never have piles.

Thorn

Christ was of a Virgin born
He was pricked by a thorn
It did never bell and swell
I trust in Jesus Christ this never will.

Then sign a cross with a thorn over the festered place. *Porlock, Exmoor, 1946.*

Appendix II

SOME SOMERSET WITCH TRIALS

The Flying Boy. South. Yeovil

A Yeovil witch in the seventeenth century threw a spell over a boy. She asked him for bread (which he probably refused) and she gave him an apple to eat, which boy-like he did regardless of all past warnings. 'Whereupon he rose in the air and flew about 300 yards' — A witness at the trial stated he was found strangely hanging above the ground with his hands flat against the sides of a great beam in the top of the room and all his body two or three feet from the ground and 'hath so remained a quarter of an hour at a time'. This witch was sentenced to death at Chard 1658.[1] *Local tradition.*

A Witch Revealed. South. Chard

Jane Brooks of Shepton Mallet met Richard Jones, aged 12, on Sunday, 15th November 1657. He was alone in the house. She asked for bread and in exchange gave him an apple and stroked his right side. Later the boy was taken ill and became speechless but recovered — his father, summoning the women of Shipton to see who was the culprit, he fell ill again as soon as he saw her. Later, again on a Sunday, he said he saw her on the wall and pointed. His cousin struck the place with a knife and the boy declared the witch's hand was cut. When accosted by the constable her hand was found to be bloody.

She and Alice Coward, her sister, were tried first at Castle Cary and then at Shepton, the boy becoming speechless, or croaking like a toad, and even hanging from a beam — which evidence brought a sentence of death upon them in 1658 at Chard.

The Trial of Elizabeth Horner, 1696. South-west. Wellington

From a letter by one Blackburne (sub-dean of Exeter) to the Bishop of Exeter.

Elizabeth Horner was arraigned on three inditements — for murdering Alice Bovet, aged 4, and pining and laming Sarah and Mary. She was accused of killing Alice by squeezing the breath out of her body, Elizabeth Bovet the mother gave evidence that Alice, ill for five days, died crying out 'Why doe you kill me' and that Sarah and Mary were

---

[1] See Willis Watson, *Somerset Life and Character*, 1925, p. 65.

threatened by the witch who made them swear and curse — that they were both very hungry and said the head of Beth Horner had entered into them, and Sarah walked up a nine foot wall several times saying Beth Horner carried her up. During her imprisonment they would vomit pins and stones and showed the marks of bites and pinches to Justice Auchester.

Alice Osborne who refused her some barm found her carefully refilled and cleansed vessel empty after 4 days tho' no one had used it, she also swore that Beth Horner threatened her children.

Margaret Armiger swore that while the witch was in prison she met her face to face in the country and Mary Stevens deposed that she had drove a red hot nail into her footprint and the witch was lame until the nail was pulled up. Elizabeth Horner bared her shoulder in court to disprove the tale of a devil's teat, she also said the Lord's prayer through, a little hesitantly, and was acquitted by My Lord Chief Justice despite the local prestige of the Bovets.[1]

The *Witches of Brewham Forest*. East. Wincanton

In 1664 a Witch Coven at Wincanton was brought to public notice and a State Trial ensued. Trister Gate was one of the meeting places for the Wincanton Coven, some of whom 'flew' there.

The most talkative of the accused was Elizabeth Style, who declared that the Devil had come to her both as a man and as a black dog. He had promised that if, like Nancy Camel of Shepton Mallet, she signed a bond in her blood and handed over her soul, and let him suck her blood when he desired it — she should have money and a long life. He asked her four times, and at length she pricked the fourth finger of her right hand on the top of the knuckle. Having now gained her body and soul, true to his reputation as a cheat, he gave her *sixpence* and vanished.

It is an accepted fact that witches are forced to betray themselves when confronted by accusers, and pay terribly for their previous sinister freedoms. Elizabeth Style is a case in point. Her confession is damning and yet she was compelled of her own volition to make it.

She used to see and meet the Devil as a man, or a dog, a cat, or a fly, and when she wished to invoke him for any harmful purposes it was by the name of Robin. When he appeared he was requested in the words 'O, Satan, give me my purpose' to harm some poor soul.

When the witches desired to harm Elizabeth Hall, a picture in wax was made and brought to be baptized by Satan, who on this occasion appeared as a man in black clothes. The figure was baptized in oil and then stuck through with thorns. Anne Bishop, Alice Duke and Mary Penny were all present and assisted in the ceremony.

[1] See A. L. Humphreys, *History of Wellington*, 1889, p. 237

Elizabeth Style also said that before attending meetings they anointed their foreheads and wrists and were soon carried there saying "Thout, tout a tout, a tout tout, throughout and about' and returned by saying 'Rentum Tormentum', sometimes in their bodies and clothes, sometimes without, yet they knew each other.

Bewitchings were made by an apple, a dish or a spoon baptized by the Evil One. Meetings took place at Lye Common, near Motcombe, and Marnhull and Trister Gate, and after their ceremonies they had wine, cakes and roast meat, and danced and made merry to the music of a pipe or cittern. At parting they said 'A boy, merry meet, merry part.'

There were 13 members of this coven.

Note: This devil was a human understudy.[1]

Eighteenth-Century Witches. North-east. Frome

In the early eighteenth century three witches, Elizabeth Currier, Margaret Coombes and Ann Moore were convicted at Bruton and placed in prison. While awaiting her trial one of them died there. The accuser was a Mary Hill, aged 18, of Beckington who, to the pride and consternation of beholders, vomited some 200 crooked pins, nails and pieces of brass. The two accused were tried at Taunton Assizes but the eighteenth century had brought an easing off on witch-hunts and the law was changing, so the vomiting of the pins came under too careful a scrutiny and, since Taunton Judges were not Mary's credulous neighbours, both women were acquitted.[2]

[1] See Poole, 1877, p. 62 Glanvil, 'Saducismus Triumphatus'.
[2] See Willis Watson, *Somerset Life and Character.* Cuming Walters, *Bygone Somerset* 1894, p. 114.

Appendix III

(a) PHANTOM HEARSES AND COACHES

FROM Cutcombe to Timberscombe on certain dread nights gallops a Phantom hearse. It has no driver and is drawn by four headless black horses. Many are the accidents it has caused, particularly by Sully or 'Devil's Elbow'. *Personal.*

'Horses are uneasy there, even in daytime.' *Walter B., Minehead, 1950.*

'Many horses with traps have bolted and caused accidents.' *Oral collection and local tradition; Minehead, Wheddon Cross, Dunster; 1906–1960.*

Porlock Hill

'The ghost horses on Porlock Hill are grey.' *Minehead bus driver, 1952.*

(Version 1.) 'Isn't that where the coach and four horses ran away? They were killed, and you see their ghosts there.' *Lewis C. (Scout), 1956.*

Is this the Cutcombe Hearse or another coach? Porlock Hill is notorious for its accidents — it may be correct.

No Man's Land. Dodington (Quantock Hills)

No Man's Land lies between Holford and the Castle of Comfort. Here every Christmas Eve at midnight a coach and four black horses drive up, turn on the green and drive away. The ghostly lady sometimes walks between Holford and Nether Stowey, and at other times rides in the coach. *Oral collection, 1937; Ash Priors W.I., 1961.*

(Version 2.) At midnight on New Year's Eve a coach drives up to No Man's Land through Walford's Gibbet, and sinks into the ground and disappears. It is drawn by black horses and has no visible driver.[1] *Oral collection, Dodington, 1951.*

There is a Fairy Coach which is sometimes seen at St. Audries. This may be the same as the above. *Seen by farmer, 1940.*

An old Black Dog patrol runs from the coast road back over the hills past Huish Barton where a phantom coach is heard to drive up to the house, about March and September. Some traditions say the Wheelmarks can be seen. This is a very uncanny area, possessing a death warning by pigeon and a 'person in silk'. *Monksilver, 1960; Bicknoller, 1960.*

On the Pawlett side of the Parrett estuary opposite Chilton Trinity, a

[1] See Willis Watson, 1925.

phantom coach complete with driver, guard and passengers used to be seen on the only lane leading to the ferry across the Parrett to Combwich from Huntspill. It is suggested that a fatal accident took place there in coaching times and all were drowned. Parrett rises at high tide over seventeen feet near the ferry. *Mr. A., Crowcombe, 1960.*

At Merriot Manor a coach is heard rumbling up to the main door. 'When we heard the wheels and clatter of hooves we used to rush to the windows to look out, but we never saw anything.' *Mrs. A., Ash Priors W.I., 1961.*

(b) THE WILD HUNT
Putsham, Dowsboro, Triscombe Stone.

Cannington Park used to be famous as the Devil's hunting ground. It is said the Wild Hunt and headless horsemen have often been encountered there.

The Devil also performs exploits on the hills around Stogursey and on Putsham Hill he rides nightly, while from Cannington Park he rides out with the Wild Hunt over the ancient track to Dowsboro and on to Crowcombe Heathfield.

The Yeff Hounds have fiery tongues, and the Rider is sometimes mounted on a headless horse.

There is also a legend, rarely mentioned, of the Wild Rider patrolling the Drove Road from Cothelstone to Quantoxhead after sunset. It is unlucky to hear him and very ill fortune to see him. *Mrs. F., cottager, Mr. D., gamekeeper, Seven Ash, Bagborough.*

The Old Roadway

Squire Thomas Musgrave of Stone Lodge died in 1780. He was a wild fellow, and was reputed to haunt his own cellars and house. He was also seen driving his coach and four on the Exford Road. On 17th December 1953 a Minehead man was driving his car down the steep dip by Suchwell Bridge when he had to swerve violently to avoid colliding with a galloping coach and four coming along the old disused road. It was during the middle morning, but there was a bit of a mist. *A resident of Stone Lodge, 1920; H. E. Kille, 1961; A Minehead driver, 1953.*

'The drive from Norton Fitzwarren Manor is haunted by the ghost of a hunting squire riding from Langford Budville to Norton Manor. He only appears on certain nights. We lived at the Lodge, but we never saw him.' *Oral, Crowcombe, 1955, local tradition.*

The Yeff Hounds, or Ghost Pack, were heard pattering through Stogumber after midnight this year, but no one looked out to see them, even nowadays. They are known to run through the village and down towards Roebuck, then on up to Wills Neck. *Member of Stogumber W.I., 1960.*

Another pack is said to hunt on Cleave Hill near Watchet. *H. E. Kille, 1961.*

Gatchell's Devil. West. Blackdown Hills

A farmer's wife needed a maid-servant, but she did not like the first applicant, who lived in the locality, and chose a girl from another village. The mother of the girl who did not get the job was already suspected of 'dark dealings' and when news came round that the farm was being haunted she was openly delighted. There was an unseen devil at the farm who broke china, made the furniture move, whisked sunbonnets from heads and made the strings of a cap hung on a chair stream out straight in an invisible wind. It talked and chuckled and gabbled to itself. Sheer terror drove the farm folk to boldness and they confronted the woman, who confessed to trickery. But as the teller of the tale said solemnly, 'There was two-three pitchforks among 'n an' nobody b'lieve 'twas all a-doed with bits of twine (cotton) or 'ool.' *A Blackdown shepherd, 1905–12.*

The Evil Eye, Ill-wishing and the evil effects of cursing

To curse loudly and intentionally is to call down Heaven's instant judgement on you. Somerset folk will still cite the following fatal cases to you.

Ruth Pierce, near Devizes, who died denying a theft and appealing to God's judgement, 1753.

A workhouse woman at Milbourne Port in 1813 and a workman at Jordans, Ilminster, in 1796, who, with a prisoner at Taunton Assizes in 1714, all used the blasphemous appeal 'God strike me dead', and so were struck.

A brutal drunken carter at Glastonbury in 1887 was reproved for maltreating his horse and replied with the same formula of defiance. The cart, loaded with stones, ran over him.

Somerset folk are very careful about cursing.

Glossary

Alices	Ulcers
Appleplexus	Apoplexy
Apple drame	Wasp
Apse	Abscess
Asker	Lizard
Bed Stick	Stick used for turning Feather-beds
Bone shave	Sciatica
Brimmles	Brambles
Broom Squires	Quantock Gipsies
Brown kitties or Brown Titus	Bronchitis
Bull-Beggar	A kind of Hobgoblin (mentioned by Reginald Scot)
Cancervells	Icicles
Catcheldy	Changeable or uncertain
Clavel tack	Mantelpiece
Cloam	Pottery
Diddiky	Rotten
Dimmet	The dusk after sunset
Dimpsies	Blindness or short sight
Dodman	Packman
Downarg	To talk (argue) down
Dowser or Jowser	Water diviner
Drang	Alleyway
Drasshle	Threshold
Drumble drone	Wild bee
Fairy Rade	The procession of the Fairies
Gad	A stick for use as a whip (goad)
Galley-Beggar	A kind of Hobgoblin (mentioned by Reginald Scot)
Gallitrap	Fairy ring
Gew-kew	Cuckoo

Griggling	Gathering apples left on the trees after the main harvest has been picked
Gullivers	Followers — i.e. masked men who followed the Hobby-horse wearing tall head-dress and carrying whip and tongs
Hoppy cough	Whooping cough
Hurd-yead	Red-head
Infloration or Information	Inflammation
Interjections	Indigestion
Jack-in-the-Hedge	Garlic mustard
Lamb's wool	Mulled ale with spiced roast apples
Lenny cocks or Lide lillies	Daffodils
Mommicks or mommets	Effigies
Mumper	Beggar
Nappy	Restive
Natomy	Skeleton
Nestle-tripe	Piglet, the youngest and weakest of the tribe
New harmoniums or Pewmoaner	Pneumonia
North eye	Squint
Nummet	Snack
Pelm or Pellum	Dust
Pin, the	Cataract
Quarter ail	Paralysis
Ruddick	Robin
Sexton's bones	Rheumatism
Spunkies	Will-o'-the-Wisps or the souls of unbaptized Children
Stumpy	Wren
Tacklacky	Running footman

Tutti	Posy
Unket	Uncanny
Whitpot	A milk pudding made of bread, cream, eggs, currants and spices

Selected List of Books Cited and Consulted

AARNE, A., and THOMPSON, STITH, *The Types of the Folktale*, F. F. Communications, Second Revision, Helsinki, 1961.

AUBREY, JOHN, *Remaines of Gentilisme and Judaisme*, 1881.

BARRETT, C. R. B., *Somerset: Highways, Byways and Waterways*. *Somersetshire, 1894.*

BAXTER, R., *Certainty of the World of Spirits*, 1691.

BOGER, E., *Myths, Scenes and Worthies of the County of Somerset*.

BOVET, R., *Pandaemonium or the Devil's Cloyster*, 1684.

BRAY, A. E., *The Borders of Tamar and Tavy*, 2 vols., 1879.

CAMDEN, WILLIAM, *Britannia*, Done into English by P. Holland, 1610.

CAMPBELL, M., *Tales from the Cloud-Walking Country*, 1958.

CAPGRAVE, J., *Nova Legenda Angliae*, 1516.

COCHRAN, V., *History of our Village*.

COLLINSON, J., *History of Somerset*, 3 vols., 1791, Index 1898.

CULPEPPER, N., *The English Physician Enlarged, or the Herbal*, 1653.

Dr. Lamb's Darling Pamphlet, 1653.

DYER, T. F. THISTLETON, *English Folk Lore*, 1884.

ELWORTHY, F. T., *Dialect of West Somerset*, 1875.

FARR, G. E., *Somerset Harbours*, 1954.

FRIEND, H., *Flowers and Flower Lore*, 1886.

GASS, D. J., *Down-Along Talks*, Somerset Folk Series No. 6, 1922.

GERARD, J., *Herball*, 1597.

GLANVIL, J., *Saducismus Triumphatus*, 1631.

GRESWELL, W. H. P., *The Forests and Deer Parks of Somerset*, 1905. *Land of the Quantocks*, 1903.

HANCOCK, F., *The Parish of Selworthy in the County of Somerset. Some Notes on its History*, Taunton, 1897.
History of Selworthy, 1897, 1903.
Minehead in the County of Somerset, Taunton, 1903.

HARTLAND, E. S., *Country Folk Lore, Gloucestershire*, 1892.

HOLINSHED, R., *Chronicles of England, Scotlande and Irelande*, 1577.

HUMPHREYS, A. L., *History of Wellington*, 1889.

HUNT, H., *Investigation at Ilchester Gaol*, 1821.

HUNT, R., *Tales and Romances of the West of England*, 1881 (reprinted 1930).
Reports of Ilchester Gaol.

IRVING, H., *Jack White's Gibbet*, Somerset Year Book, Vol. 21.

JENNINGS, J., *Observations on some of the Dialects of the West of England,* 1869.

KETTLEWELL, F. B., *Trinkum Trinkums of Fifty Years,* 1927.

KNIGHT, F. A., *Heart of Mendip,* 1915. *Sea-board of Mendips,* 1902.

LANG, ANDREW, *Historical Mysteries,* 1904.

LANGPORT WOMEN'S INSTITUTE, *Story of Our Village,* Langport Herald, 1894.

LAWRENCE, B., *Quantock Country,* 1952.

LELAND, JOHN, *The Itinerary of John Leland in or about the years 1535-1543,* edited by Tomlin Smith, 5 vols., 1906-10, Vol. I, Part II.

MATHEWS, F. W., *Tales of the Blackdown Borderland,* 1923.

MEYNELL, L. W., *Exmoor,* 1953.

MUNFORD, G. F., *The Somerset Folk Scene,* 1922.
>   *Ghosts and Legends of South Somerset,* 1922.

PAGE, J. L. WARDEN, *Exploration of Exmoor,* 1890.

PARKINSON, J., *Paradisi in Sole Paradisus Terrestris,* 1629.

POOLE, C. H., *Customs, Superstitions and Traditions of Somerset,* 1883.
>   *Pitminster, the Church of St. Mary and St. Andrew* (Pamphlet).
>   *Taunton Sessions Papers,* Taunton Museum.

SHILLIBEAR, H. B., *Ancient Customs of the Manor of Taunton Deane,* 1821.

SNELL, F. J., *Book of Exmoor,* 1903.

Memorials of Old Somerset, 1906.

Star Chamber Proceedings, 1592.

Somerset Notes and Queries (19th and 20th century).

Somerset Year Books, Vols. 1905-39.

Somerset Folk Series, Vols. 1-15.

THORNE, R. L., *Antiquities of Wellington,* 1950.

TOULMIN, F., *History of Taunton,* 1791.

WALTERS, C., *Bygone Somerset,* 1897.

WATSON, W. G. WILLIS, *Somerset Life and Character,* Somerset Folk Series No. 17, 1924.

WHISTLER, C. W., *Quantock Folk Lore,* 1907.

WILLIAM OF MALMESBURY, Bohn's Antiquarian Library, 1847.

WOOD, H. F. H., *Tales of the Polden Hills,* Somerset Folk Series, 1922.

WOOD, J., *Particular Description of Bath,* 1750.

Word Lore, Vols. 1-5.

WRIGHT, JOSEPH, *Dialect Dictionary,* Vols. 1-5.

Index

Also published by Llanerch:

The Folklore of Warwickshire
Roy palmer.

The Folklore of Plants
T. F. Thiselton Dyer.

The Folklore of the Isle of Man
A. W. Moore.

County Folklore vol. III,
Orkney and Shetlands
G. F. Black.

Lays and Legends of the English Lake Country
John Pagen White.

Celtic Folktales from Armorica
F. M. Luzel.

The Celtic Legend of the Beyond
Anatole LeBraz. ·

For a complete list of ca. 150 titles, small-press
editions and facsimile reprints, write to Llanerch
Publishers, Felinfach, Lampeter, Dyfed, SA48 8PJ.

The **Folklore Society**, original publishers of this book, was founded in 1878 and was the first learned society in the world to be devoted to the study of folklore. Its expressed aims were to encourage research and collection of traditional culture, and to make the results of this research available to scholars and the public at large.

The Society is still going strong, and organises regular conferences and other events, issues a well-respected journal and members' newsletter, publishes books on folklore topics, and maintains an extensive library and archive service which is based in University College London. Membership is open to anyone interested in furthering the Society's aims.

Information regarding the Society's activities and current subscription rates is available from **The Folklore Society, University College London, Gower Street, London WC1E 6BT (Tel 071 387 5894).**